The Atlantic economy
Britain, the US and Ireland

Denis O'Hearn

Manchester University Press

Manchester and New York

distributed exclusively in the USA by Palgrave

Copyright © Denis O'Hearn 2001

The right of Denis O'Hearn to be identified as the author of this work has been asserted by him in accordance with the Copyright, Designs and Patents Act 1988.

Published by Manchester University Press
Oxford Road, Manchester M13 9NR, UK
and Room 400, 175 Fifth Avenue, New York, NY 10010, USA
http://www.manchesteruniversitypress.co.uk

Distributed exclusively in the USA by
Palgrave, 175 Fifth Avenue, New York,
NY 10010, USA

Distributed exclusively in Canada by
UBC Press, University of British Columbia, 2029 West Mall,
Vancouver, BC, Canada V6T 1Z2

British Library Cataloguing-in-Publication Data
A catalogue record for this book is available from the British Library

Library of Congress Cataloging-in-Publication Data applied for

ISBN   0 7190 5973 9 *hardback*
       0 7190 5974 7 *paperback*

First published 2001

10 09 08 07 06 05 04 03 02 01   10 9 8 7 6 5 4 3 2 1

Typeset by Ralph J. Footring, Derby
Printed in Great Britain
by Bookcraft, Bath

Do m'athair, James O'Hearn

My final prayer: make me always a man who asks questions.
Frantz Fanon

Contents

Tables and figures

Tables

Figures

Preface

This book has been in the works for many years. It grew out of my research on the southern Irish economy since the Second World War. I began to realise, first, that you could not understand Irish industrialisation and general economic development in the late twentieth century without understanding its precedents in the nationalist industrialisation regime of the 1930s and 1940s. Once I had reached the 1930s, it became clear that one could not understand that period without a deep understanding of the political economic processes that preceded it for hundreds of years. A central theme of the book is that to explain the Irish economy (or economies) today, one must explain the long history of Irish economic change, at least since Britain incorporated Ireland as an essential part of the regional economic system over which it was establishing leadership.

As the book expanded in time, it necessarily expanded in space. My primary concern is about long historical patterns of economic change and how they affect the possibilities of poor regions to develop economically. My understanding of this theme was deepened by my years of teaching at the University of Wisconsin at Madison, especially by the influence of some of the brightest young students of economic change from around the world, including the global South. Slowly, a book about Irish economic change became a book about the Atlantic economy, which provides the context within which change in a small region like Ireland must be understood. This volume is therefore still aimed at an Irish audience but it is primarily aimed at the broad global community of scholars of economic change, who may care to consider how the Irish experience informs problems of economic and social change in other peripheral societies. This could hardly be more timely, as the 'Celtic tiger' at the turn of the century had become a sort of icon for policy makers and scholars who desire to promote neo-liberal growth strategies around the world.

Since this book concentrates on industrial development, a caveat is in order. Much of the south and west of the island of Ireland plays a peripheral role to the story after the rise of linen and, especially, the period of cotton and factory linen. This is simply because Irish industry became so concentrated in the north-eastern corner of the island, and the detailed specification of Ireland's peripheral agrarian economy is beyond the scope of this volume. The economic marginalisation of most of the island is absolutely critical to our understanding of the outcome of peripheralisation. This was indicated by the huge literature on the Irish famine that accompanied the one hundred and fiftieth anniversary of the start of that tragedy in 1995. The absence of in-depth analysis of this part of the story of Irish peripheralisation herein should not be interpreted as an absence of concern with its importance. Likewise, I have not done as detailed an analysis as I would have preferred of the northern Irish economy after partition. This is because the main story of Irish industrialisation is the rise of import substitution in the south and its eventual transformation to an industrialisation strategy that is highly dependent on transnational corporate investments. The absence of in-depth analysis of the north should not be interpreted as an absence of concern with the importance of partition in Irish life. I consider the unification of the island of Ireland and its economy to be crucial to any hope of achieving what I describe here as an articulated form of economic change, where economic growth is organically associated with greater equality and social inclusion.

Many people have helped at various stages of this project. I am indebted to colleagues at the University of Wisconsin, particularly those who participated in the Sociology of Economic Change colloquia. As director of the International Studies Center at the University of Wisconsin, Gay Seidman organised several seminars and periods of residence that provoked important discussions about my work. I am also indebted to Boaventura de Sousa Santos and scholars at the Centro de Estudos Sociais in Coimbra, Portugal, for organising a series of lectures where my work was discussed. Early support for the research came from the staff of the Sociology Department at University College Dublin, where I spent a year as a Fulbright scholar. As always, Andrew Schrank, Stephen Bunker and Douglas Hamilton read many drafts of the chapters and provided invaluable comments and criticisms. Others who commented on previous versions of chapters or who provided important materials or support include Vivek Chibber, Marilyn Cohen, Till Geiger, Jane Gray, David Jacobsen, Peadar Kirby, Russ Middleton, Lars Mjoset, Ronnie Munck, Liam O'Dowd, Jose Padin and Sally Shortall. I am also grateful to the reviewers from Manchester University Press for their comments and suggestions. Staff of the Central Statistics Office in Dublin and Cork were especially helpful in providing information that I requested, as were staff at the State Papers Office in Dublin and the University College Dublin archives. Support was also forthcoming from my colleagues at the West Belfast Economic Forum. Finally, I would like to acknowledge the patience and support of Annette, Sinéad and Caitríona, who have endured this project in one form or another for longer than anyone else.

D. O.

Beal Feirste

Abbreviations

CFR	Council on Foreign Relations
EC	European Community
ECA	Economic Cooperation Administration
EEC	European Economic Community
EFTA	European Free Trade Association
ELI	export-led industrialisation
ERP	European Recovery Program
ESM	early state module
EU	European Union
FDI	foreign direct investment
FIM	Federation of Irish Manufacturers
FTA	Free Trade Area
GATT	General Agreement on Tariffs and Trade
GDP	gross domestic product
GNP	gross national product
IBRD	International Bank for Reconstruction and Development
IDA	Industrial Development Authority
IMF	International Monetary Fund
ISI	import-substitution industrialisation
IT	information technology
ITUC	Irish Trades Union Congress
MP	member of parliament
NATO	North Atlantic Treaty Organisation
NIC	newly industrialised country
OECD	Organisation for Economic Cooperation and Development
OEEC	Organisation for European Economic Cooperation
R&D	research and development
TNC	transnational corporation
UN	United Nations

Chapter 1

Global power and local economic change

The Atlantic economy has been central to the capitalist world-system since England built and used it to rival Holland's global power in the seventeenth century. Britain controlled its trade, its industries and its raw materials to maintain competitive advantages over Europe's other colonial powers until the twentieth century. Then the US recreated the Atlantic economy, putting it at the centre of its own plans to create a 'grand area' that its industries would dominate and over which it would have hegemonic control. Even as economic power shifted toward Asia at the close of the twentieth century, cross-Atlantic trade and investments remained critical to the re-emergence of the US as the world's central economic and political power.

While Britain and the US are obvious choices for a study of the Atlantic economy, Ireland's importance may be less obvious. Ireland was a key subordinate zone to Britain during its construction of the Atlantic economy and subsequent hegemony, providing critical commodities to Britain's naval and commercial fleets, as well as its industrial population at home and its colonies abroad. After part of Ireland attained political independence in the twentieth century, it was resubordinated to the US, becoming a key point of entry for US capital which sought investments in and trade with the European market, at whose periphery Ireland lay. At the end of the twentieth century and into the twenty-first, Ireland was arguably the key intermediate zone between the US and the European Union, the place where capital in the new leading sector, information technology, agglomerated its products on their way into the single European market.

Ireland's long history in the changing Atlantic project was thus subordinate *and* critical, peripheral *and* substantial. Like many colonies, its ruling elite came from the colonial power itself, in this case England. This ascendancy and, later, Irish nationalist movements repeatedly tried to follow the English example and industrialise. But as colony and former colony, Ireland had neither the infrastructures nor the institutions it needed to compete successfully with core industrial powers. Nor did it have the necessary political power to maintain autonomous policy-making capability. It was continually peripheralised, its industrialisation transformed

1

from the potentially innovative and complex multi-linked patterns of the core nations to a limited semi-peripheral pattern that was subordinate to powerful interests within the Atlantic project. In the process, Ireland was created and recreated as an important *intermediating zone*, where England and then the US pursued their interests on, and on the 'other side of', the Atlantic.[1]

This book, then, addresses the most basic questions about uneven development: how global developmental processes, and struggles over global hegemony and competitiveness, affect the developmental choices of localities; and under what conditions localities can or cannot break out of the limitations imposed on them by such global processes. It addresses these questions concretely, by a long-term historical analysis of a key peripheral zone and its political economic relationships with the two great powers of the Atlantic economy.

Studying local change in a global context

Several themes haunt the study of economic change or 'development'. One is the relationship between *big* external forces and *small* local forces in inducing, limiting and shaping change. Another is the relationship between processes by which history structures the environment of change and others by which people create their own history. Clearly, these pairs of explanations are not mutually exclusive – they are contending forces that combine to make economic change the complex process that it is. Big external forces limit and imperfectly determine courses of change in localities. Local forces resist *and collaborate*, creating many of the contingencies that plague attempts to elaborate general theories of economic change. Histories create path dependencies, place barriers, provide favourable conjunctures and opportunities, and sow seeds of destruction in powerful industrial regions and poor agrarian regions. Remarkable people in remarkable institutions strive to transcend the limitations of history. Sometimes they exploit what history provides in remarkable ways; other times they fail.

Even if we accept – as does, for example, world-systems analysis – that the structuration and reproduction of a global hierarchy impedes the upward mobility of countries and regions, we still must explain how the global policies of core states and classes are implemented at regional and local levels to reinforce this hierarchy. Such implementation involves alliance, co-optation and compromise with, and the exercise of power over, local states, classes and other groups. It involves *imperfect* plans and actions, including failures, which explain observed variance from the central tendencies of global hierarchy and exploitation of peripheries by core institutions. This is not a world of perfect imperialist control but one where some imperialists are *effective enough* to dominate regions, exploit people and compete with other imperialists.

A major reason why imperialist control is imperfect is that each local social or economic structure has its own peculiar characteristics. Thus, global approaches to economic change must avoid the reductionist assumption that the whole system determines regional or local change. If local specificity and historical contingency matter, then strikingly different processes occur in different regions and at different times *despite* the designs of core industrial powers or the hypothesised regularities of the global system.

McMichael (1990) addresses this problem in his critique of *encompassing comparisons* of historical development, where experiences of separate regions or localities are assumed to be governed by their respective relations to the whole (world-)system. This form of thinking, he argues, is both teleological and functionalist insofar as local changes are derived from the functional needs of the whole system. Processes by which core regions establish and deepen control over other regions are analysed primarily as a means to an end rather than as contradictory and contingently unfolding historical processes. McMichael cites Wallerstein's concept of *incorporation* as an example of this mode of analysis. For Wallerstein, core powers *need* to incorporate new regions into the world economy in order to accumulate because the system can expand only by bringing fresh labour into its commodity chains.[2] This is an insufficient method of historical comparison, says McMichael, because it predetermines economic outcomes in specific regions by the nature of the whole system and, especially, its need to establish a worldwide division of labour.[3]

An alternative strategy that simultaneously explains systemic regularity *and* variation of its parts, says McMichael, is the *incorporating comparison*.[4] This method progressively constructs the whole system through comparative analysis of its spatial or temporal 'parts' as 'moments in a self-forming whole' (1990, p. 386). Both the whole and its parts form and reform across time and space. This method does not deny system, structure or recognisable patterns of change. Instead, it insists that causal regularities cannot be assumed but must be uncovered by comparing varying or convergent outcomes.

McMichael mentions two strategies of comparison to uncover such regularities. The *singular form* compares variation across or *in* space at a specific historical juncture by focusing on instances where segments from different 'social times' come together competitively in a single place, thus 'redefining' each other, with unpredictable outcomes. Two countries which meet in an uneven colonial situation, coloniser and colonised, exemplify such a combination. A most fruitful unit of analysis is social relations or institutions: the introduction of markets into subsistence agriculture, wage labour in a slave economy and so on. The historical dialectic whereby different social relations are combined and redefined to form something new and unpredictable is a singular form of incorporating comparison.

The *multiple* form of comparison compares instances of an evolving process across time. We may, for instance, follow the development of states or inter-state institutions through time; or we may follow economic change in a certain kind of region across time. Inter-temporal comparisons may reveal systemic processes and regularities, and even directions of change. For example, we may treat the 'encompassing' assumptions of world-systems analysis about a core–periphery hierarchy as contingent hypotheses to be tested or 'discovered' by multiple comparisons. Arrighi's (1994) analysis of *systemic cycles of accumulation* begins with broad world-systemic assumptions about the nature of economic and hegemonic cycles but, with the aid of secondary historical analysis, re-examines each cycle in detail to uncover what is particular about each successive hegemonic regime and what is regular across cycles.

Although incorporating comparisons concentrate on particular instances, therefore, they do not preclude generalisation and theory building. Incorporating comparisons enable the identification of a systemic whole and of regularities in the way it reproduces itself. But concrete historical processes cannot be subordinated to previously identified 'laws' of a system. Such 'laws' may be identified through dynamic world-historical analysis but they cannot determine outcomes in a given place and time, even though the unequal power structures that underlay and reproduce them may bias outcomes in certain directions.

Several important characteristics explain the outcomes of historically contingent situations. Of course, power in the form of class and state power is critical to the creation and reproduction of hierarchical systems. And the balance of power between actors and institutions in different locations will have an important impact on the outcomes of 'singular comparisons' where segments from different 'social times' come together competitively. But once we consider historical change in a regional system or a locality within it, other important factors come into play. Most importantly, social scientists have shown how historical economic change is shaped and limited through *path-dependent* mechanisms which, once introduced, 'lock in' given trajectories of economic change. Often, these mechanisms are set in train by the introduction of something – a technology, policy or social relation – that is one of several contingencies at a critical historical juncture, or turning point. The initial change may have been imposed, chosen because of short-term considerations or even introduced through chance, yet it can have significant long-term consequences that are often inefficient or disadvantageous. What is important is that a change, once made, has cumulative causality: changes in one period affect and limit what happens in subsequent periods.

Mainstream economists who discuss path dependency usually focus on a limited set of circumstances where a discrete technological 'choice' at one period affects subsequent technologies. Under certain conditions – such as increasing returns to scale due to large set-up costs or learning effects – one technology or even one producer can take over a market even though it is not efficient in the long run. Applied to trade theory, the early history of market shares among regions or countries may determine trade patterns over the long run. Industrial location is often determined by 'historical accident', locked in by decisions taken early in the history of a settlement that may be sub-optimal. Even from a relatively orthodox point of view, then, regional prosperity and uneven development can be self-reinforcing (Arthur 1988).

Path dependence in this form is still a neoclassical concept insofar as it is explained within the parameters of equilibrium economics. Special conditions create multiple equilibriums, among which sub-optimal paths may be chosen. Exit from a sub-optimal path is not possible by individual actions but takes a 'big push' by a central authority such as a developmental state, which co-ordinates actions by many individuals until they achieve exit into a new, more productive equilibrium path (Rosenstein-Rodin 1943).

But self-reinforcing processes are also common to critical theories of economic change. Dependency and world-system approaches, for example, concentrate on structural relationships that are imposed by core powers and which 'lock in' vast regions to peripheral locations within global divisions of labour. Although their specific forms of production and associated technologies may change over time, these regions remain identifiably peripheral or semi-peripheral. Whether or under what conditions peripheral states may exit to a more advantageous position through policy choice is a key debate within the study of economic change.

Haydu (1998) introduces contingency and local agency by moving beyond simple path dependency to *reiterative problem solving*. 'Continuities across temporal cases', he claims, 'can be traced in part to enduring problems, while more or less contingent solutions to these problems are seen as reflecting and regenerating the historical individuality of each period' (p. 354). Rather than focusing on how an initial change determines a cumulative subsequent trajectory, this brings choice and variability back to each critical juncture. One must explain why one solution is chosen instead of another and how this solution sets a new historical direction and limits future choices. Outcomes at a given 'switch point' are thus products of the past rather than historical 'accidents', the preferred term of path dependency. Solutions embody contradictions, create further crises and also give tools with which to confront future crises. Solutions at one time may close off future options, but they also shape future switch points and can even create new solutions in future periods.

A study that adopts such a problem-solving approach is Senghaas's analysis of how some small, predominantly agrarian European export economies evolved into mature industrial societies while others were peripheralised. Senghaas recognises that path-dependent mechanisms meant that divisions of labour established at the end of the Middle Ages 'continued to

determine the development paths of individual societies and entire con-
tinents well into the nineteenth and twentieth centuries' (1985, p. 14). But
he also insists that individual European societies went through critical
turning points where policy choices determined whether they would achieve
'autocentric' industrial development or revert into peripheralisation.

This 'turning point' came when small European countries, having been
compelled to turn toward the world market, realised the gap that had
opened up between them and the industrialised European core after the
industrial revolution. They could respond either by continuing to adapt to
an externally imposed division of labour or by trying to develop the
international competitiveness of domestic infant industries. Those who
accepted their narrow role of exporter to an associated core power –
Ireland, Portugal, Spain, Romania – were further peripheralised and failed
to industrialise. But some small countries broke out of underdevelopment,
says Senghaas, by inducing a broad-based agricultural revolution and
spreading the gains from agricultural productivity to raise the average
incomes of all sectors. By expanding and protecting the domestic market,
they created demand for new domestic industrial products, especially the
specialised processing of local agricultural produce. From such beginnings,
successful countries built up an industrial base and moved into export
markets and eventually to free trade, but only after they had gone a
substantial way toward equalising their development levels with the already
industrialised countries.

The development of linkages between economic sectors was key to the
process. Where productivity gains were sectorally limited, dualistic structures
impeded the opening up of the domestic market. Growth remained exogen-
ously determined and dependent. But the Scandinavian countries (as well as
Canada, Australia and New Zealand) switched from exports of staples to
processing and exporting finished and semi-finished manufactures. As a
result, they graduated 'in Britain's footsteps' from suppliers of raw materials
to mature capitalist economies (p. 88). They developed linked economies,
not overspecialised and dependent ones, not only improving their productivity
but also their terms of trade. Senghaas calls this 'associative–dissociative'
development because it required elements of inward-oriented protection,
which enabled the state to foster an articulated indigenous economy, and
export-orientation, which enabled such small countries to transcend the
limits of their local markets.

Unlike some critical approaches, Senghaas does not see the decision on a
turning point as being primarily imposed from outside or determined by
historical structure. Rather, in his successful European cases, 'the decision
on autocentric development or peripheralization was taken *within the
respective societies themselves*, and ... reflected different *internal* social
conditions for the processing of the opportunities and restrictions which
the world market offered' (p. 155, original emphasis). He concludes that

'the causal relationship posited by the world system approach between the *autocentric* industrial development of one group of societies and the *periphery* development of another group, does not exist at all'.

From a critical perspective this is the most contentious of his findings. It is quite a jump to analyse a limited number of European cases that had wide degrees of choice and opportunity in development policy and then to assume that other countries have similar latitude. With respect to similar attempts by small Asian countries to attain indigenous development, Cumings (1987) notes that 'many are called, few are chosen'. In other words, the image of Western wealth attracts many countries to attempt to follow a Western-style path of industrialisation. But in most cases, small countries that try to selectively protect their industries and to develop their domestic markets are sanctioned by powerful core economies. Thus, in order to succeed, countries must make the right policy choices, have the capacity to implement them *and* avoid sanctions by core powers of the world economy. Even Senghaas recognises that all of his successful cases had the 'sovereign power of self-determination', so that internal policy could respond properly to changing world economic conditions. Both structural constraints (such as colonialism) and time constraints (*when* a country attains self-determination) can undermine a country's attempts to develop.

Systemic accumulation, hegemony and incorporated local history

This study examines how Ireland's relations with Britain and the US have affected its capacity to choose its path of economic change since the sixteenth century. It examines potential 'switching points' when Irish actors attempted to redirect the country's development path toward industrialisation. It begins by analysing characteristic moments and processes of subordination, particularly Britain's incorporation of Ireland into its regional political economy. It then asks how the institutions that were built through incorporation and subsequent phases of subordination affected the abilities of Irish actors to 'switch' successfully to new trajectories of economic change.

Thus, the initial processes of incorporation and peripheralisation are examined as a 'singular form' of incorporating comparison, where segments from different 'social times' – expanding European powers and a Celtic society with its own economic and social dynamics – came together competitively in a single place and redefined each other. Subsequent critical junctures are compared across time to examine whether, or to what degree, local actors were constrained by global hierarchies and institutions that were introduced under incorporation and redefined during subsequent phases. Recurring local attempts to industrialise are analysed as iterative attempts to 'solve the problem' of industrialisation (and core reactions as iterative attempts to solve the problem of *re*subjugating recalcitrant locals).

What, then, is the approximate model of world capitalism and its core powers with which Ireland has interacted across its history of economic change? Britain's economic ascent during the sixteenth to eighteenth centuries, its status as hegemon during the eighteenth and nineteenth centuries and its replacement by the US in the twentieth century are the most important external influences on Irish economic change. The effects *in Ireland* of British and US strategies as aspirants and hegemons are central to the historical analysis of Irish economic change. To the extent that Irish agencies aspired to core-like status by imitating core industrial strategies, it is important to identify characteristics of economic ascent which assured success for Britain and the US, or the lack of which precluded Irish success.

Arrighi (1994) gives a compelling account of how successive regimes attained and lost hegemony, and identifies key characteristics which enabled their ascent and led to their eventual descent. He identifies four *systemic cycles of accumulation* centred on Genoa (from the fifteenth to the early seventeenth century), Holland (from the late sixteenth to the eighteenth century), Britain (from the last half of the eighteenth to the early twentieth century) and the US (from the late nineteenth century to the present). Each cycle included identifiable phases of *material expansion* (establishment of new trade routes and incorporation of new areas of commercial exploitation) and *financial expansion* (consolidation of capital's dominance over the enlarged world economy). A clearly identifiable class benefited from both expansions within each cycle. And each cycle included new organisational forms along with transformed revivals of previously superseded forms. These patterns of continuous and discontinuous change, expansions and restructurings were led by alliances of state and business leaders who were 'uniquely well placed to turn to their own advantage the unintended consequences of the actions of other agencies' (1994, p. 9). Because the British and US hegemonic regimes are key external actors in the history of Irish economic change, it is worth considering their specific characteristics.

British ascent to hegemony was enabled by contradictions of the previous Dutch regime. With the aid of a strong state coercive apparatus, Dutch capital successfully centralised the storage and exchange of the most strategic supplies of European and world commerce in Amsterdam, which became the central money and capital market of the European world economy. The Dutch merchant class led and governed the European capitalist engine, largely due to their control of critical trades such as Baltic grain and naval stores. Large-scale joint stock companies like the Dutch East India Company (established in 1602) exercised exclusive trading and sovereignty rights over huge overseas commercial spaces from 1610–20 to 1730–40.

But Holland's success led other Europeans to imitate its trade, war-making and state-making techniques, eventually drawing competition and falling returns. War-making increased state demands throughout Europe for money and credit, allowing the Dutch to use their competitive advantages in finance to capture rising returns. But the imperial success of the Dutch East India Company strengthened its managerial bureaucrats, who diverted the company surplus into bureaucratic expansion and managerial corruption at the expense of stockholders. As rates of return fell in Dutch enterprise, English stocks and shares became more attractive and surplus Dutch capital flowed to England, financing its ascent as an economic and military rival to Holland.

Britain followed the Dutch example by wresting control of world trade from competing European powers like the French. It bought to sell and took in to send out, but increasingly sent out goods that were reformed through manufacture. The key to British success was its use of state (especially sea) power to control and shift the core axes of trade away from Amsterdam. The English Channel became the place where American and Asian commodities met Baltic supplies. Movement toward rule of the high seas began with the consolidation of royal power after the War of Roses, accelerated with the construction of a superior English fleet under Henry VIII and Elizabeth I, and came into its own with the English defeat of the Armada in 1588.

The English beat the Dutch at their own mercantilist game. With the aid of marauding naval fleets and joint stock companies (the Levant, East India, Royal Africa and Hudson's Bay companies), the English merchant class expanded their foreign investments through privateering and adventure. Unlike Holland, England collected a far-flung empire, which was both agro-industrial and commercio-financial. Its role as clearinghouse for the world economy outlasted its role as workshop for the world, but industrialisation helped it act as entrepôt on a far larger scale than Holland.

Such a world-historical analysis is more significant for Irish economic change than models that focus inward on British industry's ability to innovate. The basis of British hegemony was its control of commerce and finance. Its recycling of plunder beginning with Elizabeth allowed England to maintain 'sound money' and long-term monetary stability. This enabled it to become creditor and financier of the world economy to a much greater extent than Holland or Genoa before. Moreover, the project was achieved by and on behalf of the merchant-adventurer class, establishing the commercio-military alliance at the centre of the British regime. The rise of plunder-financed expansion coincided with the revival of European trade in wool textiles, which provided a leading sector to impel finance, commerce and industry together. Thus began the crucial alliance between English banking capital, merchant capital and the state. As this integrated economy began to expand more rapidly at the end of the sixteenth century, industry was key 'not *per se* but as an instrument of capital accumulation' (Arrighi 1994, p. 194). In this process of material expansion, English industry moved beyond mass-produced goods into high-value luxury and armaments production: silk, glass and cannon (Hill 1967, pp. 63, 71–5). Arrighi claims that the Elizabethan strategy of redirecting industrial expansion from cloth to luxuries showed an understanding that industrial expansion translates into expansion of national wealth and power only when associated with breakthrough into high value-added activities.

English expansion, however, was still limited by its subordination to Dutch commercial supremacy. Dutch superiority in cloth dyeing and finishing shifted the centres of highest textile profitability from England to Holland. English attempts in the early 1600s to capture cloth-finishing processes failed when the Dutch simply cut off British cloth from the all-important Baltic trade. This is a clear example of the link between commerce and industry. As Israel (1989, p. 410) argues, 'Dutch superiority in dyeing, bleaching, grinding and refining was hard to challenge when it was the Dutch who had the stockpiles of dyestuffs, chemicals, drugs, and rare raw materials on which all these processes depended'. England, then, had to remove the entrepôt from Amsterdam if it was to capture competitive *industrial* advantage.

The English merchant class and its state allies finally challenged Dutch commercial supremacy by capturing the Atlantic triangular trade. This brought unprecedented material expansion based on tobacco, sugar, cotton, gold (and on the labour required to produce them) and, especially, slaves. Where Dutch commercial supremacy was based solely on a capitalist logic of power, which invested money in a given unit of territory to acquire additional money (MTM'), English commercial supremacy added a territorialist logic of power, where money was used as a means of expanding territorial control (TMT'). By limiting its territorial expansion to essential trading ports, Holland avoided problems of administering large territories and populations. But it also became dependent on the entrepreneurship and labour of foreign countries that were outside of its direct control. The English, on the other hand, built the Atlantic economy on direct colonial control of production. England used the Navigation Acts (principally those of 1651 and 1660) and other key policies to build superiority in sea commerce and gain effective control over the resources of new territories, which enabled its Atlantic commercial empire to out-compete the Dutch Baltic-centred economy.

Arrighi argues that England superseded Holland by internalising its *production costs* through industrialisation and colonisation – as Holland had superseded the Genoese in the previous cycle by internalising 'protection costs' within its armed chartered trading companies (Steensgaard 1974). England brought production within the empire and subjected it to the economising that was enabled by innovations in the organisation of commerce and industry including, crucially, economies in the transactions costs of distribution and transport. By the mid-eighteenth century these English advantages pushed the Dutch into finance and investing in English production and the British empire, even financing the Seven Years' War (1756–63), during which England established superiority over France.

English industrial/commercial ascent was a path-dependent process that spanned the previous Genoese and Dutch cycles of accumulation. Industrial ascent began with the expansion of (woollen) textiles after Edward III destroyed the Flemish textile industry. Under Elizabeth, it diversified into metal and luxury industries after England failed to capture high-profit stages of the textiles commodity chain. England became a hegemonic contender when it integrated its industrial powers with overseas commercial and territorial expansion, culminating in the industrial revolution.[5] England was more competitive in each successive phase because of the industrial, commercial and military techniques it built up in previous phases. In Arrighi's words, 'each moment of industrial expansion in England was integral to an ongoing financial expansion, restructuring, and reorganisation of the capitalist world economy, in which England was incorporated from the very start' (1994, p. 209). England, already the greatest industrial power in Europe, was unbeatable once it controlled world trade.

Despite its strength, British hegemony had its own contradictions. Its success invited rivalry. The profitability of its machino-facture, especially after the rise of the cotton industry, depended on ever-increasing supplies of raw materials *and* ever-increasing foreign markets. Its attempts to protect domestic technologies, even as it promoted global free trade in other spheres, limited the markets for British capital goods while encouraging European and US capital to produce their own technologies. Already German and US competitors were developing integrated corporate structures that would challenge British competitive advantages. But the main threat to British hegemony was inter-state rivalry, first over the territories of the non-European world and then in world wars centred on Europe itself. Such rivalries raised protection costs over and above their benefits for Britain and its European rivals. Britain's wartime demands for armaments, machinery and materials became so great that its main supplier, the US, turned from being a net debtor to build up substantial claims on British incomes and assets. US productivity outstripped that of the British and European economies, and foreign assets flowed into US ownership. By the end of the Second World War, the US enjoyed a 'virtual monopoly of world liquidity' (Arrighi 1994, p. 275). Its favourable geographic position between the Western European and Asian trading blocs and the strength of its vertically integrated corporations enabled it to exercise hegemonic control of the world-system.

At the world-systemic level, it did this through the establishment of a new regulatory regime for world trade and money – Bretton Woods, the International Monetary Fund (IMF), the World Bank. In localities and regions, it used the Marshall Plan and other regional or bilateral agreements to claim free entry not only into European and Asian markets but also into the former colonies (Bunker and O'Hearn 1993). This was material expansion within a new cycle of accumulation, centred on US foreign direct investments in manufacturing, which later was branded the *new international division of labour* (Frobel *et al.* 1980).

A major reason for US strength was that it *internalised transaction costs* through an 'organisational revolution' of corporate managerial hierarchies which began with railroads in 1850s and totally transformed US enterprises by the start of 1900s (Chandler 1977). Corporations that instituted these structures imposed organisational barriers to new entrants in leading branches of the US economy. Once they had exploited opportunities for domestic vertical integration, US corporations, with the aid of the expansionist US state, moved into foreign countries to increase their powers of accumulation. Vertically integrated corporations could economise on costs of moving intermediate inputs through commodity chains (Coase 1937, Williamson 1970, Chandler 1977). Transnational corporations (TNCs) manipulated internal transfer prices to reduce local taxes and resource royalties. Direct sourcing of raw materials and semi-fabricates enabled *economies of speed*, by which companies with greater throughput could amass surpluses even without significant advantages in average profit rates. This was especially true of sectors such as aluminium, where resource extraction and mass production could be associated with mass distribution in a single enterprise (Barham *et al.* 1995).

The US also achieved hegemonic advantage by re-externalising protection costs. Rather than controlling areas through direct or indirect colonialism, the US spread the costs of regulation across the core states through their participation in inter-state bodies, such as the General Agreement on Tariffs and Trade (GATT), the IMF, the United Nations (UN) and the North Atlantic Treaty Organisation (NATO). Costs of administering colonies and former colonies where the US opened up new investments were borne by the colonial power and the local state. Rearmament to police the new order, internally and against the Soviet threat, provided an additional economic boost for the US and for consumers of its industrial products. These factors made the period from the Korean War to the 1970s oil crises 'the most sustained and profitable period of economic growth in the history of world capitalism' (McCormick 1989, p. 99). Undoubtedly, these global changes translated locally into the south of Ireland's transformation from dependence on Britain to dependence on US investments aimed at mainland Europe.

Global change and moments of local change

Analyses like Arrighi's *cycles of accumulation* help explain hegemonic ascent and decline, but they are not sufficient to explain peripheral or semi-peripheral economic change. One must still identify with more precision how core power and economic 'success' relates to peripheral 'lack of success', and how core policies are translated in localities. Arrighi himself admits that studies of the hierarchy of world trade in terms of where large-scale profits are made tend to ignore regional factors such as class struggle and the polarisation of the world economy in core and peripheral locales (1994, p. xii). Beyond concepts like core–periphery hierarchy and global division of labour, one needs to know something about how hegemonic power enables core capitals and states to *capture* the most innovative and profitable clusters of economic activities and, conversely, to promote less profitable but often critically supportive activities elsewhere.

In order to establish and reproduce global divisions of labour, core forces must interact with local societies and ecologies to define barriers to certain activities, limit locally defined 'solutions' and shape emergent activities. Localities have been incorporated into global structures and transformed within them by state violence, settlement, plantation, direct investment and trade. Supra-national political structures which regulate inter-state economic relations such as property rights and trade may discourage certain economic activities from peripheral and semi-peripheral regions while encouraging or at least tolerating others. Yet global structures are not just an environment within which local or regional development occurs. Powerful external forces transform the localities they penetrate and, in turn, are transformed by them.

Some theorists propose that these histories of penetration may themselves show regularities. Domination may wax and wane relative to the rise and fall of local resistance. Structures of penetration and resistance may move within a deeper *rhythmic* structure of uneven global capitalist development, which appears to exhibit secular and cyclical changes as well as constancy. Chase-Dunn (1989) examines how secular changes such as the development of the forces of production (the sum of human knowledge and technique as applied to the transformation of nature) and the proletarianisation of labour interact with *cycles* or *phases* of innovation and global material expansion, trade, hegemony and war. Expansionary periods in innovation and material production increase core interests in seeking out new raw materials, labour resources and markets. Material expansion provides substantially powerful core contenders with opportunities for hegemonic consolidation while long-term decline can erode hegemonic advantages and invite competition from core contenders, often through war.[6] Phases of hegemony may be associated with different core strategies. The rise to power and the displacement of an old hegemon may require violent force, but once a core state attains hegemony it may assert control with minimum force through regulatory structures and market mechanisms such as free trade.

The effects of these secular and cyclical changes in peripheral and semi-peripheral localities are contingent. Local action may face fewer constraints during periods of global economic contraction, especially if dominant core powers lose their ability or will to control far-flung regions. Anti-colonial movements arose and semi-peripheral states established nationalist indust-rialisation regimes in the first half of the twentieth century, after Britain lost its imperial supremacy but before the establishment of *pax Americana*.[7] Hegemonic conflicts may also result in the displacement of previously dominating powers by new hegemons in a given locality. A recurring theme of this study is how the conjunction of economic and hegemonic change affects opportunities for both core penetrations of localities and peripheral resistance within them.

One would expect different core expansions and crises to induce differ-ent forms of peripheral penetration. As hegemony shifted from Holland to England to the US, the leading sectors of expansion and innovation shifted from shipbuilding to cotton to cars to microelectronics. Such shifts certainly affect the forms of incorporation and peripheralisation of dependent regions, as well as their opportunities to disincorporate and attempt to industrialise. In its post-1945 expansion, for example, the US implemented strategies to access peripheral raw materials that were spatially and logically distinct from previous or subsequent periods (Bunker and O'Hearn 1993). This hegemonic shift put paid to previous colonial and imperialist forms of peripheral control and imposed new forms of control based on economic openness and more global forms of regulation. At a shorter cyclical level, different kinds of economic crises should provoke different responses from core powers in the periphery: realisation crises (i.e., failure to sell goods in order to realise profits) may induce searches for new markets, while profits squeezes induce searches for cheaper labour or materials.

Wallerstein (1988) provides a useful structure for examining the nature of the relationships between core and peripheral change when he considers how regions are *incorporated* and *peripheralised* in the world-system. He considers three distinct moments: external arena, incorporation and periph-eralisation (1988, pp. 130, 189). A zone is external to the world-system if it is not *integral to* the commodity chains that constitute the system's division of labour. If changing local production is not fundamentally con-nected to efforts by core capitals to maximise their accumulation of capital world-wide, then the zone is external, even if it has trade links to the core.

Hall (1986), however, adds that a concentration on *effective* incorpor-ation – whereby regions are locked into the logic of global accumulation – ignores previous changes that alter those regions in crucial and irreversible ways. The introduction of the horse into the North American south-west induced irreversible changes from unmounted foraging economies even though effective incorporation was still a long way off. Such changes in *contact peripheries* can later prove crucial to effective incorporation. Early contacts change local populations in ways that facilitate deeper contact. Early Irish contacts with Vikings and Normans did not effectively incorporate the island into the European world-system, yet Viking settlements presaged the rise of towns and economic centres that would facilitate sixteenth-century incorporation, while 'old Anglo-Irish' administrative centres in the Pale were crucial footholds for later English settlements. According to Hall, 'as a region becomes more closely articulated to the world-economy, external pressures impinge more forcefully on local groups. When such pressures are sufficiently strong, and of sufficient duration, that structure of local groups is changed. If transformation is sufficiently drastic, it becomes more difficult to reverse. In other words, the more complete the previous incorporation has been, the more difficult it will be for the social structure to return to the *status quo ante*' (1986, p. 98).

Incorporation is thus the 'original' path-dependent process of globalisation. Wallerstein's *effective* incorporation, whereby a zone is 'hooked' into the world-system so that it can virtually no longer escape, is not some form of imperial original sin. Rather, it is the ultimate moment of a longer cumulative process of contact and change, which takes on world-systemic significance once an incorporating core power elaborates an effective world project and becomes powerful enough to subsume other regions within it.

Wallerstein (1988, p. 130) argues that incorporation significantly changes a society's main economic units and modes of labour acquisition, while it creates new institutional infrastructures and political institutions with relevant power and authority. Of course, the specific character of these institutional changes will be historically contingent. Not only will they differ from place to place but they will also be imperfect relative to the intentions of dominant external powers.

New *units of economic decision making*, including sites of direct production (plantations, mines, factories) and merchant collection (putters out, trade ports), have greater prospects for capital accumulation by responding to global changes. They may be bigger insofar as larger units are better able to alter production with perceived global changes. They are likely to be controlled externally or by local agents of a dominant external power (such as a settler class).

New *modes of acquiring and controlling labour* may enable economic units to acquire or shed labour with more ease in response to changing conditions. New regimes of labour control are intended to make labour more coercible. Historically, the acquisition and control of labour are two of the most difficult and contradictory projects taken on by core powers in peripheral or semi-peripheral situations.

Political institutions are important because the success of incorporation is related to the willingness and ability of local authorities to permit, abet and subsidise foreign economic penetration. Penetrating investors must be reasonably secure and able to freely transfer capital and commodities within the incorporated zone and between it and other regions. This entails them creating new *infrastructural institutions* that enable them to extend monetary and trade structures into the zone. Yet political institution-alisation may be constrained by local resistance, a fact which is amply exemplified by centuries of (ongoing) Irish resistance to foreign rule.

A longer process of peripheralisation, whereby core-oriented local trans-formations are deepened, follows incorporation. Outward-oriented economic units multiply, introducing new technologies and labour processes. Such 'deepening' varies from place to place. It may be more capital intensive in the semi-periphery than the periphery. Certain phases of peripheralisation may even involve 'backward' movement from larger to smaller economic units or from more to less proletarian social relations of production.

While incorporation and peripheralisation are important moments in local history, I suggest that other dynamic processes may be associated with the rhythms of capitalist development. *Dis*incorporation, *re*incorporation and *re*peripheralisation may accompany global economic or hegemonic shifts. Core control of a peripheral region is unlikely to be merely trans-ferred from one core power to another. New hegemons must destroy old forms of control and introduce new ones in order to reconstitute regions in their own interests. This may entail new divisions of labour, economic sectors, enterprises, labour regimes and state forms. Hegemonic transfer is further complicated by spatial limitations on core expansion, which by the late nineteenth century required the periphery's *redivision* by war (Lenin 1916).

The term *redivision*, however, implies a simple redistribution of control while reincorporation and reperipheralisation imply complex processes of recreation. New hegemons require different things from old ones. Their productive advantages concentrate in different leading sectors that utilise different technologies or materials and make different demands on periph-eral regions. They must break down old institutions from the previous hegemon. Setting up new international institutions to control trade, in-vestment and monetary structures may do this most effectively. Yet such systemic changes must be replicated throughout each peripheral region or state that is reincorporated under the new hegemonic regime. The estab-lishment of new economic units may be central to this process. The US established hegemony over previous European colonies by breaking down colonial power (supporting anti-colonial movements or transforming the nature of colonial rule) and also by creating new economic units and rules of free access to colonial resources by US corporations (Bunker and O'Hearn 1993).

In addition to hegemonic change, global recessions may present oppor-tunities for nationalist movements to *dis*incorporate. *Disincorporation* has generally had more limited goals than withdrawal from the logic of global accumulation. Historically, most subordinate regions simply hoped to escape from the constraints of peripherality by emulating characteristics of the subordinator, most often by attempting to industrialise. A longer-term objective may be to rejoin the world-system as a more equal competitor, although that objective may be pursued through uneasy alliances with groups that seek more thorough political transformation.

The outcomes of *re*incorporation may differ according to the success with which a region disincorporated during a previous period. Ireland partly escaped British control in the first half of the twentieth century, ironically leaving it more vulnerable to the US, which did not have to wrest it away. In the mid-twentieth century, Ireland arguably preferred to maintain the British link, albeit on more favourable terms, to being *re*incorporated within the emerging US–European axis of production and trade. But by the 1950s the conditions of hegemony and the logic of Atlantic production and trade had changed and the conditions of reincorporation were well beyond Ireland's control. On the other hand, regions that remained as European colonies had to be displaced from imperial control before they could be reincorporated under US hegemony (Bunker and O'Hearn 1993).

Finally, *re*incorporation and *re*peripheralisation may actually be routes of upward mobility in the world-system. Rising hegemons require new semi-peripheral zones, so a country which was peripheral in previous hierarchies may have strategic significance to a new hegemon. A region that was primarily integrated into the world economy through food commodity chains may become 'industrialised' and participate in semi-peripheral links of industrial commodity chains. I will argue that this was the most important change in Ireland's global situation after the Second World War.

Effects on local societies: exploitation and marginalisation

Two distinct but possibly related approaches analyse the effects of world-system structures and processes on local societies. Some Marxist approaches debate how core classes or regions *exploit* peripheral classes or regions (for example through unequal exchange or trade). Other analyses concentrate on whether or how the international division of labour excludes peripheral regions from innovative and profitable activities. In reality, the two processes should be related, since the structuration and reproduction of an unequal regional division of labour is a means by which core powers – states, classes and corporations – accumulate more profits while trying to assure their continuing domination of the most profitable economic activities.

Bergesen (1983) argues that the core–periphery relation is a straight-forward *world class* relation where economic zones are 'the equivalent of individuals' and, therefore, the core *exploits* the periphery. It is more useful, however, to distinguish between class relations that are based on property ownership and a regional core–periphery division of labour which cross-cuts the global class structure (Petras 1978, p. 64; Chase-Dunn 1989, pp. 38–43). This interlaced global class structure enables varieties of exploitation, whether through proletarian wage relations at the point of production (Burawoy 1979) or the appropriation of surplus labour across regions through mechanisms such as *unequal exchange* (Sweezy 1942, Baran 1957, Emmanuel 1972a, Mandel 1975). On the other hand, if different regions have uneven chances to participate in the most innovative or profitable activities, some regions may suffer more from marginalisation than from exploitation or appropriation. In this case, core regions are richer because peripheral regions are poorer – *not* because of exploitation but because core regions monopolise profitable activities and channel peripheral regions into less profitable activities. With respect to classes, Wright (1985) calls this relation *economic oppression* as distinct from exploitation. It may be caused by lack of access to *certain kinds* of assets and not simply to assets in general. Regions that are excluded from productive activities that require certain kinds of capital equipment or organisational assets suffer distinct social consequences, such as chronic underemployment, subsistence crises, famine and emigration.

There is sharp disagreement about the importance of different forms of regional oppression. Laclau (1971) and Brenner (1977) argue that transnational exploitation is small compared with local class exploitation. Resnick and Wolff (1987) appear to agree, but only because the main rationale of core activities in the periphery is to support core accumulation rather than to exploit, a situation that causes economic oppression by limiting peripheral activities and marginalising masses of peripheral people. At the other extreme, Frobel *et al.* (1980) argue that a new epoch of vastly increased direct transnational exploitation began after the Second World War. It is likely, however, that the degree of direct and indirect exploitation changes across time and space (Mandel 1975, Jenkins 1987, Chase-Dunn 1989). Only world-historical analysis can uncover whether there are spatial or temporal patterns to the predominance of one or another form of exploitation. The existence and concrete forms of exploitation are subjects of historical inquiry.

A superficial analysis of Irish economic history suggests that each form of economic oppression was most likely in different historical phases of Irish economic change. *Direct exploitation* appears likely since Ireland became dependent on TNC investments after the 1950s. *Unequal exchange* appears most likely with regard to semi-peripheral manufactures such as linen that were exchanged for English core manufactures in the seventeenth to twentieth centuries. *Marginalisation* affected large parts of the rural population during chronic subsistence crises, leading to the starvation of the 1840s. Yet chronic emigration, population decline and high unemployment indicate that marginalisation has been important across many phases of Irish history.

Both exploitation and marginalisation, however, are influenced by the core's control over which productive activities are performed in a peripheral region. This study concentrates on whether and how Ireland's incorporation into the British- or US-dominated Atlantic economy affected its ability to industrialise and, specifically, which industrial activities it performed. Parts of Ireland were semi-peripheral *industrial* regions of the British-centred global economy for hundreds of years. Cork provisioned the colonial trade; the north-east produced linen and later ships; the south now assembles US manufactures entering Europe. Thus, it is important if possible to distinguish between core and semi-peripheral industry to explain why certain industrial regimes 'succeed' in the most innovative 'leading' industries while others fail, leading to deindustrialisation and/or industrial transformation.

The world-system approach analyses the capitalist world economy as a system that contains multiple nation states and societies but a single division of labour. Core zones perform predominantly core activities, peripheral zones perform peripheral ones and semi-peripheral zones perform a balance of both kinds and possibly intermediate activities between core and peripheral (Chase-Dunn 1989, p. 211). But what concrete division of labour might this system engender? Structuralists like Galtung (1971) argue that core regions produce mainly manufactured goods and peripheral regions produce raw materials, with 'coreness' and 'peripherality' defined by the degree of processing that takes place in a region. Such definitions are problematic, since final assembly regularly happens in the semi-periphery and less processed stages of production (spinning) are often core, while more processed stages (weaving) are peripheral.

Hopkins and Wallerstein (1986) define global production as a series of *commodity chains*; these 'link raw materials, labour, the sustenance of labour, intermediate processing, final processing, transport, and final consumption' (Chase-Dunn 1989, p. 39). Core regions contain relatively high proportions of core nodes in these chains, peripheral regions contain low proportions and semi-peripheral regions are in between. Three common indicators of core nodes are higher wage rates, higher profit rates and higher capital intensity. Mandel (1975) and Amin (1975) contend that a core–periphery wage differential emerged in the 1880s, while Chase-Dunn (1989, p. 53) identifies a growing wage gap since the sixteenth century. Wallerstein (1979) expects core profit rates to exceed peripheral ones, and explains the difference by the higher capital intensity of core activities. Arrighi and Drangel (1986) empirically define the core by its relatively high gross national product (GNP) per capita. Chase-Dunn (1989, p. 207) assumes that core activities combine all three characteristics: relatively high wage rates for skilled labour working in relatively capital-intensive production, which reflects methods of production which facilitate particularly high rates of labour productivity, enabling high rates of profit.

Such differentials, however, indicate but do not define 'coreness'. One should be able to identify prior characteristics that cause each indicator to differ between core and peripheries. Arrighi and Drangel (1986) and O'Hearn

(1994), following Schumpeter, argue that this prior characteristic is the relationship of an economic activity to clusters of other activities which, taken together, comprise innovation. Schumpeter (1939) suggests that economic change occurs through a non-equilibrium, discontinuous process whereby economic activity moves to quantitatively and qualitatively different levels. At the centre of economic change are innovations which substantially increase labour productivity, making it possible to produce more output with a given level of inputs and giving rise to monopoly profits for a period. These innovative activities cluster in space and time. They concentrate unevenly in certain sectors and regions. They require significant new construction of plant and equipment and the creation of new firms or the reorganisation of old ones.

Innovation is related more to how inventions are utilised than to inventions themselves. Indeed, the reorganisation of production may be more important than technological change. Chandler (1962, 1990) proposes that larger twentieth-century firms organised production in new ways to capture economies of scale (which transform higher fixed costs into lower unit costs), technological complexity (allowing firms to combine resources in new ways) and vertical integration (reliance more on their own resources than on markets for critical inputs). New forms of corporate organisation also involve new methods of skill formation, motivation, retention of key workers and controlling the productivity gains that arise from innovation.

Mass and Lazonick (1990) and Lazonick (1991) put organisational change at the centre of innovation. They trace British competitive advantages in the cotton industry to innovations in labour costs, fixed capital costs, materials costs, marketing costs and administrative costs. Unlike entrepreneur-centred accounts, their analysis centres on the importance of developing an experienced, specialised and co-operative labour force out of pre-existing domestic and craft labour. This is a welcome change in emphasis from accounts of core entrepreneurial superiority. Yet, without a theory that elaborates the structural sources of and impediments to developing disciplined factory labour from domestic and craft labour, we run the risk of blaming peripheral labour for not 'developing capitalism', just as some analysts blame peripheral capitalists for not 'developing capitalism'. Thus, it is valuable to combine historical approaches to innovation and competitive advantage with structural approaches to global capitalism.

Mass and Lazonick also trace innovation to the development of a strong, closely linked engineering industry, which reduced the cost of producing cotton goods and increased the industry's ability to deal flexibly with changes in market demands and material supplies. Cotton's development in close proximity to the major point of entry of the raw material cheapened production and increased the stability of material supply. The advantages of empire in access to raw materials were matched by the importance of its transport and information infrastructures in opening up new markets for yarn and cloth. And the Lancashire cotton industry's centralisation around well developed input and output markets reduced the amounts of financial resources and management skills that were necessary to compete.

Finally, innovation induces wider economic growth. Schumpeter (1939) links innovation to a *primary* expansion that centres on a limited group of leading sectors; then, the prosperity generated by innovation is used to create a *secondary* expansion, where firms speculate on the primary expansion. This second wave spreads throughout a regional economy and thus can create greater general growth than the primary wave. The secondary wave resembles Hirschman's (1958) concept of linkages, where firms are induced to produce things that are needed by primary innovators, or to use their output to produce other commodities.

While innovation characterises core activities, the distinction between core and semi-peripheral industry is clarified by the concepts of *creative* and *adaptive response*. Schumpeter (1947, p. 150) proposes that economies, sectors or firms respond differently to change. Those that do something new make a *creative response* – they utilise new technologies or forms of organisation in ways that substantially increase productivity. Others respond by extending their existing practice, applying more of their existing inputs such as cheap labour. This *adaptive response* enables non-innovators to compete for a time by intensifying workers' efforts, accepting lower rates of profit and lowering wage rates. Creative response is concentrated in core activities (firms, sectors) while semi-peripheries rely on adaptive responses and are, therefore, prone to lower rates of profit, lower wages, lower capital intensity and higher rates of failure or economic stagnation.

Creative and adaptive responses are related to the Marxian concepts of absolute and relative surplus value. Like creative response, relative surplus value refers to a firm's ability to increase its rate of profit by utilising superior production techniques, so that it uses less than average labour to produce a given level of output. Surplus profits accrue to innovating firms within a sector or to whole sectors. Absolute surplus value, on the other hand, refers to firms that increase or maintain a profit rate by increasing the rate of exploitation: extending the working day, increasing the intensity of work or reducing the wage rate. This is clearly an adaptive response. Restricted access to leading-edge technology or to participation in leading sectors may consign peripheral firms to use outmoded technologies or previous innovations. Such *adaptive responses* enable them to survive in certain sectors or even to break into new *semi-peripheral* industrial sectors, albeit with lower profit and wage rates.

Finally, innovation occurs in distribution as well as production. Schumpeter (1939) and Mass and Lazonick (1990) include access to new markets and sources of material supply as important innovations.[8] By distinguishing between factor-using periods of innovative *gestation* and output-increasing periods of innovative *operation*, Schumpeter (1939, pp. 93, 99) underscores the importance of market stability and potential market expansion for extending a firm or agent's horizon.

State activities to protect markets and open up new ones are important, especially where innovation is associated with economies of scale. Bornschier (1992, p. 4) views the state as a producer or protector of innovation, referring to a 'world market for protection', which is a territorially bounded public utility and an element of the national production function. States support innovation and investments by placing their firms within national and global networks of economic transactions that are effectively protected. Hegemony, zones of influence and national protection are all means by which states try to improve the structural environment for innovation.

Sectors or commodities move in and out of 'coreness' as their relationship to centres of innovation and their sites of production change over time. Regional competitors in a single industry may be *core* or *semi-peripheral* according to whether they utilise innovations. Unlike commodity chain approaches, which define as core those nodes that receive higher average rates of profit, innovation explains the causes of surplus profits. Innovative clusters even link across different commodity chains in a region, giving coreness its spatial character.

Innovative core activities are defined in relation not just to less profitable peripheral ones, but also to other core activities. Even if a single sector in a region innovates, it is a *core* activity only if it is connected with other core activities in the region. If such linkages do not occur, the long-term stability of the activity and its ability to consistently produce innovations will be threatened. It will become dependent on outside sources of supply and on outside markets and, in the long run, will either be peripheralised or decline. Isolated local innovators are often absorbed into core firms through acquisition, a process that isolates them even further from their surrounding regional economy or even leads to their removal back to the home country of the new parent firm. Or, where foreign companies set up subsidiaries in a locality, these isolated 'innovative' activities may benefit external regions more than the regions in which they are located (for example, because of profit repatriations).

Capital dependency, externalities and the reproduction of the global hierarchy

How do core penetrations of peripheral regions relate to regional inequality? A debate in the development literature asks whether such penetration retards growth. A *capital-dependency* approach asserts that foreign penetration causes slow growth, sometimes through direct plunder but more often through profit repatriations or the squeezing out of domestic industry. Most empirical studies have found a negative association between the penetration of foreign investment and economic growth (see Bornschier *et al.* 1978; Dixon and Boswell 1996).

Firebaugh (1992) challenges these empirical findings, arguing that observed negative relationships between foreign penetration and economic growth were artefacts of incorrect measurement of foreign investment flows and capital stocks.[9] He also found, however, that domestic investments induced three times more economic growth than foreign investments, possibly because they induced more linkages, spin-offs and local reinvestments.

Dixon and Boswell (1996) respecify Firebaugh's measure of capital penetration and, as in earlier dependency studies, find that foreign penetration depresses economic growth. They explain their findings in terms of *externalities*. While stocks of foreign investments are not harmful of themselves, they are associated with structural changes in domestic economies that harm economic growth. For example, TNCs prefer freer trade where they invest, causing import penetration that threatens the viability of local firms. Dixon and Boswell cite O'Hearn (1989), who shows that the economic growth generated by TNC investments in Ireland between 1955 and 1987 was accompanied by greater free-trade-induced losses in the domestic economy. Foreign penetrations also increase the disarticulation of economies and depress levels of domestic investment.

Disarticulation, overspecialisation and the replacement of indigenous sectors by foreign-controlled ones are consistent themes of this study, through consecutive phases of Irish industrialisation and deindustrialisation from seventeenth-century woollen manufactures to protected industrialisation during the twentieth century.

What am I looking for?

I have proposed several themes about how economic activities may be distributed among regions in a structured global division of labour. Global economic change may have regularities, such as cycles and hegemonic phases. Yet there are uncertainty and variation in how these systemic patterns work out in specific places. Core powers are likely to try to restrict semi-peripheral zones from participating in the most profitable and innovative economic clusters. They may also attempt to redirect subordinate zones toward activities that serve their own global interests. How effectively they do this will depend on the relationship of numerous local factors to core interests. If core powers are effective, a pattern may emerge where local actors attempt to industrialise in contentious economic sectors, only to be redirected into less competitive, non-core activities. Ironically, semi-peripheral attempts to industrialise may actually facilitate *resubordination* by encouraging proletarianisation and breaking up social relations that impede core profitability. Specific outcomes, however, depend on the nature of local alliances, prevailing social organisation, availability of resources, and the nature and strength of the subordinating core/hegemonic project.

Other questions are also important. When or how do semi-peripheral attempts to industrialise conflict with or enhance core intentions? Are certain forms of settler industrialisation more resistant to core attempts to subordinate? Can peripheral 'success' actually invite core attempts to re-subordinate? For example, did Irish settler elites who tried to compete with English cotton manufacturers simultaneously 'invite' English attempts to transform them into factory-based linen capitalists who were, nonetheless, subordinate to English hegemony? Other questions include how core–semi-periphery relations, such as oppression or exploitation, change across time and what these changes imply for subsequent economic change. Is there path dependency in the processes whereby the world-system hierarchy is reproduced? Do disadvantages during one phase spill over into or even increase in subsequent phases?

The following chapters analyse the Irish experience of industrialisation and economic transformation within the Atlantic economy. Chapter 2 analyses English incorporation of Ireland in the sixteenth and seventeenth centuries. It examines the structural and institutional changes that took place in Irish society during the period of *contact periphery* and asks whether they enabled a more rapid phase of *effective incorporation* under the English campaigns of military suppression, plantation, confiscation and settlement. It asks how Irish economic units and activities were transformed, how they acquired labour, what kinds of political authorities were estab-lished to abet the new regime and what kinds of economic infrastructures were developed to enable new economic transactions both within Ireland and between Ireland and the outside world. Special attention is given to the developing English commercial project of the time and how its objective of establishing Atlantic maritime hegemony affected the colonial project in Ireland.

Chapter 3 examines Ireland's peripheralisation within the British-dominated Atlantic system of the seventeenth and eighteenth centuries. It places English policies in Ireland, like the cattle bills and the Wool Acts, in the context of England's broader Atlantic strategy. This first major cycle of Irish industrialisation and industrial transformation began with an attempt to compete in woollen manufactures and ended in England's encouragement of Irish provisions and linen industries. This challenges cruder conceptions of colonialist underdevelopment, yet recognition that linen and provisions were *peripheral* substitutes for *core* woollen manufacturing demonstrates how imperialism restricted Irish development in ways that would have cumulative consequences during subsequent historical phases.

The fourth chapter investigates the second cycle of attempted Irish industrialisation, in cotton manufactures, and its transformation into factory linen production (around Belfast) and peripheral depopulated pasturage (elsewhere). It compares the Irish and British cotton industries to examine how Britain captured and monopolised innovation. It shows how England's advantageous access to raw materials and export markets, which were enabled by its earlier monopolisation of sea power and trade, enabled it to compete in ways that Ireland could not. Moreover, Ireland's resubordination in an unequal free-trading political union with Britain created a dual economy – agrarian periphery and industrial semi-periphery – that created preconditions for the great starvation of the 1840s and the agrarian restructurings that accompanied and followed it, and also presaged the island's partition in the twentieth century.

The next three chapters analyse the third and most recent wave of industrialisation and transformation, in the twentieth century: southern Ireland's disincorporation from British rule, its attempt to industrialise using protectionist policies, and its reincorporation under US hegemony and transnational corporate domination. This compares with the north's economic destruction, as it remained subordinate to a declining British economy. In an analysis that has direct relevance for understanding and resolving the ongoing 'Irish question', I compare the developmental effects of peripheralisation under an ascending core power (the southern Irish case) and a descending post-hegemonic core power (the northern case). The seventh chapter analyses whether Ireland's emergence in the 1990s as a 'Celtic tiger' confirms the possibilities for regions to 'break out' of cumulative 'vicious cycles' of underdevelopment, as Senghaas argues was done by other small European nations in the late nineteenth century. Or, does the coming of the Celtic tiger denote a new cycle of subordination to the Atlantic strategies of the US, with consequences that again limit Ireland's long-term developmental opportunities?

Finally, in chapter 8 I summarise the implications of the Irish case, within a changing Atlantic economy, for our broader understanding of developmental processes. Given the changes that were analysed in the preceding chapters, I examine whether, and under what conditions, it is possible to break out of a peripheralising historical path.

Notes

1   Such global explanations go against recent trends for explaining Ireland. Since the 1950s, Irish economic historians explained Irish underdevelopment primarily as a result of market forces and inadequate Irish responses rather than imperialism (Cullen 1967, 1972). Ó Gráda, hardly a neoliberal, dismisses anti-imperialist analyses of Irish underdevelopment as 'no longer carry[ing] much conviction' (1994, p. 314). Ironically, the same period saw a turn toward a critical sociology of uneven development, but critical approaches barely touched Irish studies, leaving them inwardly obsessed and theoretically barren.

2   One tradition of Marxist development theory running from Lenin through
    (more emphatically) Luxemburg (1951) and Warren (1980) has a similar
    functionalist argument about an ongoing and unstoppable process of prolet-
    arianisation, impelled by the structural 'needs' of capitalist accumulation,
    moving inexorably toward its predestined end of a fully proletarianised
    world which, having no new regions to incorporate or exploit, is transformed
    through revolution.

3   Functionalist explanations are not necessarily wrong, as Wright (1983) shows
    in a reply to Giddens' critique of historical materialism. Functionalist explan-
    ations may be valid if they identify feedback mechanisms which impel a
    system to fulfil certain functions. Classes and class–state alliances, for example,
    construct strategies which aim to increase their abilities to extract surplus
    labour. To the extent that they succeed, the system 'functions' to help them to
    achieve those interests. In the same way, encompassing theories are not
    wrong just because they are functionalist, but they must demonstrate that
    systemic (global) processes are reproduced in localities across time to a
    degree that can explain the regularities they identify in the whole system.
    Moreover, regional or temporal variations should be examined not as threats
    to regularity but as potential sources of system instability and change. Encom-
    passing theories must therefore embed explanations of variation in their
    analyses of system regularity.

4   Unlike McMichael, I prefer the method of incorporating comparison *not*
    because it avoids functionalism but because it is the most appropriate way to
    uncover valid systemic functions and the feedback mechanisms which regu-
    late them. It provides a means to 'test' the system hypotheses generated by
    encompassing approaches such as world-systems, as well as to identify and
    explain variation.

5   Nef (1934, pp. 3–4) notes that the term 'industrial revolution' is misleading
    because equally rapid industrial expansion also took place in earlier periods,
    for example under Elizabeth I and James I.

6   The combination of economic and hegemonic cycles may produce additional
    cycles of war and trade. Krasner (1976) associates hegemony with free trade
    and indirect political control, while he associates war and co-hegemony with
    the reprotection of each co-hegemonist's zone of control (see also Bergesen
    and Schoenberg 1980). Wallerstein incorporates this association into his
    definition of hegemony as 'a situation where the products of a given core
    state are produced so efficiently that they are by and large competitive even in
    other core states, and therefore the given core state will be the primary
    beneficiary of a maximally free world market. Obviously, to take advantage
    of this productive superiority, such a state must be strong enough to prevent
    or minimise the erection of internal and external political barriers to the free
    flow of the factors of production' (1980, p. 38).

7   The association between co-hegemony and national liberation is imperfect.
    The US sometimes used its rising hegemonic power to gain control over
    colonial regions by forcing the former colonial powers out. Sometimes it
    encouraged nationalist movements but it always favoured moderate or col-
    laborationist movements over radical liberation movements. In cases such as
    Zaire, the hegemonic power went so far as to encourage a popular movement

until, having gained advantage over the competing colonial power, it outlived its usefulness and the movement or its threatening leaders were eliminated.

8 Lange (1943, p. 21), on the other hand, excludes market changes from his definition of innovations, which must be output-increasing or factor-saving.

9 More specifically, the effects of flows and stocks of foreign investments have generally been estimated by applying multiple regression analysis to a cross-section of countries for a given time period, where flows are defined as investments over a given period while stocks are defined as the accumulated capital held in foreign hands at the beginning of the period. Defined thus, foreign investment flows and capital stocks are simply the numerator and denominator, respectively, of the foreign investment rate, which is positively associated with economic growth. When the effect (coefficient) of capital stock on economic growth is estimated by multiple regression, the effect of investment flows (the other regressor) is held constant. Thus, with the numerator of the investment rate held constant, a falling foreign capital stock by definition implies a rising investment rate, which is in turn associated positively with economic growth. The negative relationship between foreign capital stock and economic growth, therefore, is a *denominator effect* produced by the fact that such a stock is the denominator of a ratio that has a strong *positive* effect on growth. Firebaugh's argument that the negative impact of capital stocks on economic growth is simply a denominator effect is demonstrated most powerfully by introducing *domestic* investment rates and stocks into the multiple regression. As with the foreign capital stocks, he finds a negative relationship between domestic capital stocks and economic growth. Unless we recognise the problem of misspecification, we are left with the absurd conclusion that both foreign *and domestic* capital stocks hinder economic growth.

Chapter 2

Incorporation and before

Whosoever commands the sea commands the trade; whosoever commands the trade of the world commands the riches of the world, and consequently the world itself.

Walter Raleigh (*History of the World*, 1616)

Irish society

In Ireland today, as in other former colonies, the British have 'plant(ed) deep in the minds of the native population the idea that before the advent of colonialism their history was one which was dominated by barbarism' (Fanon 1968, p. 213). As early as 1187, Gerald of Wales, in his *Topographia Hiberniae*, described the Irish as 'so barbarous that they cannot be said to have any culture'. They were a lazy people who had 'little use for the money-making of towns' and thought that 'the greatest pleasure is not to work and the greatest wealth is to enjoy liberty'. While this last characteristic may raise Irish 'barbarism' above contemporary capitalism, barbarism hardly describes Irish society before colonial incorporation.

People came to Ireland relatively late – probably about 9,000 years ago. By that time the entire length of the Americas had been settled and people had been in southern Britain for 250,000 years. By 6,500 BC Irish stone-toolmakers, possibly migrants from France, technically surpassed any in Britain. About 4,000 BC a more sedentary people came to Ireland with domesticated livestock, stone axes for clearing forests, flint tools for harvesting crops, grindstones (querns) to mill their grains and clay pots in which to cook and eat them. The first significant clearances of Ireland's heavily forested countryside probably began then, both to provide farmlands and to supply wood for economic activities.[1] Irish porcellanite axes were soon produced and traded throughout Ireland, Scotland, England and Wales by people who lived and quarried north of today's Belfast (Sheridan 1986). By 2,500–2,000 BC, the Irish mined copper in counties Cork and Tyrone, tin in the Mourne Mountains, and gold in Tyrone and Antrim. The earliest

28

metal axes are found in far greater number in Ireland than in Britain and other metal tools, weapons and ornaments were also produced.

During the last millennium BC a recognisable *Irish* society formed after the first Celts arrived and spread their language and culture throughout the island. Celts probably controlled major trade and ritual centres so that Irish-speakers gained preferential access to commodities and public rituals. They practised more efficient lowland agricultural techniques, milling their grain with rotary querns and 'outcompeting' native upland cereal farmers (Mallory and McNeill 1991, pp. 171–6).

The Irish population was organised politically in perhaps 100 to 150 *tuatha* (septs), each led by a *ri* (chief).[2] Eventually, mid-level 'kingdoms' exacted tributes from each *tuath* and in turn were in vague suzerainty under an *ard* (high) *ri*. *Tuatha* were divided into four main classes: royal kin, aristocrats, free farmers and bondmen.[3] A hierarchy of professionals – craftsmen, lawyers, clerics and poets – formed a fifth group, whose class location is unclear. The prosperity of a *tuath* depended on the status of its *ri*, which in turn depended on the number of clients (aristocrats and free farmers) he commanded. Lands were divided into commonage and privately held lands, the former providing a source of income for officials and professionals while each free member had a hereditary claim on land. The class relation between *ri* and client was based on granting cattle in return for a rent of produce, surplus beasts and physical labour. Untypically for Europe, clients could under certain conditions terminate their contract with one *ri* and seek a better contract with another. In this way, free commoners could become relatively wealthy, take on their own clients and even be elevated to royal kin after a few generations.[4]

The Celtic economic structure mixed pastoral and arable agriculture. Land and cattle were the basic assets. While Irish climate and soil suited pastoral agriculture (Crotty 1966, p. 70) and elites extended their power by amassing cattle, the system of client rents may have helped maintain arable agriculture. The archaeological record indicates widespread cultivation of barley, oats and wheat (Mallory and McNeill 1991, p. 190). Significant early industries included mining and metallurgy, pottery, and the production of tools, clothing and luxuries (mainly jewellery). According to Crotty (1966, p. 1), however, the Irish system of land tenure emphasised the survival and well-being of the *tuath*, a rationality that did not give way to individualism until after the sixteenth century.

Celtic society was relatively coherent. Mallory and MacNeill (1991) find little provincial differentiation of society or economy. Minor north–south artefactual differences run along a line roughly from Dublin across to Galway Bay, but the overriding archaeological impression is of a coherent culture and economy throughout the island. Likewise, historians note a unity of culture and language throughout the island from the beginning of recorded history. According to the de Paors, early Irish literature had 'a clear concept of Ireland as a nation', a concept as yet undeveloped in continental Europe (1958, p. 19).

Ireland as contact periphery

Ireland's relatively institutionalised social organisation was probably responsible for its remarkable staying power during the early centuries of incorporation. Perhaps the most important and enduring change brought to Irish society by the Christian, Viking and Norman invasions was the introduction of towns in the countryside. The Celts lived in a decentralised pattern reportedly devoid of towns (de Paor and de Paor 1958, p. 32). Although the Normans imposed their rule and extracted plunder through force, the Gaelic system of laws and economy remained largely unchanged, even within much of the Anglo Pale area around today's Dublin (Crotty 1966, p. 2). Edmund Spenser argued in the sixteenth century that Gaelic society was so resilient that it had corrupted previous English settlers, who had lapsed into 'barbarism', a fact that could be reversed only through comprehensive colonisation and severe military action bordering on genocide (Canny and Carpenter 1991, p. 172).

Notwithstanding Gaelic resilience, it is worth considering Hall's (1986) argument that decisive and irreversible changes are made in a contact periphery *despite* the failures of effective incorporation. Ó Cróinín argues that change during 400–1,200 was 'constant, sometimes rapid and often fundamental' (1995, p. 12). From the second century there were regular contacts between Britain and Ireland through trade, shipwrecks and the flight of refugees. Such contacts brought Roman practices and goods to Ireland, including weaponry, money and the written Irish script (*ogham*). Viking invasions (in the ninth and tenth centuries) and Anglo-Norman invasions (in the twelfth century) changed settlement patterns and introduced new forms of money and administration.

Political centralisation was enabled by the meeting of internal political organisation with the early church in Ireland. Gibson (1995, p. 124) argues that an early state form evolved by the twelfth century when Muirchertach Ui Briain of Thomond (Clare) moved his capital outside of his kinship area to Luimneach (Limerick). The new political centre contained an emergent bureaucracy and became the seat of the archbishopric of Munster. Most importantly, the diocesan system of territorial administration was imposed, so that political units were for the first time not co-terminous with *tuatha*. Thus, although church structures emulated the Irish social structure during the first millennium AD, they eventually abetted the establishment of centralised political authorities that would later smooth the way for the imposition of a centralised colonial authority.[5] It is important to note that this centralising process was the contingent result of local reactions to externally imposed institutions.

Norse settlements of the ninth century were confined to coastal entrepôts but they undoubtedly increased the volume of Irish trade and communication with Europe. Gibson (1995, p. 124) argues that Norse settlements introduced new weapons and fighting techniques, such as the use of ships in military campaigns, and that increased exchange may have had a crucial indirect role in promoting Irish state formation.

The Irish themselves did not live in towns until the thirteenth century, yet there was indigenous centralisation of settlements in the form of the *ri*'s homestead, which usually consisted of a ring fort and a church or monastery. By the eleventh century, towns like Armagh combined monastic and secular functions, including small-scale industry, streets, houses and commercial establishments (Mallory and McNeill 1991, pp. 238–42).

The establishment of towns and markets increased considerably during the twelfth to sixteenth centuries as English earls attempted to convert Irish lands into medieval-style estates in order to grow corn for English and continental markets. The Normans slowly expanded their holdings through force until they nominally controlled two-thirds of Irish land in the fourteenth century. Their wooden castles (motte and bailey) were scattered throughout the countryside along with mills, especially in south-eastern Ireland, ruled by agents who acted as military officers, local justices and advisers. Although the native population eventually overcame and Hibernicised these 'old English', Norman institutions and land-use patterns remained. Mallory and McNeill (1991, p. 263) note that Norman mottes often coincide with places that are still centres.[6]

Besides introducing mill-based economic centres, the Normans established towns with market institutions and communities of people 'whose principal source of income was commerce, rather than crafts servicing a monastery or the aristocrats of the area' (Mallory and McNeill 1991, p. 264). Towns had transport infrastructures connecting them to the surrounding hinterland. Coastal towns had harbours that were points of import and export, tying the hinterlands to global markets. Irish hides and wool were important exports to the European continent. Markets in the town centres traded both Irish and foreign goods and created a general marketisation of the island. Wine-filled pots imported from France were followed by French and English craftspeople who taught pot-making and stone masonry to locals. Similar movements of skilled craftspeople featured in later Irish economic change, especially in linen. Although the Norman period was marked by political instability, this had little effect on the new commercial relations or the growth of towns and markets, which undoubtedly laid important foundations for the later effective incorporation of the island by England.

Finally, Tudor political institutions, although restricted to centres like Dublin, were direct forerunners of the political institutions that abetted subsequent English regimes. A dependent Dublin parliament was established and the colonial governor was invented in Ireland in 1172, along with various governor's councils. The four courts (chancery, king's bench, common pleas, exchequer) which Cromwell later re-established as the basis of the peripheral judiciary originated in Tudor Dublin. Tudor offices became the basis of the rural administration of Ireland by the Protestant ascendancy during subsequent centuries of English rule: sheriffs, town magistrates, justices of the peace and other local officials (Quinn 1945).

The emerging Atlantic project and the context of effective incorporation

Despite these changes, Irish land tenure was scarcely influenced by transformations of European economic organisation. During the sixteenth and seventeenth centuries, however, successive waves of violent English conquest transformed the Irish economy and Irish society. Clan members were stripped of their legal right to lands and chieftains were made absolute landowners through a policy called *surrender and regrant*. Lands were confiscated and resettled and power in the towns transformed. This created a highly unequal and ethnically segmented class hierarchy between the native Irish (called today by their predominant religion, Catholics) and settler or absentee English, Anglo-Irish and Scots-Irish (predominantly Protestant). The new system enabled a small ascendancy to seek wealth at the expense of stability for the masses on the land. Wealth was appropriated by introducing new farming techniques and productive organisation and by reducing Irish peasants to tenants and labourers. The ascendancy in Ireland achieved their position *both* through the exploitation of native and settler labour *and* through the marginalisation of large numbers of native Irish, who were banished or impoverished, or emigrated.

For those with political and economic interests in Ireland, subjugation was necessary to clear the way for new colonial projects. For the pious settlers of the sixteenth century (and motivations were not mutually exclusive), the Irish and recusant old Anglo-Irish were subhuman: 'all so universally blinded through corruption of nature, evil bringing up, continual acquaintance and customs of sin that they be void of all knowledge of God ... drowned in idolatry and infidelity with disobedience to God and their prince'; 'worse than horse and mule that have no understanding' (contemporaries quoted in Bradshaw 1978, p. 489). Reforming planters like Edmund Spenser wanted the Irish 'reduced to the point that they would forget their very ancestry and their historical memory' and turn to the modern pursuits of arable agriculture and Protestantism. The English administration in Ireland did use torture, fines, imprisonment and murder to 'reduce the Irish to civility' (Canny and Carpenter 1991, p. 172). Gaelic resistance increased this strategic interest in subjugation. Yet despite appalling state violence, reduction failed at this time, largely because the London government was unwilling to commit the necessary resources to subjugate the Irish fully.[7] Such resources were slowly released as it became clear how important Ireland was to England's emerging Atlantic project. Yet, in this context, the strategy would be to subjugate and transform Ireland, not to 'reduce' it.

In order to explain the character of England's effective incorporation of Ireland during the seventeenth century, one must understand its dominant global economic and political project of the time. This is not to say that England always succeeded in its plans for peripheral regions like Ireland, nor even that its strategies were always consistent. Rather, English policies were consistent and successful *enough* to transform peripheral regions in ways that favoured English economic power and eventual hegemony, while severely constraining peripheral developmental possibilities.

The project that proved so powerful aimed to enhance English economic might by opening up new lines of commerce and stabilising others; this eventually led to England establishing commercial and maritime supremacy over Holland and other European competitors. This project transformed the key axes of world production and trade: spatially, from the Baltics and East Indies to North America and the Levant; and sectorally, from exports of traditional textiles to exports of new textiles and imports of new industrial raw materials. This also involved a transition from one dominant class to another.

English global expansion began before the seventeenth century with the rise of a class of merchant adventurers who formed the great joint stock companies along the lines of the Dutch. Yet Brenner (1993) identifies an emerging English coalition of *new merchants* in the early seventeenth century who consolidated their power from the 1620s, pushed the legislative revolution of 1641 and, eventually, emerged victorious in the establishment of the Commonwealth, the reconstruction of English naval supremacy, the defeat of Dutch hegemony and the construction of an integrated global division of labour centred in the British empire and co-ordinated by English commerce. The coalition consisted of colonial, interloping merchants, domestic traders, shopkeepers and artisans. Most of the new merchants were involved in the Atlantic trade and opposed the older English monopolies like the East India Company. They used the City of London's political, financial and military resources to achieve their programme in an uneasy coalition with parliament against the crown. Their economic interests – for naval power in the new Atlantic trade routes, against prohibitive crown customs and taxes, and against the commercial barriers maintained by trading monopolies and the City's old order – were strengthened by their ideological organisation in London's independent Puritan churches. As the coalition's power developed, it engaged in semi-privatised commercio-military adventures of imperial conquest in Ireland and the Caribbean, and against the trading monopolies through an East Indian interloping venture. Simultaneously, they pushed for parliamentary supremacy against the king.

In 1648–49 the coalition established the Commonwealth. Their aims, elaborated in works like those of the London political independent Hugh Peter,[8] gave extraordinary prominence to the long-term strategic interests of English commerce. Their first priority was to invade Ireland to 'teach the peasants liberty', thereby suppressing them as a hostile force while bringing Irish resources into English hands. Ultimately, this gave them the necessary control to transform Irish economic activities and make them more compatible with English imperial interests. In the shorter term, Irish conquest united Presbyterians and political independents in their common interest of sharing out Irish lands.

A second strategic problem was the nature of hegemony. One option was a pan north European Protestant alliance, led by a strong English navy.[9] This would unite the north European Protestant powers against their southern Catholic rivals. Failing such a coalition, which depended on the Dutch accepting second place in a British-led global regime, the English state would attempt singular hegemony. In either scenario, building English naval power to establish and control commercial sea routes would be the top priority.

On the other side of the Atlantic and further abroad, a large-scale imperialist campaign involved a two-pronged attack on the West and East Indies. According to Hugh Peter, Protestant imperial warfare would have long since occupied England's energies 'were we not more effeminate than our predecessors in Queen Elizabeth's time.... I must confess I am divided between Ireland and the Palatinate, only I quiet myself in this that we may do both' (quoted in Brenner 1993, p. 506). Once the Commonwealth was established, Peter pleaded in *A Word for the Armie* 'that the work of Ireland may not thus still be made a mock work, but that the business be carried on strenuously and vigorously by men to be confided [in]'. He also called on the state to renew its imperial action in the Americas to establish full control of the trade routes between the West Indies and Europe.

The Commonwealth was extremely successful in commerce, military/ naval consolidation and diplomacy because its leaders saw a direct connection between their domestic political interests and overseas commercio-military power. According to Brenner (1993, p. 580), 'government support for commercial development tended, under the Commonwealth, to be raised almost to the level of a principle'.

The Commonwealth's first military project was the subjection of Ireland in 1649–50. The aim was ostensibly to wipe out 'royalist privateers' but Brenner (1993, p. 581) contends that the Irish campaign was a first step in a process whereby the Commonwealth 'was increasingly able to frame objectives for its naval campaigns against the royalists that furthered not only the immediate military defence of the new state, *but also the improvement of conditions for the pursuit of commerce*' (my emphasis). Operations initially designed for defence were turned toward commercial expansion and maritime hegemony. Since royalist privateers had succeeded in partially paralysing English trade, the struggle against them was also a struggle to control commerce on the seas. In this respect, the Irish campaign can be placed alongside Penn and Blake's naval campaigns against Portuguese and French privateers to reopen English trade routes, ending in the humiliating peace terms which forced Portugal to open its colonies to English trade, gave England use of Spanish ports throughout the Mediterranean and generally showed by example what happens to those who hindered English commerce.

The campaign for commercial supremacy was led by a reorganised parliamentary navy which commanded the support of almost all royal navy officers, along with their ships. Traders with American dominated the Commons Committee which oversaw finance and expansion of the naval fleet. Besides financing the navy through a new customs commission, the regime regularly hired private armed merchant vessels from new merchants.

Once the regime defeated the royalists at sea in 1650, it turned its full attention to commerce. This meant bringing back into English commerce the American colonists who, alienated by English customs laws, attempted to disincorporate during the English wars. This partial disincorporation provided an opportunity for the new merchants, since it swept away political royalism in the North American colonies. There and in the West Indies, old customs and trading systems were replaced by a new trading regime more fitting to the requirements of the new merchants. It was here that English navigation law came into prominence, culminating in the famous Navigation Acts.[10]

The act of 3 October 1650, intended to enhance English merchant hegemony throughout the British empire, forbade 'all ships of any foreign nation whatsoever, to come to, or trade in, or traffic with any of the English plantations in America, or any islands or places thereof, which are planted by and in possession of this Commonwealth, without licence first had from the Parliament and Council of State'. The act was aimed not just at the Dutch but also at royals and other competitors from within the empire.

Merchant activities in the Americas followed a pattern already tested in Ireland and the West Indies during the 1640s: new merchants requested permission to suppress colonial revolt and subjugate a colony, followed by land grants and rights to trade there. By 1652 royalist revolts were suppressed throughout the colonies, the Dutch were excluded from colonial trade and parliamentary commissions were established to ensure good conditions for merchant-led colonial 'development' (Brenner 1993, pp. 597–8).

These new regimes changed the nature of trade. Previous English trade was primarily bilateral, dominated by cloth-exporting merchant adventurers, and English customs were designed to raise money for the crown while protecting merchant monopolies. The new traders, however, set up multilateral (triangular) trades involving wider varieties of goods. Customs on re-exports were seen as unacceptable restraints of trade. Re-exporting Dutch middlemen were viewed as parasites who profited from merchants. This new attitude realigned imperial policies in individual colonies because it sent the merchants and the English state on an empire-wide hunt for new sources of critical materials. In Ireland, the most important of these would be naval provisions and linen.

The acute necessity of bringing supplies into the empire was increased by events of the mid-seventeenth century. During long periods of war, the Dutch used their competitive advantages in shipping and their customs-free entrepôt in Amsterdam to eliminate English competition and recapture near-monopolies of crucial re-export trades, most notably of Baltic raw materials. The Dutch also made inroads in the Americas and retained their dominant position in the East Indies. After the peace between Holland and Spain, Dutch competition encroached on all the dynamic trades that England had developed since Elizabeth. Overcoming Dutch competition was thus at the top of the Commonwealth's policy-making agenda.

It would be a mistake, however, to conclude from the persistent use of private armies and adventurers that the English state was unimportant in the new regime. The reorganisation of English commerce and, eventually, the erection of English hegemony required state intervention to organise the economy, protect English trade and shipping, and ultimately to destroy Dutch competition through war. A national coalition of class and state interests emerged where, for the first time, English fiscal policies aimed to serve commerce rather than vice versa. Moreover, new merchant commercial needs corresponded to 'national commercial needs' in a way that monopoly trade interests had not. In short, national policy was now commercial policy.

If anything, the Commonwealth government learned that the 'secret of commercial success – as revealed by the Dutch example – [was] the state's systematic support of trade' (Brenner 1993, p. 627). As Benjamin Worsley noted in *The Advocate* (1651), 'it is by trade, and the due ordering and governing of it [by the state] and by no other means that wealth and shipping can ... be increased and upheld, and consequently by no other [means] that the power of any nation can be sustained by land or sea, it not being possible ... for any nation ... to make itself powerful in either of these without trade or a thorough inspection into trade and the course of it'. The Dutch had achieved competitive advantages not just by building better ships but also by state management and direction of trade, protection of merchant fleets and willingness to forego customs revenues to keep shipping costs low. The Dutch government also used selective protection to encourage Dutch manufactures and to manage which foreign commodities were imported and which were discouraged (Brenner 1993, p. 627).

The mid-seventeenth-century transition of the English class structure thoroughly changed English commerce and commercial policy, which in turn affected regional economic, political and social structures world-wide. Some changes were direct: the subjugation of Ireland or the West Indies through war and plunder, and the subsequent forceful changes in their land tenancy, markets, legal regimes and other social structures. Other changes were more indirect. Policies like the Navigation Acts were intended primarily to achieve hegemonic ends like outcompeting the Dutch. Nonetheless, they deeply affected local political economies. On the other hand, while English hegemonic competition required defeating the Dutch, this in turn required improved material supply and market networks that could be attained only by subjugating imperial colonies.

Effective incorporation

How, then, did England's drive for commercial superiority and hegemony affect Irish economic change? Following Wallerstein (1988), key moments of incorporation and peripheralisation can be classified into four categories: transforming the key economic units of countryside and town, finding new ways to acquire and control labour, creating supportive institutions of public authority, and establishing commercial infrastructures.

New economic units in countryside and town

Ireland's fluid land tenure relations resisted invasions because they efficiently provided pastoral subsistence. They finally began to break down in the sixteenth century, when English fears that continental rivals might attack through Ireland induced Henry VIII to resurrect a policy of subjugation. Hegemonic conflicts in the developing European state system thus raised Ireland's importance in English eyes. England first tried to transform Irish *ri* and Norman landholders to feudal landlords by confiscating former clan lands and regranting them with private title. Several historians contend that this policy's failure disabused English regimes of the notion that the Irish could be cajoled into complying with English law (Bottigheimer 1971).

If the Irish would not comply, then the alternative was to import a loyal population. Anglicising Ireland became the aim of Elizabeth's conquest, beginning with a 1556 project to confiscate all lands in counties Laois and Offaly and plant them with new English settlers. Indigenous resistance brought more anti-Irish terms of plantation, demanding adherence to English language, manners, customs and dress and prohibiting intermarriage between settlers and Irish.

Plantation met two problems which would hound English control of Ireland for centuries. First, the indigenous Irish resisted it. Second, most suitable English planters considered settling in Ireland to be too risky and the returns too low. Although the first plantation was largely a failure, further schemes followed. In the late 1560s young West Country Englishmen like Walter Raleigh, Humphrey Gilbert and Richard Grenville came to the southern province of Munster to seek opportunity. Raleigh's case suggests that westward movement to Ireland was part of a broader English expansion into the Atlantic, which would soon become the heart of British global hegemony. One planter, Peter Carew, claimed two million acres (5–10 per cent of all the land of Ireland) in counties Carlow, Cork, Kerry and Waterford. Such wild claims, backed by the English state, became a foundation of the use of English law to devastate customary Irish tenure. Yet such titles were insecure due to Irish resistance. The Desmond rebellions (1569–1583) and O'Neill rebellion (1594–1603) spread throughout Ireland and were put down only by Elizabeth's policy of scorched earth and mass murder. According to Mountjoy, who devastated Ulster in his war against the Irish under Hugh O'Neill, 'when plough and breeding of cattle shall cease, then will the rebellion end' (quoted by Foster 1988, p. 34).

Military defeat of the rebels did not achieve security. For this purpose the English required a more significant transformation of the Irish class structure and an effective and loyal state administration. Rebellion, however, became the rationale for English confiscation of Irish land. When the Desmond rebels were convicted of treason, the crown confiscated 574,645 acres of their land, which Elizabeth then gave to Scottish soldiers who took part in Ulster's pacification. Horsemen were each granted 400 acres of conquered Irish land and foot soldiers 200 acres (Bottigheimer 1971, pp. 10, 14). Over time, the definition of Irish 'guilt' expanded to fit English desires to confiscate new lands. After the Desmond rebellion, repeated calls were made to remove the native Irish from Munster and replace them with English settlers.

Labour acquisition, however, remained the major problem with such schemes. Plantation rules barred settlers from allowing Irish tenants on the confiscated lands but English colonists were unwilling to emigrate in adequate numbers. Colonists like Raleigh hired cheap and plentiful Irish labour to work their large estates. As a result, the Munster plantation shrank to about a third of its original size and was then virtually swept away by the 1598 rebellion. Rabid colonialists like Edmund Spenser complained that colonists who hired Irish labourers 'thrust out the English' and he suggested that the native population should be eliminated. But Spenser had no workable alternatives for accessing labour.

As the O'Neill rebellion ended with the abject surrender of the last Irish *ri* in Ulster, Scottish planters intensified their colonisation. Still advocating colonisation on the cheap, Elizabeth's Ulster plantation was organised and financed by the City of London. Moody (1939) and Bottigheimer (1971, p. 22) argue that, unlike North America, where corporations willingly pursued profit, the crown foisted Irish projects on the City. Nonetheless, the Irish projects in time became important to the wider profitability of the Atlantic project, including the Americas. In the meantime, conflict between crown and commerce culminated in the Star Chamber proceedings of 1633–35, which fined the City and withdrew its Irish charter over charges of profiteering.

Conditions in England changed, however, with the rise of an independent parliament and a coalition of new merchants and puritans. Their desires to confiscate more Irish lands were not served by the absence of rebellion, so new excuses were made for confiscation. Not surprisingly, this provoked fresh rebellion. Where earlier plantations took mainly Celtic lands, Anglo-Irish lands were confiscated in the 1630s. This laid the conditions for their coalition with the native Irish and, eventually, for rebellion in 1641. In a familiar escalation, the English reacted to rebellion with further subjection.

By the 1640s the emergence of an English hegemonic project made Ireland important enough to warrant wholesale subjection. After centuries as a contact periphery, Ireland was incorporated in a surprisingly short period. Between 1640 and 1688, the share of Irish land held by the Scottish and English nearly doubled from 41 per cent to 78 per cent, an increment of seven million acres, which laid the foundation for a new Protestant ascendancy (Bottigheimer 1971, p. 3). Most of this revolution took place during 1652–60, under acts of 1652 and 1653 that followed Cromwell's campaign.

By all accounts the Irish rebellion of 1641 was unexpected in England (Trevor-Roper 1964, p. 96). It was concentrated in Ulster and, since hostilities were initially aimed at Protestant settlers, the English parliament was not overly concerned. Crown and parliament were preoccupied with their own disputes and Pym, the puritan parliamentary leader, reportedly was prepared to sacrifice Irish Protestants to the general interests of English reform. Even a flood of publicity about atrocities against Protestant settlers (many of which were fabricated) failed to move parliament. English indecision was increased by difficulties in raising men to fight in Ireland: Ulster was already heavily settled and had little available land to confiscate as payment for adventure.

But the alliance of the southern Anglo-Irish gentry in rebellion brought new lands into the conflict that were ripe for confiscation. London merchants, some with estates in Ireland, offered to finance actions against the Irish in return for Irish lands and commercial opportunities. In December 1641, parliament presented a 'grand remonstrance' to the king, stating that the rebellions were part of a Papist conspiracy throughout the islands. In February 1642 London merchants offered to 'reduce' Ireland with their own money on four conditions: the right to name their own officers, power to enlist soldiers and to impress if necessary, state supply of arms and ammunition, and satisfaction out of the rebels' estates.

The king assented with an act for the 'speedy and effectual reducing' of the Irish rebels. To satisfy the fourth condition, he promised a fifth of

Ireland's total acreage. Although rebellion was largely confined to the north and east, land was to be confiscated equally from each of the four provinces, thus holding all Irish equally 'guilty'. The act provided that four to twelve shillings of adventure would buy an acre, depending on the quality of land. Two and a half million Irish acres were to secure a million pounds of adventure. The merchants justified this with the dubious claim that Irish owners still held ten million acres, of which they were only asking a fourth (Bottigheimer 1971, pp. 43, 49).

In mid-April, parliament sanctioned the 'Additional Sea Adventure', under which fifteen named Londoners (mainly merchants) mounted an expedition to 'take, surprise, vanquish, destroy, or kill' any Irish rebels they encountered and to destroy rebel shipping. The promoters organised the expedition privately and handpicked the officers. Most of the 171 adventurers were the same colonial interlopers and City militants who backed North American adventures (Brenner 1993). Simultaneously with the Irish adventure, they financed an impressive venture to wrest control of the West Indies from the Spanish.

Within two weeks of parliamentary approval, the merchants mobilised 1,000 foot soldiers, 500 seamen and 15 ships for six months of private plunder in Ireland. By its random violence the adventure probably brought more Irish into resistance than it suppressed. Yet it demonstrated the ability of the new merchant alliance to mobilise men, money and materials for further Irish adventures. The presence of parliamentarians like Oliver Cromwell indicated that the coalition could articulate an imperialist ideology based on material interest, anti-royalism and independent Puritanism.

Habakkuk (1962) sees the adventure as the germ of Cromwell's claim on Ireland because it initiated a state debt that could be repaid only with Irish land. After this, the English project explicitly aimed not just to conquer Ireland but also to confiscate its lands. The part to be confiscated grew not only with the costs of suppressing Ireland but also with the rising costs of the English civil war. As the debts of the Commonwealth rose, claims on Irish land became so big that wholesale confiscations were necessary and a negotiated settlement with the Irish resistance became impossible. Apart from adventurers, over 40,000 unpaid troops served the English parliament in Ireland, which thereby accumulated an additional debt that would have to be paid in land. Eventually, in the words of the royalist Edward Hyde, 'Ireland was the great capital out of which all debts were paid, all services rewarded, and all acts of bounty performed' (Brenner 1993, p. 401).

The Irish adventure was primarily a big commercial venture by expansionary merchants. Irish land, obtained through adventure at eight shillings per acre, was absurdly underpriced. Thus, adventure not only solved the problem of subjugating Ireland within the emerging Atlantic economy, but it did so at a handsome profit. English and Scottish adventurers and soldiers became the new colonial class in Ireland.[11] Adventurers lent the

English state £306,718 for Irish campaigns, three times the amount invested in Irish plantations and more than any contemporary English colonial project save the East India Company (Rabb 1967, p. 66). Bottigheimer calculates that 750 of 1,533 adventurer investors were from London, providing two-thirds of the £258,000 raised under the original act of 1642; three-fifths of the £43,000 pounds raised under the Sea Ordinance of 1642; and nine-tenths of the money raised under the Doubling Act of 1643. Of the 928 adventurers whose vocation is listed, 689 were 'merchant or urban' (Bottigheimer 1971, p. 65).[12] In terms of direct political power, eighty present and future members of parliament – mostly independents – subscribed to the adventure (MacCormack 1956, p. 33).

As the Irish interests of the adventurers increased, negotiated peace became impossible. The adventurers pressed Cromwell to intensify the war because they feared that their lands would be devalued by the time they got them. To speed up the conquest, soldiers were promised even more Irish lands, but at a level that remained constant regardless of how long the war went on (Bottigheimer 1971, p. 96). Cromwell accomplished quick conquest by a mass terror campaign between August 1649 and May 1650. He accepted no limit to the amount of Irish land that would be confiscated to pay off the costs of conquest. By the end of the campaign, Irish lands were promised to 1,500 adventurers, who had invested £360,000, and 35,000 soldiers, who were owed £1,500,000 in back pay. William Petty's survey shows that Cromwell confiscated eleven million of twenty million acres in Ireland,[13] more than three times the amount envisaged in the original act. Barony tables list 1,043 adventurers, mostly London merchants, who were given average holdings of 1,100 English acres.[14] One merchant, Thomas Vincent, received 19,000 of the best acres in Leinster, double the size of the biggest estate under Elizabeth's plantation (Bottigheimer 1971, pp. 139–40).

The English incorporation of Irish land was completed after 1689, when William III defeated the Jacobites in the western front of England's European war. For a decade after the Williamite victory, those who had failed to explicitly support William were indicted for 'high treason' and their lands were summarily confiscated and transferred to settlers (Simms 1956, p. 193). Estimates of Irish lands still in Catholic hands after the Williamite settlement range from a fifteenth (Butler 1917, p. 202) to a seventh (Simms 1956). Soon thereafter, penal laws decreased native landholdings further still.

In summary, the second half of the seventeenth century saw an astounding transformation of Irish land ownership. The Catholic share of land fell from 59 per cent in 1641 to 22 per cent in 1688, 14 per cent in 1703 and 5 per cent by 1776. Catholics lost six million of the six and a half million profitable Irish acres they owned in 1641. This massive forced transfer was the final episode in a longer process of transforming Ireland's Gaelic society and economy into one that was more amenable to the emerging England-centred Atlantic project. Confiscations installed a new aristocracy on the island that was sympathetic to the expansionary English commercial project. But this project required more than the transformation of land ownership. New landowners required ways of acquiring, shedding and controlling labour. The whole project required new commercial and political structures to abet further transformations and limitations of Irish economic activities.

Acquisition and control of labour

The average adventurer held 700 acres after Cromwell's settlement. Even under pasturage, such estates required substantial numbers of workers and few English were queuing to settle them. In 1652 the English government proposed that settled areas must be cleared of Irish and an act of that year established categories of Irish guilt for rebellion. An act of 1653 banished all indigenous Irish, whether innocent or 'guilty', to the barren lands west of the Shannon River. Yet most adventurers desired cheap Irish labourers, who would pay higher rents than English settlers. Many stayed east of the Shannon to work the estates of the new owners. Retaining Irish tenants provided an informal solution to the problem of acquiring labour but, given the obvious potential of such an uneven relationship for resistance, this 'solution' would provide the most abiding problem for English control of Ireland.

Over time, labour problems emerged and re-emerged. Forms of labour control varied as regions experienced different histories of industrialisation, deindustrialisation, industrial transformation and class struggle. These changes will be analysed in subsequent chapters. Incorporation itself, however, established a regional pattern. Regions where colonial settlement failed were marked by absentee ownership, rack renting (the insertion of middlemen between lord and tenant, each driving up the tenant's final rent), insecurity of tenure, disincentives to improvement and small-plot subsistence centred on the potato. Regions where settlement was more successful developed semi-proletarian domestic forms of production which combined subsistence production of foodstuffs and industrial raw materials (flax and wool) with textile production. Throughout the island, incorporation launched a system of forced emigration, which became a means of shedding surplus labour even while rural underemployment depressed wages and incomes.[15]

Public administration: the creation of an aiding and abetting authority

The institutional pillar of Ireland's political incorporation under England was the replacement of native *brehon* law by English law. This process began in the Pale in the twelfth century but only in the seventeenth was the island divided into counties, with English courts and judges, and *brehon* law declared illegal. Even then, martial law, if any English law, administered most of the island until Cromwell extended administrative institutions throughout the island and strengthened offices, which were filled by Commonwealth supporters. Revenue commissioners were recruited from the ranks of soldiers and recent settlers and given wide-ranging powers to collect taxes and enforce laws, especially those that punished the native Irish. Justices of the peace were reinstated as the main officers of local civil law. The four courts were re-established in 1655 and competing regional courts dissolved.[16] The court of chancery confirmed the registration of confiscated properties, thus validating the new private property relations of the Protestant ascendancy. New judges and barristers from England were appointed to extend law enforcement throughout the island. English replaced Irish as the sole language of law and administration (Barnard 1979, pp. 281–2).

Since most historians of the Elizabethan and Cromwellian periods have emphasised the transformation of Irish agrarian society, few have analysed the transformation of Irish towns. Yet the removal of Catholic merchants and their attempted replacement by Protestants had crucial consequences on subsequent Irish class structure and economic change. Elizabeth used plantation towns to extend English authority in Ireland. Town patrons were given grants, along with powers to hold markets, fairs and courts and to retain their profits (Hunter 1971, pp. 41, 48–9). Schemes to attract tradespeople and merchants had limited success. Local government in these plantation towns was in the hands of a small, self-electing group who made byelaws, set up civil courts, imposed fines and punishments and sent members to the Dublin parliament. Yet these towns grew only slowly, because the English lacked administrative commitment to them.

Pre-plantation towns, on the other hand, were stronger and grew more organically. They were centres of local government, military defence, trade and commerce. They already had systems of administration and commerce, including courts, justices of the peace and local political institutions centred on corporate guilds. Apart from Protestant-dominated Dublin and Belfast, however, most towns were dominated by political 'unreliables' like the indigenous Irish and old Anglo-Irish Catholics. Catholics controlled administration and commerce in Cork, Galway, Waterford, Kilkenny and Limerick.[17]

Cromwell transferred urban economic and political power to more 'reliable' citizens. He not only barred Catholics from local government and merchant trades, he also physically removed them from Irish towns. Special byelaws disenfranchised anyone who spoke Irish or did not attend Protestant worship. Citizens who used Irish dress, language and other customs were subject to harsh and degrading punishment. Many were expelled and even shipped to the West Indies. Their houses and properties were confiscated and given to Protestants. Attempts were made to bring settlers to towns and by 1660, according to a contemporary source, 'the corporate towns [were] mostly inhabited by English and Protestants and governed by them, whereas before the war, it was difficult for a Protestant to get office in any town' (quoted in Barnard 1979, p. 67). Corporations and guilds were given extended power over economic and political life. They controlled local trade and enforced laws concerning public health, apprenticeship, weights and measures, and poor relief. Later, penal laws completed the process of turning the indigenous population into non-citizens. Acts of 1695 and 1704 disarmed Catholics; forbade them to go abroad for schooling; forbade their ownership of horses over a certain value; banished Catholic clergy; consolidated the exclusion of the native Irish from property and professions; and created sacramental tests and oaths of allegiance for public office. Foster (1988, p. 153) maintains that penalisation of the native Irish was the 'foundation of the ascendancy' because it removed their claims to property or position.

As in the countryside, however, the English found it difficult to attract Protestant merchants and tradespeople. Cromwell's close financial supporter Martin Noel was granted 200 houses in Wexford, where he established a lucrative preserving business and gained further wealth as a customs farmer. But such men were rare and most towns found themselves lacking in commerce and trade. Barnard cites evidence that the modal town settler was a failed English businessman who sought new opportunity in Ireland. A contemporary dismissed Galway's settlers as 'a few mechanick barbers and taylers' and 'mean persons unfit to carry on the trade of soe great a porte' (Barnard 1979, pp. 57, 59, 60).

This is not to say that the settlers were incapable of maintaining urban power. Although some Catholics side-stepped the law, Protestant councils regularly enacted new byelaws to expel them. Later, when James II threatened to reverse the Protestant monopoly of municipal power, settler resistance was a key factor in his overthrow. Protestant power in the towns is indicated by the fact that electors returned only one Catholic to the restored Irish House of Commons of 1661. Barnard (1979, p. 71) claims that Protestant domination of Irish borough governments became one of the most enduring Cromwellian legacies in Ireland.

The installation of Protestants in positions of urban power and commerce was essential to English attempts to create reliable local authorities. The removal of Catholics from Irish towns contributed to an equally important goal: the destruction of independent economic structures, making Ireland more dependent on England's core economy. Before Cromwell, Catholic merchants controlled Ireland's small merchant fleet and dominated a dynamic trade with Europe and the Americas. Galway merchants, for instance, had considerable trade with Spain, Portugal, France and the West Indies.

The removal of these contacts increased Ireland's dependence on trade with England and it reduced English fears that continental incursions would follow trade. Most importantly for Ireland's long-term development, Cromwell practically obliterated its equivalent of the English new merchant class and the exclusion of native Irish from merchant and industrial activities was copper-fastened by penal laws. Along with the trade and shipping restrictions of the Navigation Acts, the destruction of the indigenous Irish merchant class, a rather invisible episode in Irish colonial history, created a negative path dependence that severely reduced its long-term development options and capabilities.

Finally, Cromwellian policies centralised political and economic life in Dublin. Smaller towns which could not sufficiently replace their Catholic middle classes declined. Dublin's centrality increased as Irish trade and production became more dependent on and subordinate to England.[18] Administration, law, education and other state functions were increasingly concentrated there. Thus, Dublin became a point of intermediation between the English core and the peripheral Irish countryside, a centre of import–export trade as well as law, administration and taxation.

The creation of an abetting authority was not without contradiction. As with any white settler administration, there were inherent conflicts between competing groups of settlers and between the settlers and their associated core power. Acts aimed at Catholics also excluded northern Dissenters from corporation offices. As the numbers of Dissenters in Ulster swelled, this exclusion became a basis of northern anti-systemic movements during the eighteenth century (Foster 1988, p. 157; Clark and Donnelly 1983).

Another conflict involved the settlers' legislative independence. The erosion of settler claims to legislative independence after 1660 culminated in the 1720 Act for Better Securing the Dependency of Ireland, which abolished the Irish House of Lords' right of appellate jurisdiction, thus making Ireland a fully dependent colony of England. This became a major bone of contention between the settler ascendancy and the English core later in the century, and led to new claims of legislative independence when English rule was weakened by the North American War of Independence.

Institutional infrastructures: international commerce and the Navigation Acts

Irish property relations and state institutions were bilateral matters involving Ireland and England. Incorporating Ireland into the Atlantic-based *world* economy required its integration into multilateral institutions. New international economic and political infrastructures governed who traded what with whom and in whose vessels.

The seventeenth century was a period of emerging British control of the seas, especially transatlantic commerce, by direct military force and through regulatory infrastructures like the Navigation Acts. These acts did not greatly affect Ireland's trade outside the empire. Under the first acts, Irish ships and seamen were even considered 'English' with respect to coastal trade and imports from outside the empire (with the crucial exceptions of Holland and Germany). Irish continental trade was damaged more by the destruction of its traditional commercial classes, with their European trade contacts, than by law. The major intent of the acts with respect to Ireland was to restrict and channel its trade with the empire (just as the acts were meant to broadly regulate global trade affecting the empire).

English merchants resisted Ireland's status under the act of 1660 as a place to which enumerated colonial goods could be sent directly. Thus, acts of 1663, 1670 and 1671 excluded Ireland from trading directly with the American plantations for enumerated products including cotton-wool, indigoes, sugar, tobacco, coffee, coconuts, silks, hides, skins and many other items – in short, 'practically ... all commodities exported from the plantations' (Murray 1903, p. 43). This made Irish export trades less attractive because Irish merchants could not directly import plantation goods in return. After further pressure from English merchants, acts of 1696 excluded even non-enumerated colonial goods from direct import into Ireland. These laws were primarily intended to restrict English imports of East Indian silks and calicoes and to restrain the emerging Irish woollen industry.

At their broadest level, the Navigation Acts were meant to restrict foreign (especially Dutch) competition in commerce on the high seas, a key to achieving global hegemony (Modelski and Thompson 1988). Harper (1939) argued that the major effect of the Navigation Acts was to exclude Dutch shipping from the English plantation trades. Before 1660, the Dutch entrepôt carried out much of that trade, but the 1660 act enumerated nearly all of the goods that the Dutch could carry profitably. Consequently, Harper finds almost no mention of Dutch vessels arriving at empire ports from anywhere other than Holland after that date. English records are corroborated by Danish records of ships passing the Øresund. 'The decline in Dutch entries', writes Harper, 'is accompanied by an increase in England's ships and in those of the other countries with which she traded' (1939, p. 300). English shipping also gained considerably in its share of the trade with Holland.

British naval and merchant marine domination increased over the century following the acts. By the beginning of the North American War of Independence, 3,730 of the 7,694 ships trading in Britain were built in Britain, 199 in Ireland, 2,342 in the thirteen colonies, 163 in other colonies, and 1,260 in foreign countries (Harper 1939, p. 361). Ships from other colonies and foreign countries accounted for only 18 per cent of ships trading in Britain.

Ireland's merchant marine declined after the sixteenth century owing to the twin damages of core sea domination and the decimation of Ireland's native merchant class. Irish ships were originally replaced by Dutch ships, which dominated Irish trade until the 1660s. By 1698, however, the Dutch were replaced by English ships. Out of 120,728 tons of recorded Irish trade, 21,532 tons (17.8 per cent) were carried in Irish ships, 76,044 (63.0 per cent) in English ships and 23,152 (19.2 per cent) in foreign vessels (Harper 1939, p. 283). Also by this time, the bulk of Irish trade was with England rather than the continent, and was restricted by British limitations on Irish exports (see chapter 3).

Neoclassical economic historians like Cullen (1972) argue that state policies had little to do with the decline of Irish shipping and the rise of British sea power. Yet there is compelling evidence that the Navigation Acts were effective. Irish customs officials may have been relatively lax in enforcing the laws, because of their initial ambiguity but also because questionable plantation trades brought them high revenues. Yet special English commissions and officials enforced the laws and seized offending ships and assets. Irish resistance was reportedly significant when the acts were changed in 1670/71 to disallow direct Irish trade. But Harper claims that 'vigorous efforts' stamped out most illegal trade. As early as 1673, the English Lord Treasurer sent agents to the Isle of Man and Ireland to 'prevent abuses in the Plantation Trade' and enforce the new act. In 1678–81 alone, more than 100 vessels were seized for illegal direct trading to Ireland and nearly 100 admiralty trials were held concerning illegal trade between Ireland and America. By 1682, the Treasury claimed that violations of restrictions on direct trade were 'a mere nuisance' (Harper 1939, pp. 117, 155, 261). Further evidence of enforcement of the acts are numerous recorded cases of ships seized for illegally unloading in Ireland, merchants who were impoverished by penalties for illegal import trade, legitimate traders who had great difficulty getting around restrictions, and so on (Harper 1939, pp. 119, 123, 128, 152).

One might conclude that these cases prove the size of the smuggling trade. Cullen (1972, p. 18) asserts that there was 'widespread evasion', but gives no hard evidence. Yet Lee (1981) finds that smuggling has been vastly overestimated. Harper (1939, p. 248) argues that most recorded smuggling cases were marginal infringements concerning interpretation of the acts rather than real smuggling.

The acts surely damaged the competitiveness of incipient Irish industries during the century following their enactment. Vessels that stopped in England before continuing to Ireland, in compliance with the laws, faced significant additional transactions costs. A typical ship that entered port in Bristol, for instance, lost 5 per cent of its earnings in payments to enter and clear for pilotage, mayor's dues, reporting and clearing at the custom house, lights, anchorage and moorage, surveyors and so on. Another 2 per cent went on commission for the English factor. But extra transactions costs were only one price of the requirement to enter goods first in England. Seamen regularly complained that favourable winds could shift during an English stop (Harper 1939, p. 246). Alternatively, smuggling was expensive given the high losses of ships and goods to British enforcement of the acts.

en insists that the Navigation Acts were not problematic for
ise they 'were a grievance to the Irish merchant rather than to
' (Cullen 1972, pp. 38, 18). Since Cullen's only evidence is
.h imports of tobacco and sugar (by law, through England),
...s conclusions appear to be an ideological denial that state actions can
effectively reverse market-determined outcomes. His throwaway admission
on merchants, however, is telling because English policy caused major long-
term damage to Irish developmental prospects *precisely* through its distortion
of Irish class formation. Irish merchants, who were restricted in their ability
to import, surely lost motivation to export. The costs of directly exporting
in indigenous ships was prohibitive without the ability to take on imports
for return journeys. Without exports, a central motor for developing industry
and increasing the productivity of labour is removed, especially from an
island economy with a small internal market. The Navigation Acts thus
took trade and shipping out of the hands of Irish merchants and gave them
to the English merchant class, limiting Ireland's development potentials as
they enhanced the class power of a driving force of English capitalism.

But another crucial point must be emphasised. The *exceptions* to the
Navigation Acts affected Irish economic change as much as their restrictions. Under the Staple Act of 1663, only servants, horses and Irish victuals
could be shipped directly from Ireland to the colonies. Direct shipments of
Irish linen were allowed after 1705. Even when the Navigation Acts were
mostly removed in 1778, the Irish could not directly export wool, woollen
and cotton manufactures, hats, glass, hops, gunpowder or coal to the
colonies. Nor could English woollens or glass be exported from Ireland to
the colonies, while iron exports paid a duty (Harper 1939, pp. 401–2). In
all these instances, trade restrictions were designed not only to suppress
Ireland's activities in competitive products but *to encourage the production
of commodities and services that were crucial to England's Atlantic commercial project*. In chapter 3, we shall examine the effects of these policies
on Irish industrial transformation.

Transformation rather than impoverishment was certainly the main
objective of English policies toward Ireland. Perhaps nationalist historians
like O'Brien (1919) overemphasised England's impoverishing intent toward
Ireland (although 'reduction' of the native population *was* intended by
early English policies and later Irish poverty hardly caused overriding
policy concern in the English state).[19] Yet impoverishment hardly makes
sense as a policy goal anyway when English settlers, including the sons of
merchants and aristocrats, would have numbered among the impoverished.
The truth was a much more complex one of contradictory alliances and
conflicts between the most powerful English classes and the ascendancy in
Ireland.

Yet this complicated reality does not mean that policies such as the
Navigation Acts were neutral with regard to Ireland. While English policies

encouraged certain activities in place of others, there were clear differences between what was restricted and what was encouraged. Horses, provisions and servants (!) were hardly equivalents to woollen manufactures, England's leading industrial sector. They were *peripheral* products that Britain required for the maintenance of empire. Over the following centuries, emerging Irish industries were consistently restricted and replaced by other economic activities, *not* to impoverish but to discourage Irish competition in leading core sectors in favour of less expansive semi-peripheral activities that were nonetheless important to core projects for economic ascent and hegemony.

Conclusions: effective incorporation as the basis for peripheralisation

Taken in isolation, events in seventeenth-century Ireland appear as most historians have viewed them: either a succession of horrific violations of Irish people and society by an external aggressor, an unfortunate example of the people of one region being caught up in the political conflicts of another region; or the expansion of dynamic modernising agents who could not be contained within the territory of a single country. Elements of each story ring true. Yet complete understanding is impossible without comprehending the nature of England's global project and how it competed with other European powers to implement that project. Ireland was incorporated into an Atlantic project that was becoming central to the changing capitalist world-system.

The process of incorporation utterly changed Ireland's basic economic units through confiscation and settlement, while it transformed its class structure. It provided the basis for a tenant–landlord system of labour acquisition throughout most of the island, along with combined industrial/agrarian production in the north-east. It established an abetting political authority based on settler ascendancy which, nonetheless, continually came into conflict with the English core over its rights of political sovereignty and economic inclusion. It brought Ireland (in a subordinate position) into emerging international infrastructures of trade, investment and monetary flows that would prove crucial to English competitive advantage over the following two centuries.

The pace and extent of incorporation was dizzying. Seldom had the world seen such wholesale transfers of land ownership and control in such a short period as the Cromwellian settlement. Yet the pace of this phase of *effective* incorporation obscures the centuries during which Ireland was transformed as a contact periphery. Gaelic society was irreversibly changed by Christian, Viking and Norman settlements. Towns were established, market relations instituted and foreign trade expanded. From the twelfth century onward, incursions and settlers chipped away at Gaelic land tenure, class structure and political administration. Without the creation of the

Pale, the imposition of the old Anglo elite, the subsequent centralisation of Gaelic political power and the subjugation of *rianna*, incorporation could not have been achieved as quickly or systematically as it was in the century between Elizabeth I and William of Orange.

England's incorporation of Ireland into its Atlantic-centred global project created an ethno-class division on the land that became the main basis of inequality in Ireland. But incorporation and peripheralisation also provided the basis of regional inequality between Ireland, England and the rest of Europe. Although incorporation increased Irish agricultural productivity and enriched its settler elites, agriculture remained concentrated in pasturage: 70 per cent pasture and 15 per cent tillage compared with 50 per cent tillage and 30 per cent pasture in Europe (Crotty 1966, p. 4).[20] The limited 'modernisation' that accompanied changing land tenure thus increased the efficiency with which agriculture produced the same things it had already been producing, while reorienting production away from indigenous subsistence toward external markets.

The combination of individual land holdings and pasturage threatened the masses of Irish on the land. Adventurers, soldiers and other settlers came to Ireland from an England that had already been transformed from tillage to shepherding in response to higher prices for wool and increased trade during the fifteenth century. Individual land holding and sheep pasturage together promised large profits, but only for a few landowners, whose returns increased as they displaced more people from their lands. Thus, English soldiers and planters came to Ireland, in Crotty's (1966, p. 6) words, as 'apostles of the new order of individualism', with little regard for the security of the masses. Any notion that these 'apostles' evaluated the productivity of existing agrarian activities and changed them to modernise the native population hardly jibes with subsequent policies of banishment, penal laws and tenancy. Most importantly, modern individualism cannot explain why these apostles' subsequent productive activities diverged so distinctly from those in the place from whence they came. For this, we must examine how the changing nature of England's global project affected economic change in Ireland itself.

Notes

1   The Belfast master chronology of tree rings dates to 5400 BC, one of the longest in the world (Mallory and McNeill 1991, p. 2).

2   Among these *tuatha*, archaeologists claim that Ireland is remarkable in this period for having tens of thousands of sites or settlements, more than all of continental Europe north of the Alps (Mallory and McNeill 1991, p. 185).

3   Legally, Irish society was divided into seven classes, although in terms of their relationships to property these seven collapse into four main classes.

4   Thus, the old Irish saying *nil uasal na iseal ach thuas seal thios seal* (neither up nor down but up for a spell and down for a spell) may have been more true of relatively fluid Gaelic class relations than of capitalist Ireland where inter-class mobility is much less.

5   Gibson's contention that the centralisation of Gaelic political units was equivalent to early state formation goes against traditional perceptions that Irish centres of government were never states since they lacked large bureaucracies and nucleated settlements. In addition, political power was transitory, ebbing and flowing as individual leaders were replaced. No leader was able to unite the whole island into a single polity before the colonialist destruction of the Gaelic system and aristocracy in the late seventeenth century. The Irish case also differs considerably from Renfrew's (1984) notion of *early state module* (ESM). While Renfrew's ESMs average about 1,500 square kilometres, Muirchertach's 'state' was six times larger (9,600 square kilometres). Gibson, however, convincingly argues that Irish ESMs were larger because they were based on an agro-pastoral mode of production, unlike Renfrew's cases of vegetable agriculture. The land intensity of pastoralism led to lower population densities in Ireland and, conversely, larger political units. In addition, political control over such large areas without nucleated settlement was organised differently: indirectly through the creation of debt, which underpinned client relations. The state expropriated livestock, food and labour from its base population through patron–client relationships. Clientship also existed among higher and lower *rianna* (chieftans), so larger political units took on 'federate character'. Long distances and the broken landscape of the pastoral economy, which increased costs of transport and communication, impeded direct managerial control. Moreover, there was less need for direct control because there was little demand for public works that required management, like terraces and irrigation systems, as in horticulture. Finally, territorial administration may have been partly entrusted to church officials, so that the system required fewer bureaucrats (Gibson 1995, pp. 125–6). In such an agro-pastoral mode of production, Gibson contends, a more centralised state structure with direct class control was likely only if it was introduced by an external force, such as English colonialism.

6   The physical character of such a contact periphery is described as follows (the description is for Ulster, but may not have differed substantially in other areas of Ireland): 'If we were to visit a knight living in Ulster in 1300, we should perhaps have found him living, not like an English knight in a hall with a large farmyard set beside it, and set within, or at the edge of, a village of peasants who worked the land around. Instead in Ulster he might be living in a more or less isolated hall, perhaps set on a motte, or else beside one ... near to a mill, but with his peasants scattered over the countryside in no such close relationship as a village. It is in fact quite likely that many of these would be the descendants of the families who had worked the land before the English came, simply carrying on under a system not greatly changed' (Mallory and McNeill 1991, pp. 263–4)

7   Lest the potential for genocide be underestimated, Canny (1978) analyses the direct links between England's policies for Ireland and its subsequent treatment of North American indigenous populations.

8   See, for example, Peter's *Last Report of the English Wars*. According to Brenner (1993, p. 541), Peter played a 'pivotal role as link between, and mouthpiece for, the allied army, City, and parliamentary radical leaderships'.

9   The concept of *bigemonie* was introduced quite recently by Bergsten (1987), of the pro-imperialist Council on Foreign Relations in the US, who applied it to the possible hegemonic coalition of the US and Japan in the 1980s and 1990s. It applies quite well, however, to the period of prospective alliance between England and Holland.

10 On the effects of the Navigation Acts in North America see Sawers (1992).

11 This explains Marx's later support of Irish nationalism, on the grounds that the English ruling class could be most effectively hit in Ireland, where it was most vulnerable (Marx and Engels 1971, pp. 406–7).

12 Rabb (1967) and Brenner (1993) reach similar findings on colonial trading ventures in general.

13 Some of the adventurers and soldiers may have had no involvement whatever in the Irish campaign. According to Bottigheimer, it is 'impossible to know how much of its debt the revolutionary government in England managed to pay out of those lands, or to what extent it was paying the costs of revolution at home as well as repression abroad' (1971, pp. 139–40). Ironically, the form of payment in land would come to matter. Soldiers who were paid in English land were paid largely in crown lands, which reverted to the crown with the restoration. Lands confiscated in Ireland remained with soldiers and adventurers despite restoration (Firth 1962, p. 207).

14 This equals 700 Irish acres – there are 1.58 English acres to an Irish acre.

15 This is similar to the situation described by Lewis (1954) as 'economic development with unlimited supplies of labour', although, in the Irish case, surplus labour and semi-proletarianisation continue to depress incomes not only in the industrial sectors of the 'dual' local economy but also in the labour markets to which they emigrate.

16 While the dissolution of the court of Munster appeared to go against the interests of the new Commonwealth administration and the reforming programme of the English army, its replacement by the old four-courts system became important in the process of peripheralisation because it centralised judicial power in Dublin.

17 Despite this Catholic dominance, Lord Deputy Arthur Chichester in 1610 claimed that the native Irish were 'indisposed and unapt' to town life (Hunter 1971, p. 43).

18 Dublin's rise as a comprador centre was notable during the English invasions, as local political and religious independents supplied the English army. Some of these local 'new merchants' gained political power as Dublin aldermen along with wealth during this time.

19 The latter, many would argue, was the case with English attitudes toward the great hunger of the 1840s. For such a recent point of view see Kinealy (1995).

20 Indeed, the transition from tillage to pasture was one that would endure through the centuries. The percentage of Irish agricultural land in pasture rose continually, to 79 per cent in 1871, 86 per cent in 1911 and 88 per cent in 1933 (Beddy 1943–44, p. 195).

Chapter 3

The first cycle of industrial transformation: wool to linen

Chapter 2 examined how Ireland was incorporated into a global economy with an ascending English project at its core. The emergent *global* division of labour between England, Ireland, the Atlantic colonies and the Levant was organised *primarily* by a coalition of expansionist English merchants and the English state. Their policies took different forms among colonies and trading partners. In Ireland, they limited trade (and, thereby, profitability), established new economic units through confiscation and resettlement, established abetting authorities in the towns and countryside, and repressed the native people. How did this affect Irish economic change? This chapter examines Irish industrial change in the seventeenth and eighteenth centuries. In a relatively short period, nascent cattle and woollen export sectors were diverted into provisions and linen production, new *peripheral* sectors that would last, in altered forms, for more than 200 years.

An early transformation and a new problem: cattle to provisions and sheep

At the start of the seventeenth century, the English landed gentry held sufficient political power to protect their interests from external threat. Their cattle bills of the 1660s restricted Irish beef exports, the first direct blow against economic expansion by the new settler gentry in Ireland. Exports of live Irish cattle to England expanded rapidly after the Cromwellian resettlement. Lean Irish cattle were exported to southern England, fattened and sold to the growing English urban populations. It was a familiar way for the new settlers to profit. Southern English graziers, their kith and kin, provided familiar trading networks for their product. But breeders from northern and western English counties complained that Irish cattle glutted their markets, made their trade unprofitable and lowered their rents. Since these counties were overrepresented in parliament relative to the demographically booming south-east, the breeders were a powerful political force.

The first cattle bill was part of the second Navigation Act, of 1663, the ironically named Act for the Encouragement of Trade. Apart from requiring imports from plantations to land first in England, the act placed a prohibitively high duty on Irish cattle exports to England during the trading season. It was extended in 1665 to totally prohibit Irish cattle, sheep and provisions exports to England, then three-quarters of Ireland's exports. Parliament used the new act to increase its popularity against the crown by providing that half the forfeited value of contraband animals went to the poor of the parish where they were found. The other half went to whoever made the seizure (previous convention gave half the value of contraband to the monarch).[1] The cattle bills were renewed periodically until they were made permanent in 1680.

Broader English commercial interests opposed the bills. Some said the ban would ruin south-western English graziers and raise the cost of beef in London. Others claimed that they would reduce Irish foreign exchange earnings, thus barring settlers from buying English manufactured exports. Irish opposition ran along similar lines. Irish Lord Lieutenant James Butler argued that the impoverished Irish 'could not take the English manufactures unless the English took their cattle'. The Irish were already banned from exporting wool *outside* England, to countries where they could make a 'mighty profit'; now they were prohibited from sending live cattle *to* England, 'whither they can only send them with advantage'. In 1666 he argued that the bills had caused such poverty that it was 'past the skill or power of the government to supply a remedy' (quoted by O'Donovan 1940, pp. 51, 52).

English parliament was unmoved by such protestations. When Irish representatives came to the English parliament to oppose the 1665 act they were given just thirty minutes to read it and prepare a response. They refused these terms and the bill passed without their input. Lord Annesley, angered by such treatment, claimed that the act was passed not for the benefit of English landlords but simply 'to domineer over that distressed Kingdom of Ireland'. Ironically, since so many settlers got their properties by supporting the Puritan cause against the king, the overriding *political* reason for the cattle bills was English parliament's desire to get at the king's main representative in Ireland (Butler) by attacking the wealth of Irish breeders.

Edie (1970, p. 5) argues that the cattle bills were a watershed in the English treatment of Ireland as a colony. They were 'an early and an important indication that in so far as it was within English power to do so, Irish interests were to be subordinated to the political and economic needs of England'. The bills also indicated the establishment of a powerful civil society in England, where dominant classes exercised political power through parliament to the detriment of crown power. Royal policy was to encourage and tax Irish cattle exports, so the Irish looked to the crown for support.

Parliamentary debates over the cattle bills clearly show that the leading English classes intended to subjugate the Irish economy. They argued about how best to do this and whether certain forms of subjugation were more costly to English imperial interests, then they returned to narrow class interests. The solution was to merge narrow interests with the broad interests of empire by encouraging the Irish to leave the (more profitable) live cattle trade for the (less profitable) provisions trade.

The subjugating intent of all sides is clearly shown by Solicitor General Heneage Finch's arguments against the cattle bills. 'I confesse Ireland is a conquered Nacon', he argued, 'but [it] must not be soe treated for the Conquerors inhabite there.... Wee punish ourselves'. Finch was especially concerned that, since the Irish gentry spent their incomes on English manufactured goods, the embargo on cattle exports would encourage them to buy manufactured goods elsewhere, thus making them independent, against 'state policye to make kingdoms dependent upon ours'. Ireland could not be kept 'in a totall dependence upon England ... unlesse their cheife and onely Trade bee with England'. Finch insisted that Ireland must be kept dependent on England, but asked 'can it depend without Trade, or Trade without Cattle?' (quoted by Edie 1970, pp. 19, 20, 24).

When the acts were passed, cattle comprised over half of Ireland's exports. Cattle, sheep and wool together comprised three-quarters of Irish exports, practically all of which went to England (O'Donovan 1940, p. 53). As table 3.1 shows, live cattle exports practically stopped following the 1665 act, falling from 37,544 in 1665 to 1,054 in 1669. This huge fall in exports forced Ireland to turn to the provisioning trade as the only way new settlers could dispose of their beef. Proponents and opponents of the cattle bills both proposed giving Ireland provisioning contracts for the English navy (Edie 1970, pp. 21, 22). In early 1667, Irish Lord Lieutenant Butler and his council petitioned the king with a list of requests to offset the effects of the cattle bills, among them that Ireland be allowed to victual the English navy. The Privy Council agreed, suggesting that such a trade with friendly countries would keep Ireland from reopening its trade with the English plantations in America (O'Donovan 1940, p. 62; Edie 1970, p. 36).

The transition to provisions was not easy and there is little indication it would have occurred without the negative inducement of the cattle bills. In 1664 the Council of Trade concluded that the Irish were not suited for the provisions trade because they slaughtered their cattle too young for barrelling (O'Donovan 1940, p. 51). Yet by 1670 Ireland barrelled and exported its beef to England, to continental European countries and to the American plantations. Irish barrelled beef reportedly sold in Holland for a penny a pound, while butter, tallow and hides undersold English products by about half. Despite Ireland's poor transport and commercial infrastructures, it undercut English produce because Irish rents were a tenth of English levels and its labour considerably cheaper.

Table 3.1 Exports of livestock and provisions from Ireland in selected years, 1641–1800

Year	Live cattle (number)	Beef (barrels)	Butter (hundredweight)	Pork (barrels)
1641	45,605	15,215	34,817	0
1665	37,544	29,204	26,413	1,252
1669	1,054	51,793	58,041	771
1685	n.a.	75,231	134,712	2,514
1704	494	70,833	92,219	13,727
1708	34	66,105	111,498	2,848
1712	150	85,532	140,265	3,986
1716	210	110,288	186,978	8,202
1720	231	117,966	186,449	7,794
1724	376	133,597	147,452	8,575
1728	307	135,064	175,749	10,545
1732	110	145,208	153,727	12,206
1736	47	148,962	147,121	11,530
1740	14	150,495	161,212	11,640
1744	128	127,990	154,310	11,820
1748	23	123,846	201,666	16,092
1752	6	176,325	237,345	20,063
1756	29	163,525	206,307	34,910
1760	1,029	161,235	207,246	37,138
1764	2,344	195,869	237,564	49,101
1768	1,299	193,435	283,681	43,138
1772	1,012	203,869	276,286	42,805
1776	3,654	197,206	269,762	56,630
1780	4,178	171,486	248,585	79,291
1784	2,425	171,158	251,293	89,118
1788	18,858	144,861	299,569	86,528
1792	23,764	120,728	308,823	92,723
1796	12,078	121,083	293,661	131,663
1800	19,712	130,480	291,041	141,186

n.a. = not available.
Source of data: O'Donovan (1940, pp. 63, 104, 111, 112, 116).

Table 3.1 shows how quickly salted and barrelled cattle replaced live cattle exports.[2] In 1665, only 28 per cent of Irish cattle were exported in barrels; by 1669, 96 per cent were barrelled. Even this may understate the effects of the cattle bills. Only 14 per cent of cattle exports were barrelled in 1641 and much of the decrease in live cattle exports between then and 1665 probably happened between 1663 and 1665.

Table 3.1 also indicates that the cattle bills seriously affected Irish economic well-being. Not only did livestock exports fall after 1665, but *total* cattle exports, live or barrelled, fell by half and did not reach 1665 levels again until 1716. Some cows were probably kept for their milk and butter; Irish butter exports rose several times over between 1665 and 1700. On the other hand, milk and milk products (butter, buttermilk, curds and whey) were a staple of the native Irish diet, and any shift from subsistence production to exports may have decreased their nutritional intake and contributed to chronic subsistence crises.

Irish exports went mainly to the Atlantic maritime trade. In 1685, 33 per cent of barrelled beef, 40 per cent of barrelled pork and 28 per cent of butter exports were sold to English merchant ships (O'Donovan 1940, p. 71). French merchants took the cheapest (and worst) Irish meat to feed their colonial slaves. Colonies like Martinique were supplied exclusively by Irish provisions (O'Donovan 1940, pp. 105–6). Portugal and Holland and their colonies were other major customers.

Although most of Munster, Connaught and Leinster were turned over to grazing for the provisions trade, the trade itself was concentrated around Cork. As the last port between England or continental Europe and the Americas, Cork was a convenient place for ships to load up with victuals for their Atlantic runs. By the 1730s, Cork was the largest centre for provisions exports in Ireland or Britain. During 1772–1800, more than half of Irish beef exports went from Cork, while much of the rest came from nearby Waterford (O'Donovan 1940, p. 117). But Agnew (1994) shows that the provisions trade was also an important source of the development of the merchant community in Belfast, which would later be the crucial segment of Irish industrial capital.

Irish provisions were now an important part of the Atlantic commercial infrastructure but their control was not yet an effective instrument of English hegemony. As long as Ireland provided crucial commodities to the other colonial players in the Atlantic, it was not working fully to the advantage of English commercial supremacy. Continental ships that bought Irish victuals also sold manufactures that the Irish had previously purchased from England. Moreover, while south-eastern English victuallers lost considerable business to Ireland, the English navy continued to stock up in England at much higher prices than continental ships paid in Ireland. We can safely assume that English prices rose even further once Irish cattle were excluded from its stockyards (Edie 1970, p. 42). Such a situation was unsatisfactory for landed class interests in southern England and even less satisfactory to English commerce and the navy, who provisioned at a substantial disadvantage to England's hegemonic competitors, Holland and France.

The transformation of the Irish trade to English hegemonic interests exemplifies how imperial power can give flexibility to a core state, enabling it to turn contradictory relationships to its advantage in ways that peripheral states cannot. Although the Irish sold cheap provisions to France and Holland, they did so from within the British empire. Following the Dutch example, the English state was thus able to make its imperial rivals dependent on supplies over which it had control. This gave England the power of *strategic withdrawal* of key commodities in times of hegemonic competition such as war.

During the 1670s, English interests recognised the importance of controlling Irish trade more strictly. William Temple reflected the common English sentiment when he wrote that Irish interests should not interfere with English interests, 'to which it is subordinate'. Competing activities, he argued, should be 'either declined or moderated, and so give way to the Interest and Trade of England, upon the health and vigour thereof, the strength, Riches and glory of His Majesties Crowns seem chiefly to depend'. Temple suggested that the best way to divert Ireland from competing activities was to encourage others that would be useful to England, specifically linen and horses (Edie 1970, p. 44). Edward Harley, in support of the cattle bills, claimed likewise that 'Ireland is but a colony of England' which had been 'rescued' at great expense. Thus, Irish settlers should not be indulged at the expense of the well-being of England, 'the territory from whence they came' (Edie 1970, p. 47).

Opponents of the cattle bills made similar arguments about the necessity to divert Ireland from any new competing activities such as woollen manufactures, saying that it would be much less harmful to allow them to resume exporting livestock. John Maynard called for the repeal of the cattle bills because they induced a flourishing Irish woollen industry and decreased Irish dependence on England. William Coventry argued that the bills raised beef prices paid by English townspeople and the English navy (Edie 1970, p. 47). A 1677 London pamphlet (*Reasons for a Limited Exportation of Wool*) argued that Irish provisions threatened English interests far more than live cattle exports:

> This Act is injurious to the nation by sending our own and foreign merchant ships to victual in Ireland; by want of returns from thence, by loss of our trade for hops, hides, butter and cheese, which trades are now taken up by the Irish to the ruin of many counties of England, by discouraging navigation, for it is said that a hundred of our ships were continually employed in this traffic of lean cattle.

The pamphlet went on to argue that Irish provisioning harmed English competitiveness because cheaper victuals kept Dutch labour costs low, enabling Dutch textiles to compete with English textiles (quoted by Edie 1970, p. 65).

A more eloquent and, ultimately, more persuasive argument about English hegemonic interests came from the prominent London merchant Thomas Papillon, who is worth quoting at length:

> The State of the Question is, What the true Interest of England is in Reference to Ireland, which certainly is, to make Ireland serviceable and advantageous

to England, and not to set up Ireland in Competition with England. It is a Consideration worthy of an English Parliament to make Ireland profitable to England. This cannot be done by excluding them from a Trade to England, that's to make them independent of England, and to force them to a Trade with foreign Countries, and so to a Familiarity and Correspondence with them. The Way for England to make Ireland advantageous, is, that England should be Master of all the Commodities of Ireland, and no Commodities whatsoever to be transported out of Ireland to any other Parts of the World. (Quoted in Edie 1970, p. 48)

With a shrewd eye for hegemonic advantage, Papillon added that if England controlled French and Dutch supplies, it would have the tremendous strategic weapon of cutting them off during wartime.

Such contemporary recognition of the connections between English strategic and commercial interests is notable, especially since so few modern Irish historians recognise them. Viewed in the context of the Navigation Acts and other measures to establish English control of world trade, the cattle bills and the subsequent encouragement of the Irish provisions industry were an important local manifestation of global hegemonic strategy. 'If all the Commodities of Ireland must pass thro' England', Papillon wrote, 'then all foreign Commodities that Ireland wants would be supplied in the same Way, which would be of great Advantage to England' (Edie 1970, p. 48). Instead of simply restricting Irish trade, he argued that it should be transformed to England's advantage. Ireland should produce linen for the English navy and provisions for English commerce, while Irish wool should be prohibited because it would destroy English trade.

This was an early form of flexible accumulation. Just as late-twentieth-century firms and states found it strategically profitable to subcontract crucial but unstable products, thus shifting risk on to other providers, the southern Irish regions were forced to depend on unstable *peripheral subcontracting* in provisions. Considerable instability was created by hegemonic conflict itself. Sometimes war simply disrupted the provisions trade. But, periodically, England found a strategic advantage in cutting off provisions to Holland or France. This it did at great cost to Ireland rather than England. Indeed, since embargoes created surpluses of Irish provisions, the English profited doubly because their merchants and navies could buy Irish victuals at especially cheap prices.

By the 1700s England regularly used Irish provisions as a strategic weapon. During its war with Spain in 1739 and the Austrian War of Succession in 1741 it laid embargoes on Irish exports to Spain and France. This kept them out of French and Spanish hands and cheapened them for the English navy, which got its provisions at 'absurdly low' prices (Murray 1903, p. 71). Since cattle products still consistently made up 40–50 per cent of the value of its exports, this was a massive economic blow to Ireland. From 1770, England embargoed Irish provisions and linen exports to

France and the American colonies due to the American War of Independence. From 1776, Irish provisions could be exported only to England,
which re-exported them to the colonies. Finally, in 1778 there was a complete embargo on Irish provisions exports even in British ships, totally
stopping the provisions trade for six months, after which Ireland could ship
them to the dominions but not to Britain. The effects of these restrictions
were severe. Barrelled beef exports fell by 40 per cent between 1772 and
1792 and never recovered. Exports to France, which made up a third of beef
exports in 1764, fell practically to zero in 1780 (O'Donovan 1940, p. 125).

The severity of Ireland's position was relieved by the removal of restrictions on Irish exports to England, where, according to Arthur Young
(1780, p. 246), the interests of the English war effort had been sacrificed to
'three or four London contractors'. The opening of the English food
markets increased Irish butter, ham and bacon exports, although barrelled
beef exports continued to decline. The provisions trade was a political
football and Irish accumulation on such an unstable basis was practically
impossible.

Regional accumulation was also limited by the fact that provisions
production had lower profitability than cattle. This, argues Crotty (1966),
is proven by the rapid switch of Irish production back into cattle when the
cattle bills were repealed in 1759. A more robust indicator of the sector's
peripherality is the degree to which it depended on the adaptive response of
cheap labour costs rather than innovation. Irish provisions consistently
undersold English provisions because of cheap Irish labour (O'Donnell
1940, p. 66; Edie 1970, p. 41).

It could be claimed that the provisions trade induced wider development
through its linkages to tanning and barrelling. Yet even these were highly
labour-intensive peripheral trades which had disastrous consequences for
Ireland's economic development. Cooperage, tanning and iron smelting
destroyed Irish woodlands. Oak and ash near navigable rivers were cleared
for staves, hazel and willow were cut for hoops and inland timber was
converted into charcoal for smelting iron ore. Unlike in England, Irish
woods were not preserved because landlords desired to clear lands for
grazing. Leases required their tenants to clear a certain amount of timber
each year (McCracken 1971, pp. 57, 95).[3] Such 'development' was clearly
unsustainable.

Irish deforestation for stave making began in the early 1600s, when
Walter Raleigh used his influence with the Privy Council to ship staves to
England, despite a 1596 injunction forbidding their export from Ireland.[4]
Boyle, who bought Raleigh's lands, recorded transactions involving four
million staves (about 500,000 cubic feet of wood) during 1616–28. The
East India Company owned woods in south Cork which they used to
make staves and build ships until the 1640s. They also contracted with

landowners for staves, despite a new prohibition on their export in 1615 (McCracken 1971, pp. 100–1). In 1625, another attempt to control Irish stave exports failed owing to opposition by influential landowners.

Timber exported as casks for provisions rose from 59,100 to 204,500 cubic feet during 1641–1717. Additional staves were exported to England and Scotland. The provisions trade used 4,500 tons of wood annually during 1700–50, rising to 7,000 tons in 1800 (McCracken 1971, pp. 110, 119). By this time Irish deforestation was nearly complete. The Chevalier de Latocnayne, in his 'walk through Ireland' in the 1790s, found 'they had not left wood enough to make a toothpick in many places' (quoted in Neeson 1991, p. 65). By one estimate, an eighth of Irish lands were forested in 1600 but only 2 per cent remained so in 1800 because of the exploitative clearances that accompanied the Cromwellian confiscations and settlements and the transition of southern Irish production from livestock to provisions (McCracken 1971, p. 15).[5]

The Navigation Acts and cattle bills must be viewed together to understand their significance to Anglo-Irish colonial relations. England passed the Navigation Acts to control empire trade and, through it, production in imperial regions. Within this context, the cattle bills were specifically aimed to control Irish production and trade. In a sense, the cattle bills were an exception that proved the rule of imperial power. They probably did not increase the wealth of the northern breeders who urged their passing. They may not have *directly* served the cause of empire and hegemony very much, a question that was at the heart of parliamentary debates about increasing Ireland's dependence on England. The key advantage of core global power, however, is the flexibility it gives a regime to turn peripheral challenges to its own benefit. Ireland's take-over of the provisions trade clashed with important landed interests in England but it became extremely useful to the emergent imperial merchant class because it lowered the price of provisions while ensuring their stable production within the empire. Soon, Irish provisions became a weapon in England's hegemonic conflict with rival continental powers.

Although it took until 1759 to remove the cattle bills, the predominant English class that forced the legislation was already at the end of its ascendancy by the late 1600s. The new merchants and wool manufacturers became more powerful than landed cattle interests and the eighteenth century would be the century of wool (Deane and Coale 1962, p. 68). Textile manufacturers in south-western England (competing with Irish wool producers) and East Anglia (competing with Indian silks and calicoes) began to press their own demands on the state. Their success began a cyclical pattern whereby emergent Irish industries were transformed in the interests of Ireland's associated core power, a pattern which arguably continues today.

The first industrial transformation: wool to linen

Marx said that Ireland was colonised as a sheepwalk for England. Apart from being a source of British food supply, sheep were also the basis of the first great modern industry. The relationship between Irish shepherds and the English wool industry is best examined in the context of the cattle bills. Irish sheep were important to the growing woollen industries of England because they supplied their basic raw material. While seventeenth-century Irish records are sketchy, cattle exports outnumbered sheep exports until the middle of the century. Exports of live Irish sheep to south-western English ports were not great during the first half of the century, but there were significant exports of wool (Woodward 1973). Then, sheep exports nearly tripled, at the expense of wool, between 1641 and 1665 (O'Donovan 1940, p. 63). Irish tenant farmers, whose lands were too small to carry many cattle, herded sheep instead.

English policy repeatedly manipulated the Irish wool trade from the beginning of the seventeenth century. Irish wool exports were forbidden in 1614. In 1615 they were allowed into England only by licence. Some Irish ports were licensed to export wool to England in 1617, a measure designed to stop Ireland from supplying England's continental competitors (O'Donovan 1940, p. 41). After 1619, exports were allowed to England only by special warrant, and there were continuous Irish complaints that not enough warrants were issued. After 1632, however, the lord deputy of Ireland granted export licences more freely, on the grounds that discouraging wool exports would encourage the Irish to develop home-grown woollen manufactures (O'Donovan 1940, pp. 42–3).[6] In 1641 an Irish request to export wool, skins and yarn to England was granted, the first of many cases where the English encouraged Irish home spinning of yarn for the English weaving industry.

After the restoration, English policy discouraged the emerging Irish woollen industry. In 1660 high import duties effectively stopped Irish woollens from entering the English market. Although Ireland could ship wool to the rest of the world after obtaining a licence, it had to be sent to England first and shipped in English ships. In 1662, Charles II instructed the lord lieutenant to grant licences freely for wool exports for fear that Ireland would otherwise make up its own woollen fabrics and compete with England manufacturers. 'The same would be of incomparable inconvenience to the trade of clothing in Our Kingdom of England', the king wrote, 'considering that wools being cheaper in Ireland than here, our subjects there might undersell our subjects here and consequently much decay the trade of clothing in this Our Kingdom, which we must not admit' (O'Donovan 1940, pp. 77–8).

The cattle bill of 1667 restricted Irish sheep exports but, ironically, had the immediate effect of encouraging the Irish to hold sheep instead of cattle

because Irish shepherds could still export wool to English woollen manufacturers (Murray 1903, p. 38; O'Donovan 1940, p. 79). Thus, the bill
increased the supply of cheap wool to England's leading industry.

Ireland's peripheralisation into sheep, however, was land intensive and
increased the underemployment of Irish labour. Commentators of the time
refer to the degree to which Irish peasants were unoccupied (see Cullen
1972, p. 23). This destabilised subsistence and repressed Irish incomes,
which in turn induced the larger sheep farmers to seek profits by linking
forward into wool manufacture. Wool, the leading core industry of the
time, was still relatively labour intensive and could be produced with
rudimentary capital equipment using underemployed rural labour. Thus,
Ireland's advantage in labour costs gave it competitive advantages over
even the most progressive English manufacturers. When the Irish parliament enacted protectionist duties to help local manufacturers increase their
share of the Irish market in the 1670s, a cottage industry in woollens grew
rapidly. By the 1680s, Irish woollen products were competing on English
markets. Exports of Irish frieze rose from 279,722 yards in 1641, to
444,381 in 1665, 753,189 in 1683 and 1,129,716 in 1687 (Murray 1903,
p. 104; Cullen 1972, p. 23).

Ireland's textile industry thus began in woollens and expanded rapidly
after 1670. This was doubly dangerous for English industrialists and merchants. Not only did Irish woollen goods compete on English markets, but
they also used up raw wool that was needed by the English industry. Thus,
London merchants petitioned the crown to stifle the Irish infant industry in
1676. Edie (1970, p. 51) shows that the common political sentiment in
England was to crush competitive Irish trades and make Ireland a supplier
of raw materials and a consumer of English goods. Protectionist pressures
intensified in the mid-1690s after the Irish industry recovered from the
Jacobite war and economic crisis hit the English wool industry (Kelly
1980). Bristol economist John Cary's influential 1695 pamphlet *Essay on
Trade* proposed the restriction of imports of Irish woollens and Indian
calicoes and silks. Cary also favoured diverting Irish production into linen,
a common English theme of the time.

The first attempt in the English parliament to prevent Irish exports of
woollen manufactures failed to be passed in 1697. There was substantial
support for restrictions, but members of parliament (MPs) disagreed about
whether to restrict or ban Irish woollen exports and about what to do with
Irish producers who were forced out of woollen manufactures. Moreover, a
problem was that the Irish parliament was made up of English settlers who
were jealous of their new-found wealth in manufacturing woollens. The
domestic organisation of woollen manufacturing fit well into Ireland's
peripheral social organisation: spinning and weaving complemented farming's seasonality and its gendered division of labour. Profits from woollens
increased landlords' incomes beyond what they could obtain from rents.

Outward-oriented sections of the English state were naturally reluctant to alienate their settler agents in Ireland, England's most important peripheral zone.

The 'moderate' English plan, pushed by the Board of Trade and the ruling Whig Junto, was to compensate the loss of woollen profits by encouraging Irish linen production. This was hardly a benevolent sentiment. When the English Board of Trade was set up in 1696, it was instructed to find a way to acquire linen from within the empire to relieve English dependence on Baltic linen (Kelly 1980). Even then, linen was peripheral in terms of its relative labour intensity. It was profitable only in areas with low labour costs and core English producers were not interested in its manufacture. Yet England required it as a low-cost and durable way of clothing its military. Most of all, diversion into linen was considered to be the surest way of breaking the Irish woollen industry. Bristol MPs wrote in a letter to John Cary in 1695, 'we cannot think any thing will hinder Ireland's increase in the Woollen Manufactures so much as by setting up a Linnen Manufactury there, and reduceing that Kingdome to the terms of a colony ... anything less than this will be but doing the business by halves' (quoted in Kelly 1980, p. 28).

In 1696, the English parliament removed import duties on Irish linens. In the same year, John Locke inquired in Dublin about the Irish manufacture of linen on behalf of the Board of Trade (Kearney 1959). The following year, Locke proposed a 'moderate' scheme for the gradual discouragement of Irish woollen manufacture by increasing import duties on wool, subsidising flax growing, obliging everyone not on the poor rate to produce a stated quantity of flax and yarn, and setting up working schools and competitions to increase weaving and spinning skills. The Board reported to the king later that year, reaffirming its support for reserving the woollen industry for England by transforming Irish production to the manufacture of linen (Kelly 1980).

The preferred route of action was to get the Irish themselves to dismantle their woollen trade. The secretary of state for Ireland in the English Privy Council had a bill drawn up for the Irish parliament which aimed to divert Irish production from wool to linen. He was very clear that the intent of the bill was to divert the Irish from the woollen trade, which the English were 'so jealous of', and warned that failure to pass it would invite stricter measures in the English parliament (Kearney 1959, p. 488).

The Irish parliament did not pass the bill. Irish woollen manufacturers would not agree to their own demise. They were English settlers, but Irish linen manufacture was already concentrating among Scottish Presbyterian settlers in Ulster (Kearney 1959). The divergent interests (religion- and class-wise) of English Protestant settlers and Scots Presbyterian settlers thus turned the Irish parliament against encouraging linen at the expense of the woollen industry. Yet the interests of the ascendant bourgeoisie of western

England broke the power of English settlers in Ireland. Their class support for stern measures coincided with a political desire to neutralise the Irish parliament, which was leaning dangerously toward separation from England by its encouragement of the Irish woollen industry and its threats to defy English parliamentary rule.[7]

The English parliament passed its Woollen Act in 1699, prohibiting Irish woollen exports.[8] Although some Irish historians argue that the act was not meant to subjugate Irish industry (Cullen 1969; Kelly 1980), English economic historians are less forgiving. Ellison (1886) claims English woollen interests had an easy victory over Irish interests because the latter had no powerful equivalent of the East India Company to represent it. He provides extensive quotes from English parliamentary debates to demonstrate a clear British intent to replace Irish woollens with linen and provisions. He also documents repeated English government recommendations to Irish viceroys, from the 1650s to the 1690s, that they should encourage linen, provisions and fisheries in place of woollens. The transition to linen was finally ensured by the Woollen Act.

Kearney (1959) makes a great deal of the fact that mercantilism was not a fully coherent set of policies carried through by unified English governments. This ignores the reality of class struggle and class–state relations in seventeenth-century capitalism generally and England in particular. The English state was an arena of competition among divergent landed and commercial interests. The targets of mercantilism changed as relative class power changed. The Woollen Act and accompanying linen measures were no less mercantilist just because a coalition of woollen manufacturers and new merchants forced them through parliament against the wishes of the monarch. Nor was the campaign launched at the same time by East Anglian and London silk weavers against the East India Company any less mercantilist because it originated among ascendant sections of capital against opposition from others. Each of the resulting legislative measures was intended to facilitate ascendant sections of English industry by reducing foreign competition.

Taken together, the discouragement of Irish woollens and the encouragement of linen are a prime example of regional peripheralisation in the interests not just of leading core capitalists but of the global system as a whole. The 1699 Woollen Act directly subordinated Irish production by forbidding exports of Irish cloth to England *and* its colonial markets. Irish woollen goods were thereafter confined to the Irish market until the law was revoked eighty years later under the pressure of war, recession and the next phase of Irish separatism. In 1701, Asian silks and calicoes were also forbidden entry into England.

Ireland went into recession soon after the Woollen Act. Cullen (1972) insists that the act did not cause this recession because it did not start until 1702, three years after the act. He argues that the Irish economic crisis was

caused by Irish monetary revaluation in 1701 – which raised Irish commodity prices to foreign importers, who then stopped buying Irish goods,
in turn causing a general deflation – on the basis that this happened
between the Woollen Act and recession. This argument confuses long-term
with short-term effects, structural with cyclical crises and agrarian crisis
with industrial stagnation. Short-term recession was a proximate cause of
economic distress in the woollen industry. Yet the industry's long-term
ability to weather recession and to expand in better times had already been
crippled by English protectionism. Long-term economic crisis was primarily
a result of Irish dependence on agriculture and agricultural exports, which
was intensified by restrictions on diversification into industry. The importance of the Woollen Act was not any immediate short-term economic crisis
it may have caused but its long-term structural effects on Irish industrialisation.

What, then, happened to the long-term structure of Irish industry after
1699? The value of total Irish exports rose from £814,746 in 1700 to
£1,043,052 in 1731. Yet this was entirely due to the rise of linen exports to
England from practically nil in 1700 to £254,000 (over 25 per cent of total
exports) in 1731. Non-linen exports declined by 3 per cent to £789,037,
including declines in raw wool and woollen exports (Cullen 1972, pp. 40–
1, 48).

We know with certainty that Ireland's woollen industry stagnated in the
first half of the eighteenth century. Production for the Irish market may
have risen slightly. But *with the aid of* (not solely because of) protective
legislation against Irish and Asian textiles, the English woollen industry –
the leading sector of early-eighteenth-century core capital – boomed, promoting the development of English capitalism and laying the groundwork
for the later and more critical rise of cotton. Woollens were England's largest
industrial sector in 1770, comprising more than 30 per cent of value-added
in industry (Crafts 1985, table 2.3). They still dominated English industry
into the nineteenth century (Berg 1994, p. 40). Meanwhile, *primarily
because of* restrictions on Irish exports of woollen manufactures and the
encouragement of linen, the Irish woollen industry failed to expand significantly and, indeed, probably declined.

It is irrelevant whether Irish woollens survived English mercantilism in
some form, because what 'survived' was marginal compared with the
expanding provisions and linen sectors, which became the centres of Irish
industry. The crucial fact is that the Irish economy was transformed, in the
interests of the English core, from a producer of food and woollen manufactures to a producer of food and linen.

What was the nature of this transformation? Apologists for imperialism
like Clark (1934, p. 305) assume that it was a transformation of equals: 'If
the English had wished to impoverish Ireland they would not have lacked
an excuse for restricting the Irish linen trade as they had restricted the Irish

woollen trade. So far from doing all this they promised to encourage it by all possible means, as an equivalent for the lost opportunities for the woollen manufacture. They kept their promise.'

Such arguments are pitched against a nationalist 'straw person' claiming that England wanted to 'destroy Ireland'. But of course England never intended to 'destroy' Ireland but to transform and subordinate it. To this end, it is important to compare wool and linen, to examine whether the replacement of the former by the latter was an exchange of 'an equivalent' or an unequal trade of an innovative core industry for a peripheral one.

Characteristics and evolution of the linen industry

There is no doubt that England encouraged Irish linen as it discouraged woollens after the 1690s. Violations of the Woollen Act carried harsh fines, half of which were to be used to encourage Irish linen production. An act of 1696 allowed plain Irish linen to enter England duty free and a linen board was established in 1711. In 1700, England funded a colony of Huguenot weavers in a scheme to boost linen production around Belfast. Other skilled immigrants with experience in producing broadcloth textiles and capital to set up their production were also attracted to Ireland (Gill 1925; Cohen 1990). Crawford (1972) argues that the subsequent expansion of linen was due less to the efforts of immigrants than to the removal of English duties on linen in 1696. Either way, the transformation of Irish industry from wool to linen was facilitated by English policies that were directly aimed at that result. Additionally, the negative incentive of prohibiting wool provoked movement into linen early in the eighteenth century.

The arrival of Scottish settlers in north-eastern Ireland enabled relations of production that flexibly combined domestic linen production with farming. The relatively stable tenure given to the north-eastern settler population encouraged considerably more capital investment and improvement than the notoriously unstable native Irish tenancies. Dowling (1999) argues convincingly that the British state aimed its linen policies at Ulster with the precise purpose of stabilising the landed estate system there.

The production relations of linen were different from those of woollens. The landed Anglo-Irish gentry of Munster and Leinster, like their counterparts in the English West Riding, had organised woollen production among their tenants in a putting-out system. Linen was produced mostly in Ulster in a more decentralised domestic production system that was organised around regional and gendered unequal exchanges involving Scottish and Quaker settlers as well as native Irish tenants.

This distinction is important beyond the geographic shift it induced in Irish textile production. The shift to linen is important because it was a shift away from an industry with the potential to develop core production relations to one that clearly induced the expansion of semi-peripheral domestic production. The manufactures which eventually became leading core industrial sectors, specifically woollens and cotton textiles, began under rural putting-out systems (*Verlagssystem*). Merchants and landed interests organised the supply of the raw material, which was not readily available to spinners or weavers, and put it out to households or small 'factories' for a piece-rate. While weaving was often concentrated in factories, the bottlenecks encountered in spinning required more and more extensive putting-out, which in turn imposed expenses that eventually encouraged the mechanisation of yarn production. It does not follow that the Irish woollens industry would, likewise, have been inevitably transformed into competitive full-scale industry had it been allowed to flourish under the putting-out system. Disadvantages with regard to raw material supply, participation in sea commerce and access to markets – the results of imperial policy – would have crippled the Irish woollens industry in export markets. Still, the substitution of linen for woollens was also the substitution of potentially 'progressive' relations of production for others with less proletarianising potential.

The *Kaufsystem* predominated in linen: cottage producers cultivated their own raw materials, which they processed and wove into textiles in an integrated domestic production system, until they sold the cloth to merchants in the marketplace.[9] Merchant capital accumulation remained concentrated in the later links of the commodity chain, such as bleaching, while households remained remarkably resistant to capitalist incursions into raw material supply, spinning or weaving. Irish linen production remained organised in households while English textiles came under the control of emergent capitalists. Although this system left petty producers formally independent, it enabled their 'exploitation through trade' or *unequal exchange* (Dobb 1963, p. 209).

I will examine Irish linen production in greater detail below, but first it is important to examine why England encouraged Irish linen. Before the rise of English power in the Atlantic economy, Dutch hegemony was based on Amsterdam's role as a centre for trading systems centred on the Baltics and the East. Dutch merchants controlled flows of critical raw materials, enabling them to amass industrial and commercial profits. Amsterdam was where 'Baltic, Mediterranean, Atlantic, and Indian Ocean supplies met and turned into one another's demand' (Arrighi 1994). Arguably, Holland's most important trading asset was its control of Baltic products, including flax, which it manufactured into linen and sold throughout the world. Beginning with Elizabeth, English hegemonic strategy centred on the diversion of trade from Amsterdam, from eastern trading networks to English-controlled networks in the Atlantic and the Levant (Braudel 1984; Arrighi 1994, pp. 174–213).

Linen was a critical supply for the burgeoning English naval and commercial fleets, as well as its new Atlantic colonies. Yet Holland's role as broker for flax and linen destabilised English access. The English state could not induce sufficient domestic production of linen since woollen (and later cotton) manufactures were far more profitable and less labour intensive. English farmers considered flax to be a burdensome crop and much less profitable than other products. Securing a stable supply of linen and, if possible, flax under English control was thus important to the emerging English hegemonic project. Such was the commercial environment in which England discouraged Irish woollen manufactures and encouraged its export-oriented linen and provisions industries.

From the Irish perspective, the *dependent* nature of the linen industry is crucial. For the next 200 years, it depended almost entirely on English markets for home consumption or re-export. There it faced largely disadvantageous competition from other textiles, most notably cotton. High value-added stages of production such as printing and dyeing remained in England. And linkages to sectors like machine building and transport – which made woollens and cotton so valuable to English industrialisation – came late and were substantially fewer in linen. The Irish industry depended on English inputs, technologies, transport, distribution and finance. Linen was limited geographically; limited in its ability to induce the rates of technical, organisational and material change that we associate with the rise of capitalism elsewhere; and particularly limited in its ability to act as a 'leading sector' by inducing new linkages to other regional economic activities.

As I have indicated, the predominant organisational characteristic of linen was the long survival of its domestic system of production. It was spread throughout the countryside among farmers who also spun or wove. This contrasts with English textile industries from woollens on, which concentrated in towns, creating an industrial working class. This is not to blame a 'backward' or undifferentiated Irish peasantry for the pace and kind of change. Lower as well as higher classes of Irish experimented with new forms of productive organisation and tried new things. But the Atlantic-centred system of which Irish linen and agriculture were a small part limited the degrees and kinds of change that could be profitably introduced.

Gill, writing in 1925, noted the importance of hand weaving 'even today' (p. 1). He described a piecework system that fits more readily in the eighteenth or nineteenth centuries than the twentieth. While domestic relations of production did not dominate the industry in the twentieth century, their survival reflects the slow and incomplete proletarianisation and mechanisation of linen relative to other textiles. Domestic production predominated in the linen industry until well after 1820. While the production of other textiles was largely mechanised early in the nineteenth century, hand weaving still played a central role in Irish linen in the 1870s. A literature on *proto-industrialisation* (Collins 1982; Cohen 1990; Gray 1993) shows that Irish linen had its own dynamic, but this dynamic was dependent and *semi-peripheral*, with lower profit rates and rates of expansion relative

to core industrial agglomerations; semi-proletarian production relations
and lower wages; slower rates of technical/organisational change and lower
capital intensity; and fewer linkages to other local economic sectors (Arrighi
and Drangel 1986; O'Hearn 1994). As Gray (1993) shows, the organisation
of the Irish industry was based on unequal exchange between unevenly
developed stages of linen production that were arranged in a gendered
division of labour.

The process of linen production

In order to understand the nature of the linen industry and its changes, it is
important to outline its organisation of production and marketing in a
comparative context. Flax culture was widespread geographically because
the crop was relatively simple to grow on small plots. Yet, despite state
encouragement, most flax was imported. Local cultivation was reportedly
limited because farmers considered flax to be a 'scourging crop', which also
took considerable time and energy to grow, harvest and prepare. Stripping
the bolls, winnowing the seed and steeping the flax were 'greatly disliked'
by small farmers (Durie 1976, p. 90). Moreover, there was no correlation
between harvests in Ireland/Scotland and the continent, so a bad crop
would not be repaid by a higher price, as would be likely in wheat or
barley. Because of limitations on local production, the price of imported
flax rose considerably along with demand (Gill 1925, p. 223; Durie 1976,
p. 90). Freight and insurance rates were considerable and during wartime
there were massive problems with securing flax or flax seed at any price.
This contrasts directly with the successes of the British Board of Trade and
British traders in securing raw cotton from the Americas in quantities that
expanded even more rapidly than European demand, so that its price fell
considerably and consistently during the first half of the 1800s (Gill 1925,
p. 224).

Since some flax was grown by weavers, the early linen economy was a
relatively integrated system of production from flax and its preparation
through spinning and weaving, until the raw cloth was sold to a trader for
finishing and export. As time went on and distribution improved, systems
of production and distribution became more specialised, even while they
remained largely domestic. Families who spun and wove mixed home-
grown flax with supplies from elsewhere.

Gill suggests why capitalist development occurred in some industries
while the domestic *Kaufsystem* tenaciously remained in Irish linen: 'the
cotton trade early developed a capitalistic organisation, since all the raw
material had to be imported, and in later years those who controlled the
import became the ruling "junta" of merchants and spinners' (1925, p. 34).
Large Lancashire spinners, through their favourable relations with cotton

importers, introduced many of the most noted innovations in cotton factory organisation and labour control (O'Hearn 1994). By contrast, Irish linen had no such impulse at the upstream end of the commodity chain, so that the major impulse toward mechanisation began downstream, in bleaching, and proceeded much more slowly.

Unlike cotton farming, the expansion of which was aided by the introduction of the cotton gin, the harvest and preparation of flax continued by hand. Even compared with hand-sheared wool, this was a laborious and tedious procedure. Stalks had to be carefully pulled by hand and laid out for the laborious process of *retting*, a natural process of decay which separates the outer stalk from the fibre. This requirement for careful hand labour in harvesting and preparing flax is often cited as the reason why it is especially suited to smallholdings such as predominated in Ireland. After retting, the flax was *dried* in the air, in ovens or over open fires. Then came the particularly onerous job of *scutching*, where the flax stems were beaten with a wooden knife to separate the fibre from the husk. The strands were then *beetled* (hammered) to make them finer, and finally *hackled* or combed to remove impurities and draw the fibre into even finer strands. Shorter flax fibres (*tow*), including those removed during hackling, were prepared for spinning by *carding*. All of this preparation was carried out by the grower or by households who bought rough flax and processed it themselves (Gill 1925, p. 37). Many of these jobs were still done by hand in the twentieth century.

Water-powered mechanisation first occurred in Ireland in scutching, *after* 1817, when not only most cotton processes were mechanised but after mechanised scutching was routine in Scotland and England. Mechanised scutching happened in Ireland only after the Linen Board intervened directly by importing machinery from Scotland or England and providing grants for scutching mills (Gill 1925, pp. 265–95).

Markets for flax were notoriously unstable, leading some commentators to emphasise the importance of women's labour to household subsistence where spinning was combined with growing (Collins 1997; Gray 1997). Spinners were primarily women who spun either for weavers in their households or for sale (mainly in the so-called 'yarn counties' to the west and south). They were 'super-exploited' in the sense that their minuscule incomes from spinning were less than the costs of reproducing their labour. This predominance of women survived the rise of factory spinning in Ireland to a much greater degree than in English or Scottish textiles (Boyle 1979).

The typical Irish male linen worker was the *farmer-weaver*. Observers repeatedly note that attempts by larger landowners to centralise production in factories or weaving sheds were mostly unsuccessful (Gill 1925, p. 44; Crawford 1988, p. 34). This indicates that the industry survived because its participants flexibly moved in and out of farming and weaving, growing flax or food as markets and seasons changed. Young remarked that the weaver became a farmer during a slump, returning to weaving only when conditions improved (Young 1780, pp. 118, 139). In this way, Irish agriculture 'both encouraged the growth of industry and determined its limits' (Gill 1925, p. 49).

In the last decades of the eighteenth century, some wealthy peasants accumulated enough capital to set up weavers (often from their own families) in cottages or weaving sheds, supplying them with yarn and selling their cloth output in markets. But this variant of capitalist transformation 'from below' never made the transition from very small-scale, family-based production to full-scale capitalist factory production.[10]

Crawford (1988) also questions whether upstream investments by drapers and bleachers in weaving sheds and putting-out operations had any enduring effect on the concentration of linen production. A similar class of 'industrial employers' concentrated English woollens before 1700 by organising production and collecting goods for merchants. Gill (1925, p. 144) seems to be searching in vain for similar capitalist development in Ireland when he discusses how bleachers put out yarn to Ulster linen weavers who had settled around 'bleach greens' by the late eighteenth century.[11] But Crawford shows that the vast majority of weavers were still spread around the countryside and most cloth was still sold in open markets as late as 1830. Putting-out yarn for weaving dominated Irish cotton, but not linen.

At the start of the seventeenth century, many weavers bleached (whitened) their cloth. But as they spent more of their time weaving to meet the rising demand of export markets, they had less time for bleaching. Instead, brown linens were either sent abroad or, increasingly, to bleach-works in Ireland. As technical improvements brought increased economies of scale, bleaching concentrated before any other linen sector. The first bleach-works were set up in the early 1700s by Quaker, Huguenot and possibly Dutch immigrants (Gill 1925, p. 50; Cohen 1990, p. 422). By the 1720s, the Linen Board paid considerable capital grants to set up bleach greens. A class of middlemen (*drapers*) arose who bought brown linen for bleachers and in many cases became bleachers themselves.

While bleaching brought profits to some Irish merchants, the most profitable and technically demanding finishing processes remained in England. Practically all Irish linens, both brown and white, were exported to England, where they were printed or dyed, made up and exported. The English legislature in 1696 removed its duties only on imports of coarse white and brown linens from Ireland but remaining duties prohibited coloured linen imports. When England finally allowed Ireland to export linens to the colonies in 1705, it again restricted exports to white and brown linens (and, of course, the Navigation Acts restricted Ireland from directly importing anything in return). New English duties imposed in 1711 excluded Irish coloured linens from the English market in the interests of local dyers, while problems with Irish credit and capital accumulation, as well as the concentration of machinery and chemical trades in England, increased English competitive advantage. Machine (cylinder) printing and factory dying thus remained concentrated in England, to the disadvantage of the Irish industry.

Irish customs data from 1780–1800 show that coloured linens made up a minute proportion of total linen exports: on average, about one-half of 1 per cent (Irish Customs, various years). In the first quarter of the nineteenth century, this fell further, to about one-tenth of 1 per cent. Moreover, exports of cambric and lawns were only 1–2 per cent of the level of those of coloured linens because English manufacturers retained these profitable trades. Britain also controlled the manufacture of Irish sailcloth on the principle that England should be as self-sufficient as possible in naval stores, a principle that was relaxed for plain linen and provisions because sufficient production could never be induced in England. In the early eighteenth century, the English parliament granted bounties for the re-export of Irish sailcoth from Britain. But when English manufacturers protested against Irish competition, the bounties were removed and Irish imports were excluded from Britain by a duty. In general, bounties for Irish linen exports were always restricted to certain varieties, while bounties on the rest were restricted to British manufacturers. Moreover, bounties were of limited use to Irish manufacturers so long as the bulk of Irish linens were consumed in Britain rather than being re-exported and receiving a bounty. Even in the best years, less than a fifth of Irish exports received a bounty (calculated from Murray 1903, pp. 128, 130).

The early structure of linen and flax markets was determined by the decentralised organisation of the industry and by its dependency on English markets and productive inputs. The first outlets for linen fabrics were periodic fairs (held two to three times a year) but as the trade increased markets became more frequent and numerous. At the upstream end of the industry, *jobbers* or *grey merchants* traded flax, yarn and cloth among producers and buyers. Jobbers carried goods from scattered individual producers and small local markets to larger markets, and supplied raw materials and productive inputs in return. But jobbers also created a system of dependence, where small weavers who relied on them for access to yarn and markets had to weave at disadvantageous fixed rates and buy yarn or flax at exorbitant prices (Crawford 1972, p. 25).

The cloth markets themselves – *brown linen markets*, from the colour of the unbleached fabric that was sold in them – may have emerged from the relatively well organised Ulster farm markets. Gill (1925, p. 27) surmises that specialised linen markets grew from the attendance of farmer-weavers at fairs and markets before the linen trade had grown to be of importance. Jobbers generally paid cash to spinners and then transported the yarn to markets to sell directly to weavers. Yarn markets were often tied to linen markets so that the weavers could buy yarn and sell cloth at the same time. Although the linen industry was concentrated in Ulster, cloth was usually taken by road to Dublin during the eighteenth century and sold by Irish exporters to English buyers from London, Bristol and Chester.

It could be argued that the market characteristics for linen were more important, relative to the characteristics of production, than they would be during the second phase of linen expansion, in the nineteenth century. Technological and organisational change even in leading sectors such as woollens was relatively slow, so that the extension of production to new regions was the main source of capitalist expansion. Profitability was, therefore, not only constrained by but in some cases even determined by market access.

Linen was far surpassed by woollens as the chief manufactured commodity of mass consumption and global export, Arthur Young's 'sacred staple and foundation of all [English] wealth' (quoted in Pawson 1979, p. 106). Yet the Irish linen sector grew rapidly during the eighteenth century and was easily the most important source of Irish economic expansion. By mid-century, linen exports surpassed livestock and provisions in value and by the end of the century linen exports were more than twice as valuable as livestock and provisions. Despite this rate of expansion, however, Irish linen was *peripheral* because it was subordinated to English control. It was extremely dependent on the English market, England restricted the parts of the industry in which Ireland could engage and local producers were subordinated to settler classes.

The English market consistently bought more than 90 per cent of Irish exports during the eighteenth century. Even Cullen (1972, p. 59) notes that 'access to the English market had been the very condition of [Irish linen] expansion'. While English demand induced rapid rates of growth of Irish linen production throughout the eighteenth century, however, English producers still monopolised the most profitable parts of the industry. Wool was the 'engine' of English growth in the pre-cotton era. But British linen production still exceeded Irish linen production when cotton took off in the 1770s, even though linen then generated less than 1.5 per cent of England's national income (Deane and Cole 1969, p. 203).

The reason for Ireland's market dependence was neither laziness nor lack of desire to export abroad on the part of Irish merchants. For two centuries after the suppression of the native merchant class in the seventeenth century, Irish merchants still tried to reach American and continental markets in linen and other manufactures. But more than a century of English maritime policy and the Navigation Acts gave British traders competitive advantages that the Irish could not overcome. In addition, the underdevelopment of Irish industry as a whole left Irish merchants unable to secure the economies of scale and lower transactions costs that were crucial to success in overseas trade. Ireland exported only meat, butter and corn in any quantity – and these predominantly to England – so that Irish shippers could not mix loads to make long-distance trade profitable. Irish poverty and dependence on English imports – as well as the fact that the greatest 'Irish' consumers, its absentee landlords, did their consuming in England – meant that Irish exporters were unable to make up return loads even after the repeal of the Navigation Acts allowed them to import directly from the colonies. Irish demand for tobacco, sugar, rum, or even flax seed or raw cotton was too small to sustain a profitable return trade from the Americas. Finally, undeveloped commerce and banking meant that Irish merchants could only give short-term credit – two months as opposed to eight months given by English merchants – leaving them at a distinct disadvantage. Even with its linen 'industry', the dependent and disarticulated Irish economy could not create the many broader linked activities in shipping and distribution that were induced by core English industries.

Conclusions: initial industrial transformations

Ireland was not long incorporated into the English-centred Atlantic economy when the limitations of its position on economic change became apparent. Despite the recent English origins of most landholders and entrepreneurs in seventeenth-century Ireland, they could not carry on the same economic activities they left behind in England. Those who tried to compete by breeding cattle were barred from exporting them. Many responded by raising sheep, hoping to increase their income by putting-out wool for their tenants to spin and weave. The English response was to restrict Irish woollen exports. In each case, when certain Irish economic activities were restricted others were induced in their place: provisions for cattle, linen for woollens.

Although it has become fashionable among Irish economic historians to emphasise the new opportunities provided by British colonial policy, this ignores two important features of these transformations. First, while each restriction was initiated by a small English class faction which called on the state for protection against Irish competition, each transformation induced a new critical product for the broad English imperial project. Those with the clearest interests in protection were not necessarily most interested in inducing the new trades. Restrictions of Irish industry generally responded to narrow English class interests, while transformation was intended to meet the broader interest of imperial ascent, led by an alliance of the English state and the new merchants. England built its economic ascent in the seventeenth century, and eventually its hegemony in the eighteenth and nineteenth centuries, on its control of the Atlantic economy. Its success shifted the nexus of world-system power from Holland and the Baltic trade to England and its Atlantic triangular trade. Sea power, Atlantic commerce and the American plantation economies were crucial to this trade. Provisions and linen were critical to each of these. Ireland was thus a key source of commodities and services for the emergent empire. It provided them to English commerce and English colonies, and withheld them from England's competitors.

Second, the original and transformed industries had different development potentials. While one cannot say that the woollens trade *would have* led broad Irish industrial development, it did so in England. Provisions and linen, however, had limited potential for innovation. Cheap and plentiful Irish labour made it rational to compete by extending the use of labour and intensifying exploitation rather than by introducing new technologies or forms of productive organisation. Domestic spinning and weaving required little capital, at most a spinning wheel or handloom; only bleaching and finishing required substantial capital (Crawford 1972, p. 33). Nearly all increases in linen output in the eighteenth century were thus the result of using more labour rather than mechanisation or organisational innovation.[12] Most Irish weavers were male farmers and cottiers who wove during the winter months and outside of farming hours. Women spun while they were not farming. With few exceptions, even the most skilled linen weavers remained farmers throughout the eighteenth century.

The developmental contribution of linen and provisions was limited by their raw material supply and markets. Both had restricted markets. Irish linen, especially, had few linkages to other industrial sectors. Its disarticulation was noted in 1641 by Lewis Roberts, in his book *The Treasure of Traffic*: 'The town of Manchester buys the linen yarn of the Irish in great quantity, and, weaving it, returns the same again to Ireland to sell' (quoted in Ellison 1886, p. 6). While this division of labour would change over time, the disarticulated nature of linen remained. Both linen and provisions faced long-term problems of raw material supply, because of limitations to domestic flax cultivation and, in the case of provisions, the destruction of resources such as timber. Unlike England, Ireland had no imperial reach with which it could ease supply problems. These characteristics of *semi-peripherality*, as we shall see in chapter 4, limited the industry's expansion even more during the period of factory production in the nineteenth century. Industries such as linen and provisions were insufficient to promote broader economic development of the region. Not only was Irish industrial participation limited to semi-peripheral industries such as linen, but even within linen the Irish were restricted to the more labour-intensive stages of production.

The peripheral character of early Irish industry was not the fault of the Irish themselves, or even of particular Irish classes. It was quite rational for Irish capital to compete with cheap labour instead of innovating. Their options were limited by their subjugation to the interests of an England-centred global system, in which the most profitable and expansive economic activities were reserved for core regions. The English state repeatedly protected the expansive and predatory activities of its capital by sea power, by hegemonic control of world trade and by legally restricting competing industries outside England (e.g., Irish cattle and wool). When its industries achieved clear competitive advantage or England desired free access to materials and markets, the same state staunchly defended free trade – by force, if necessary.

The different abilities of local capitalists to organise state protection may be the ultimate systemic distinction between core and peripheral industry during the eighteenth century. Critics of nationalist arguments about deindustrialisation are correct to stress that the 'Irish' capitalists of the fledgling woollen trade – Cromwell's landlords – were really English settlers. Yet such colonial settlers are contradictory, both in how they pursue their own interests and in their relations to their sponsoring 'mother country' (Emmanuel 1972b). They are potential rebels against core control when it interferes with their economic interests. The Anglo-Irish settlers of the late seventeenth century attempted to organise woollen production on core terms, in competition with the powerful woollen interests of south-western England. To this end, they mobilised for parliamentary independence and against the right of England to make laws for Ireland. The Woollen Act was a decisive blow against settler aspirations to create an independent Irish parliament that could protect their industries as a core state would do.

A close-up analysis of interactions between subjugating core alliances and peripheral classes shows that peripheralisation, like incorporation, is complex and usually contradictory. Ireland's settler merchant-entrepreneurs were peripheralised and never allowed to protect their industrial interests. England controlled what they could produce and where they could sell it. They depended almost entirely on English markets and could create few linkages. Despite surface appearances, the trade of Irish woollens for a linen industry was never a trade of equivalents.

Yet colonial suppression created unintended outcomes and continually met resistance in many forms. By the end of the eighteenth century, many Irish organised the United Irish movement to replace British rule with an Irish republic along the lines of the enlightenment. At the same time, Irish men of property took the opportunities presented by England's difficulties in the Americas to press for legislative independence. Along with it, they again attempted to establish a range of Irish manufactures, including cotton, which would again bring them into conflict with the interests of English capital at the core of Atlantic economy.

Notes

1 The regulation of Irish cattle exports was not new. In February 1621, in a parliamentary debate about the reasons for a lack of coin in England, the

secretary of parliament blamed 'the great number of cattle that are every year brought out of Ireland, for which much and only money is exported out of this kingdom'. An 'Act against the importation of Irish cattle into England, and the exporting of coin out of England into Ireland' got its first reading in April 1621 but the parliamentary session ended before the bill was passed (Edie 1970, p. 7). In 1627 the duty on Irish cattle exports was doubled. Consistent Irish petitions to the king finally succeeded in reducing the duties in 1641.

2   The data in table 3.1 are based on O'Donovan's (1940, p. 104) assumptions that one ox provided two barrels of beef.

3   Neeson (1991, p. 59) notes that few Irish historians have recognised the importance of a continuing supply of timber to England's economic expansion during 1600–1862. Yet English historians such as Albion clearly recognise that 'the relationship of ship timber to sea-power gave it an importance far above ordinary articles of commerce', especially in England where 'timber supply was inseparably connected with sea-power' (Albion 1926, pp. viii, x). Neeson claims that Irish colonisation was a 'prototype for the basic English policy of colonisation in Canada and part of New England; to secure the timber supply' (1991, pp. 59–60).

4   Legislation against staves was not meant to preserve woods but rather was passed because timber which parliament thought should go for ships was being used for the more profitable stave trade (Neeson 1991, p. 339).

5   An additional reason for deforestation, especially in Ulster, was reportedly to clear the woods where native Irish and rebels hid. Thus, there were three main reasons for felling trees: 'security of person, security of pocket, and land' (Neeson 1991, p. 63). At the same time as they were intended to unmask rebels, however, clearances ironically incited rebellion. The encroachment of pasture ruined villages and enclosed commons. Locals in Tipperary reacted by establishing the Whiteboys, the first of a number of popular secret agrarian movements which destroyed fences and cattle and took actions against extortionate tithe collectors and landlords.

6   Although Lord Deputy Wentworth stated his desire to 'make every Irishman a loyal and prosperous English citizen', even by Foster's revisionist reckoning he 'encouraged some Irish industries but discouraged others to keep Ireland dependent' (1988, p. 55).

7   This was implied in Molyneux's famous pamphlet of 1698, which refuted England's right to legislate for Ireland. Kelly (1980) cites evidence of a significant body of influential English opinion in favour of the abolition of the Irish parliament.

8   While the Woollen Act was the most directly prohibitive piece of English legislation of its time, it should be considered in the context of a series of new restrictive policies that were introduced in the 1690s to cut off Irish trading with the outside world. English commercial interests were especially concerned to cut off Irish trade with France during periods of hegemonic conflict.

9   See Kriedte *et al.* (1981, pp. 98–101). The distinctions between the *Verlagssystem* and the *Kaufsystem* in Irish and Scottish linen production, and their relation to theories of *proto-industrialisation*, are discussed in detail by Gray (1997).

10   As I will argue below, the transition to factory linen production in Ireland was marked by the rather sudden displacement of a rural proto-industry by larger-scale investments that were concentrated in a completely different region, often by former cotton entrepreneurs. I am not convinced that this really matters (i.e., that the latter were the 'wrong kind' of capitalists), since there was also a rather rapid displacement of rural English textiles by the emergent Lancashire cotton economy. Rather, the decisive limitations of linen development were produced by the semi-peripheral nature of the industry itself – including its raw-material and market limitations – which precluded the economies of scale and scope that would induce clusters of innovations in English cotton, including the rapid expansions of linked productive and distributive activities.

11   Cohen (1990) shows that bleach greens in limited specific areas, such as around the Bann River, acted as magnets for settlement during the middle of the eighteenth century.

12   Although machinery was available from the 1730s, Irish flax was scutched by hand. Mechanisation of spinning and weaving followed cotton by decades. The only major gains in productivity before 1800 were from substituting the spinning wheel for the distaff or rock and the modification of handlooms. Even the spinning wheel did not reach some remote areas until the 1790s (Durie 1976).

Chapter 4

The second cycle of industrial transformation: cotton to linen

In chapters 2 and 3 I analysed how England established commercial superiority by displacing Holland from its position at the centre of world trade. It moved the central axes of world trade to the Atlantic, where it used its superior sea power and commercial infrastructures to put territorial expansion at the service of its industries' needs for raw materials and expanding markets. From the mid- to late seventeenth century, England and France competed to replace Holland as the centre of world commercial and industrial power.

By the late eighteenth century, after the end of the Seven Years' War (1756–63), England had clearly won its battle with France for world supremacy. But the world-system it inherited was far from secure. Britain became *hegemonic* by creating order out of the chaos of the late eighteenth century: the American and French revolutions, the Irish rebellion, slave rebellions in the Americas and renewed war with France under Napoleon (Arrighi 1994, p. 51). It organised a reordering of the world-system, sometimes by force (as in Ireland), and reintegrated regions into a division of labour where it had clear domination of the high-value stages of production. Most crucially, it organised regions including the insurgent North American colonies to supply critical raw materials like cotton wool. Steady supplies of such raw materials enabled innovations that gave England insurmountable competitive advantages in the most profitable stages of industry.

In Europe, England re-established the Concert of Europe as a form of regulating inter-state relations among the great powers, with itself at the centre of governance (Polanyi 1957; Arrighi 1994, p. 53). It reorganised its imperial rule in such a way that even the newly independent North American regions played a productive part in the regional division of labour. And it used this combination of territorial and productive power to recirculate the wealth and materials of empire into rapidly expanding circuits of accumulation centred in England. Free-trade imperialism, the regime emphasised by Gallagher and Robinson (1953), would not arrive as a multilateral system until after 1860 – and then for only a few years (Bairoch 1976; Senghaas 1985). In the meantime England used bilateral free trading relations to exploit its own competitive advantages to the maximum. As Arrighi (1994, p. 55) puts it, 'by opening up their domestic market, British rulers created world-wide networks of dependence on, and allegiance to, the expansion of wealth and power of the United Kingdom'. Really, however, it was *England* where this expansion of wealth and power was concentrated; as I will show, the integration of Ireland into the 'United Kingdom' was precisely a way of subjugating it within a 'network of dependence'.

The cycle of accumulation that England created in the early nineteenth century was the result of its efforts to create a territorially based economy that combined access to raw materials and markets with the production of a broad cluster of linked industrial products. Much more than woollen manufactures, England's economic expansion of the nineteenth century extended far beyond cotton, particularly into iron and the capital goods that used it. McNeill (1982) argues that the 'overexpansion' of iron production forced English companies to find new uses for it; in a classic case of Hirschmanian *forward linkages* (Hirschman 1958), new uses for iron were found not just in machinery but also in railways and ships. The growth of engineering, in a sense, created its own demand (no wonder Say's Law emerged in this period), with the expansion of rail and sea transport inducing new projects to move raw materials which, in turn, induced yet new industries that used the raw materials. The liberalisation of world trade enabled this expansive phase to continue into the latter half of the nineteenth century, but in conditions that would not have been possible had England not already gained control of the Atlantic economy, its resources and trade through mercantilism and forceful territorial expansion. As Nef (1934) argued, English advantages did not begin with the 'industrial revolution' or even the 'commercial revolution' that vastly increased the size of markets in the late eighteenth century. Rather, English industry and commerce had grown together in a 'revolutionary' way since the sixteenth-century reformation.

Nef, however, wondered about the hiatus in English industrial expansion that occurred during the seventeenth century. English woollen textile manufactures expanded rapidly in the late fourteenth and early fifteenth centuries; English metal industries expanded in the late sixteenth and early seventeenth centuries. Yet the spurt of activities that is usually identified with English hegemony, a combined expansion of textile and metal industries, did not begin until the late eighteenth century. Arrighi (1994) explains the long lag between England's economic restructuring under Elizabeth and its world domination two centuries later by the necessity to create world commercial supremacy, which ultimately made the synthesis of capitalism and territorialism work.

This process of creating commercial supremacy, which required control over peripheral regions like Ireland, was analysed in depth in chapter 3. In this chapter, I explore how the process of combining territorial control with capitalism affected industrial competitiveness. From early in the seventeenth century, English state policies aimed at moving English manufactures into the most profitable stages of industry. Holland dyed and finished English textiles, for example, enabling it to draw off a large part of the profits of English manufactures (Israel 1989). Without commercial supremacy, the English state could do little about this. When it restricted exports of undyed cloth so that English industry might be induced into the profitable stages of dyeing and finishing, Holland used its power as entrepôt to retaliate by closing off markets to English cloth exports (dyed or undyed). Moreover, Holland could stockpile critical raw materials that it controlled through its commercial supremacy, giving its industries advantages in the high value-added trades. Therefore, England had to displace Holland as the centre of world commerce in order for its capital to move into the most highly profitable trades.

England finally broke Holland's hold on important commodities like tobacco, sugar, slaves and codfish with the Anglo-Dutch wars of 1652–78 (Hill 1967, pp. 123–4). Most importantly, it took over the Atlantic triangular trade. This chapter examines how commercial supremacy affected the abilities of English industry to establish unbeatable competitive advantages in the highest value-added stages of industry, particularly within the cotton industry and in the broad cluster of linked industries that together enabled and comprised England's innovative surge of the nineteenth century. I will pay particular attention to the way England competed against Irish forces which attempted to expand in the cotton industry and, in so doing, subjugated and transformed the Irish industry. In the process, the Irish textile industry was once again peripheralised from a potentially competitive leading sector to one that was lacking in innovations and linkages, and whose development was again largely subordinated to the processes of British accumulation within the Atlantic economy.

Cotton and English supremacy

Cotton by itself did not comprise England's industrial rise; it was at the centre of a series of linked innovations which made up the 'industrial revolution'. Cotton never exceeded 11–12 per cent of British GNP (Farnie 1979, p. 24),[1] but it nonetheless had a great impact on overall English industrialisation (Berg 1994). Cotton was a *leading sector*, the centre of a wide cluster of innovations and a wider network of expansionary impulses, inducing technical spin-offs in mechanical engineering, chemicals and steam power (Musson and Robinson 1969). It was a bulwark of the English export trade, with important linkages to shipping (Davis 1962).[2] And the rise of Manchester and Liverpool induced the development of shipping, canal and rail technologies and the improvement of post and communications (Redford 1934, pp. 188–204).

Farnie (1979, pp. 27–36) uses a linkage approach to assess the impact of cotton on British economic change before and after 1830. Before 1830, the greatest growth effects from cotton were in spinning, where changes in technique, productive organisation and supply of the raw material were centred. There were important backward linkages in engineering and transport, but forward linkages were limited to weaving and finishing. Weaving was still performed primarily on hand looms in homes or small workshops. The finishing trades were more capital intensive but were not yet linked to the chemical and dye industries, which would become prominent later in the nineteenth century.

After 1830, spinning induced changes that transformed the whole economy. The introduction of power looms added impetus to mechanical engineering. Transportation requirements stimulated the introduction and expansion of the Lancashire rail system. William Fairburn and others revolutionised mill-building technologies in Lancashire. Cotton may have consumed half of the increment in steel production and fabrication through its demand for power looms, printing cylinders, steam engines and boilers (not to mention the steel consumption of transport and mining machinery). Other linkages included machine oils, wooden bobbins, chemicals and dyes, and rubber and leather machine belts. Murray (1870) estimates that 154 ancillary industries supplied the cotton sector by 1870. To this we may add the consumer demand generated by the industry's workers.

The control of machinery and concentration of engineering in Lancashire was explicit British policy. Cotton merchants and manufacturers, including the otherwise vehement Manchester free traders, opposed machinery exports and the emigration of skilled machinists to forestall foreign competition. The British state complied with comprehensive and rigorously enforced legislation (Redford 1934, pp. 131, 133; Musson and Robinson 1969).

Rates of change of technology, productive organisation, wage rates, skill levels and profitability were uneven among subsectors of the cotton industry. Before 1830, the most innovative processes were in earlier links of the cotton commodity chain. The major technical innovations – the water frame, the mule and the jenny – were all in spinning. Moreover, spinning first combined these new technologies with factory-based production. Most authors agree that the stimulus for change in spinning was the bottleneck it created to weaving. Without sufficient cheap labour of the kind that induced the *extensive* growth of Irish flax cultivation and spinning to increase the supply to linen weavers, English capital required other means to increase the supply of cotton yarn. These included a remarkable series of technical innovations in the late eighteenth century and the centralisation of spinning in factories.

Even with this vast increase in yarn supply, however, weaving never became a bottleneck on spinning. Rather, factory spinners *encouraged* traditional social relations in weaving by using the export market as a vent for their surplus yarn. Thus, in the terms used to discuss innovation in chapter 1, spinning before 1830 was the centre of *creative response* and weaving a centre of *adaptive response*. As mechanised mill spinning increased yarn output, rural hand weaving was extended through the putting-out system until the 1840s (Landes 1969, pp. 42–4). A significant proportion of factory-spun yarn was put out to Ireland, which had a network of weavers scattered throughout the countryside and a rudimentary commercial network in the form of brown linen markets that could be adapted to the putting-out system. Ironically, although the *Verlagssystem* never took hold in linen, it was introduced widely by combined English and Irish commercial interests in cotton as a response to the rapidly expanding capacity of the mechanised English spinning industry.

Access to the raw material and innovation

Access to key raw materials was essential for English industrial growth. Since raw cotton cannot be grown in Europe, its access was a potential constraint on the growth of the industry, most immediately on spinning. Unlike the inelastic supply of flax and wool, however, American cotton planters in the late eighteenth century increased their supply of cotton even faster than its rapidly growing demand. England's advantageous access to this supply, and Ireland's disadvantageous access, was a crucial reason why it could capture and localise innovations while peripheralising the Irish industry.

Advantageous access to materials was a direct result of English control of the Atlantic economy. I have already discussed how the Navigation Acts forced English colonies to channel their trade with each other through England, restricting them from developing a cross-Atlantic merchant marine and commercial infrastructure. Even after US independence and the repeal of the Navigation Acts, England maintained important competitive advantages in direct access to raw materials.

These advantages were not an automatic result of English restrictions. They were increased by the actions of the British state, such as the British Board of Trade's efforts to induce cotton cultivation in Asia, Africa and America. From the 1780s, American planters reportedly got the idea that the British would do practically anything to secure a steady supply of cotton wool (Redford 1934, p. 217). Within a decade after the saw gin made it economical to process upland cotton, the southern US went from exporting no cotton to become Britain's major source of cotton in 1803 (Baines 1835, p. 302). When British consumption exceeded US supply, the Board of Trade generated extra supplies from India, Brazil, Egypt and elsewhere (Ellison 1886, p. 87; Redford 1934, 217 ff.).

In the 1790s, as spinners increased their demands for consistent supplies of raw cotton and the importance of importers being close to spinners increased, cotton supplies were centralised in Liverpool and the organis-ation of supply improved (Edwards 1967, pp. 107, 110). Before 1800, dealers bought raw cotton at the docks and resold it to spinners by auction or private sale, mostly in small lots of one or two bags. But as spinners got bigger they bought in bigger lots and demanded price discounts (Edwards 1967, p. 113). Brokers replaced dealers, selling large lots of cotton at a discount to large spinners, who could afford shorter credit terms. Small spinners, who required longer-term credit, could not compete.

The brokerage system required improved organisation of supply in favour of larger spinners, who economised and increased their flexibility by keeping expensive cotton stocks in the hands of brokers (an early example of just-in-time delivery) and by selling off their extra supplies to dependent smaller spinners (Edwards 1967, p. 104). Increasingly, brokers sold cotton by sending samples to spinners on approval (Edwards 1967, p. 103). This system considerably increased the speed of cotton distribution but it also increased the supply advantages of the biggest spinners close to Liverpool. A broker sent samples to his favoured customers early in the day and kept the cotton from competitors until a purchasing decision was made (Ellison 1886, p. 177).[3]

A consistently diverse supply of cotton was crucial for the competitive advantage of larger Lancashire spinners. Their ability to spin a variety of weights of yarn gave them market flexibility when coarse yarns were in oversupply. Bigger scale, better technology and skilled machine operatives enabled them to switch production more easily to different weights of yarn. They maintained access to cotton of various lengths and qualities by employing several brokers (Edwards 1967, p. 121). By 1800, there was a hierarchy of supply of raw cotton by the buyer's size and proximity to Liverpool: the most consistent and cheapest supply in Lancashire, higher prices in outlying English counties and in Glasgow, and the highest prices and most uneven quality in Ireland and beyond (Edwards 1967, pp. 107, 110). Canal and rail transport systems in Lancashire further increased these differences.

Innovation in British and peripheralisation in Irish cotton

British prohibitions on Irish cattle and wool exports led to their supplant-ation by linen and provisions. But linen's semi-peripheral character and the instability of its markets made it an unreliable staple industry. When war and rising prices disrupted flax supply, farmer-spinners and farmer-weavers moved into subsistence farming (Crawford 1969, pp. 27–8; Durie 1976, p. 91). Up to three-quarters of the linen looms in the north of Ireland were reportedly idle during the depression of 1773 (Monaghan 1942, p. 1). Unlike core English textile sectors, Irish linen entrepreneurs could not compete by introducing technology or factory organisation. Their advantages

lay in cheap domestic labour, which was cheapened further by supplement-
ing a 'family wage' with subsistence farming. Limitations of raw material
supply and final demand gave Irish capital little rationale to innovate.

An Irish cotton industry, on the other hand, was established during a
period of relative autonomy from Britain. In response to mobilisation by
the Irish Volunteers and under pressure in colonial North America, Britain
repealed some of its more egregious restrictions on Irish trade and industry
(although a century of the Navigation and Woollen Acts, and more than a
century of class transformation, left Irish commerce underdeveloped). As
linen stagnated during 1770–80, the semi-independent Irish parliament
encouraged cotton manufactures with bounties and protection against
English calico and muslin. New spinning technology, including water-driven
mills, was introduced. Cotton progressively replaced linen in north-eastern
Ireland. Monaghan (1942, p. 3) reports that in 1760 there were 400 linen
looms and no cotton looms in the Belfast region, while an 1810 census
reported 860 cotton looms and six linen looms. Merchants and landlords
also attempted with varying degrees of success to set up cotton manufactures elsewhere in Ireland.

Why cotton? Irish merchants and other prospective capitalists were
aware of linen's unstable markets and the tenacity of its domestic production
relations. Mid-eighteenth-century attempts by some northern bleachers and
drapers to set up linen-weaving factories in the vicinities of their works
achieved only limited success. The vast majority of their fabric continued to
come from domestic weavers through the brown linen markets. Thus,
textile capitalists accumulated capital but were hardly encouraged to reinvest in linen. On the other hand, they knew through their economic and
social networks that cotton had already begun to induce industrial growth
in England beyond the levels achieved by wool, not simply because of its
mass consumption character but also its factory organisation and new
technologies. Irish capital recognised the potentials of cotton compared
with linen and attempted to follow the English path of development, as
they had tried before in cattle and woollens.

Although small by English standards, Irish cotton production expanded
rapidly before 1800. Because all of the raw material for the industry was
imported, rates of growth of Irish and British cotton production can be
estimated from their retained imports of cotton wool.[4] Figure 4.1 shows the
logged output of the British and Irish industries between 1782 (the first
year of normal activity after the start of the American War of Independence)
and 1822 (the last year for which separate Irish data are available). Using
autocorrelation models, O'Hearn (1994) found that the overall rates of
growth in the Irish and British industries were similar over the forty-year
period. The British industry grew by 6 per cent per year and the Irish
industry by 5 per cent, so at this level of generality the two cotton industries
appear to be nearly equivalent.

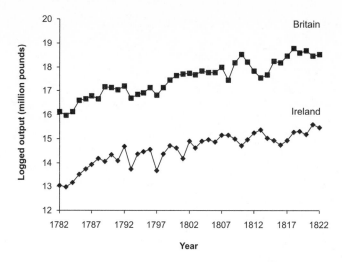

Figure 4.1 Logged output (in weight) of the Irish and British cotton industries, 1782–1822. (See note 4 for sources of data.)

A closer look, however, indicates that the Irish cotton industry went through two phases. Cotton output grew rapidly and relatively smoothly until the mid-1790s and thereafter became slower and more erratic.[5] Before 1801, the British cotton industry grew by 7.1 per cent annually and Irish cotton output by 7 per cent. But after 1801 British cotton continued to grow relatively rapidly, at 5.1 per cent, while the Irish growth rate fell dramatically, to 2.6 per cent.[6] Moreover, Irish output displayed much more variance after 1802, indicating that Irish cotton output was more unstable, with periods of high output and equally distinctive slump. Instability and recession in the British industry were less severe.

The early success of the Irish cotton industry is reflected in the English response to Prime Minister Pitt's 1785 proposals to introduce limited free trade between Ireland and England. In his commercial propositions, Pitt suggested normalising trade duties between the two countries and allowing the Irish to trade in colonial goods, in return for higher Irish contributions to the costs of empire and in hopes of moderating Irish demands for legislative independence. While the plan satisfied Pitt's overriding concern with budgetary solvency, he also hoped it would reverse Irish discontent, which had already led to a semi-independent Dublin parliament and, worse, escalated with the creation of a republican movement led by dissenting settlers. The last thing Pitt wanted was another North American-type scenario of rebellion (O'Brien 1987, pp. 63–84).

Lancashire cotton manufacturers rejected Pitt's proposals outright, regarding Ireland as a commercial threat because of its abundant low-wage labour, plentiful waterpower and state incentives to industry (Edwards 1967, p. 11). Robert Peel even threatened to move his cotton manufactures to Ireland if the propositions were enacted. English industrial capital organised solidly against Pitt and defeated the proposals.[7]

Fifteen years later the English manufacturers' attitude had changed. They pressed Pitt to withdraw Irish cotton duties immediately under the 1801 Act of Union of Ireland with Britain, in order to gain free access to Irish markets. The Manchester Chamber of Commerce argued that 'the removal of all restrictions would tend to direct the capital and industry of both countries to prosecuting those various manufactures for which each possessed the greatest natural qualifications' (Redford 1934, p. 142). After delays due to political considerations, Irish duties on cotton yarn were eliminated in 1816 and on cotton cloth in 1824.

In 1785, British industrial capital rejected free trade with Ireland because it had too many 'natural qualifications' to produce cotton manufactures. By 1801, the same class demanded immediate free trade because England enjoyed distinct competitive advantages in producing cotton. The localisation of innovation in the cotton industry around Lancashire and the peripheralisation of the Irish industry explain this apparent anomaly. The English industry became a centre of *creative response*, introducing new technologies and, more importantly, exploiting new forms of productive and commercial organisation. The Irish industry, on the other hand, employed the *adaptive response* of extending its labour-intensive system of putting-out in weaving, which became a subsidiary sector to English spinning. Ireland's peripherality is indicated by its concentration in weaving rather than spinning, its unfavourable access to the raw material, its lack of linkages to other innovating sectors and its unfavourable access to external and even domestic markets.

For a time, Ireland's relative advantages in cheap labour costs and waterpower enabled it to remain competitive with Britain, despite its continued reliance on adaptive responses. But in the adverse commercial conditions of the early nineteenth century, including war and global economic instability, the strength of England's innovative sectors enabled them to survive and expand more rapidly than the Irish. England's innovations were not a national event, however. They required state sponsorship and the advantages of empire. The subordination of the Irish textile industry gave large English spinners the flexibility to move in and out of the Irish market, dumping their surplus yarn in periods of slumping demand while using cheap Irish weaving labour to cheapen the cloth England sold throughout the world. This explains the rising instability of the Irish industry after 1801. England's innovations and creative responses and, ultimately, rapid rates of growth and relative market stability came at the cost of Irish adaptive response, instability and periodic stagnation.

Spinning and weaving: creative and adaptive responses

The key innovations during 1780–1820 were centred in cotton spinning, which was clearly the leading sector of the world-economy. New spinning technologies were combined with innovations in factory organisation to radically increase throughput and labour productivity. Linked capital-intensive sectors such as finishing, machine building, shipping and distribution were increasingly mechanised. Yet weaving was still primarily done in homes and small weaving sheds. Expansion of yarn output was achieved primarily by increasing labour productivity through innovations in technique, organis- ation, productive scale and material supply (a *creative response*). Expansion of weaving was achieved primarily by adding more labour and equipment (an *adaptive response*). Some spinners competed for a time by intensifying labour exploitation and accepting lower profit rates; weavers in general adapted to the increased supply of yarn by extending their existing practice through the putting-out system. In world-system terms, cotton spinning was at the centre of core industry while weaving was a semi-peripheral link of the cotton commodity chain.

During the early cotton period, little capital was required to begin either spinning or weaving. Yet the organisation of production into factories was concentrated in spinning, culminating in the predominance of large spinning mills in the early nineteenth century (Edwards 1967, p. 9). A small spinner could produce with relatively little capital outlay but the large mill, which combined power mules and multiple spindles with the advantages of buying large lots of cotton wool, massively increased throughput. Factory innovations turned spinning from being a bottleneck on weaving to inducing its rapid expansion.[8] But weaving did not expand by increasing its labour productivity through innovation. Rather, a series of middlemen intermediated between the large yarn producers and multiple weavers spread out over large areas.

Low wages gave Irish weavers a great advantage over the British. But English spinners retained the best cotton for their own use (Mann 1860, p. 88). Moreover, British supplies of raw cotton were more stable than supplies to Ireland. O'Hearn (1994) finds that not only was the rate of growth of British cotton imports higher during 1782–1822, but also that cotton wool imports varied much more from year to year in Ireland, particularly after 1800. This increasing disadvantage in access to the key raw material for the spinning sector, a cumulative outcome of English mercantilist policies and the uneven development of supply networks in England and Ireland, soured the Irish environment for innovation. This happened regardless of efforts by the Irish state and its prospective industrial class. Under such conditions, Irish spinning could survive only if low wages compensated for technical disadvantages and higher material costs.[9]

Lower wages were maintained by continuing the Irish agrarian-based domestic relations of production, which reduced the subsistence costs of farmer-spinners and farmer-weavers. But the persistence of this agrarian-based organisation of production precluded the wide-scale introduction of factory-based spinning that was revolutionising the English industry.[10] Thus, Irish entrepreneurs used relatively labour-intensive processes including putting-out to compete for a time with Lancashire spinners but, as a result, Irish spinning eventually declined and weaving predominated.

Weaving was clearly semi-peripheral. Weavers' wages were extremely low (see below) and cloth markets were unstable. It was usually the first textile sector to feel the effects of a recession (Ellison 1886, pp. 78–9). Since weaving sheds required far less capital than spinning mills of corresponding dimensions, there were few economies of scale or speed. And weavers were often tied to buyers, while the larger spinners moved back and forth between home markets and export (Ellison 1886, p. 79; Edwards 1967, pp. 27, 50).

Yet spinning firms did not automatically achieve the diversified market access necessary to realise economies of scale. This had to be created. Throughout the world-system, England established market access through its use of sea power to dominate international commerce and to regulate its imperial trade laws and practices. Free trade (in Ireland as throughout the world-system) enabled spinners to dump their yarn abroad during difficult periods. During the wartime period after 1803, reportedly, 'the export effort sometimes resembled a gigantic dumping operation; the outcome of desperate attempts by manufacturers to fight off idle capacity illustrating their dependence on the foreign market for their successful expansion' (Edwards 1967, p. 74). English dumping was especially important in the finer yarns, where stocks tied up huge amounts of capital (Edwards 1967, pp. 128–30).

As the English industry became concentrated into fewer, larger enterprises, smaller spinners came to depend on large spinners and dealers with market contacts to sell their yarn. In time, they became 'controlled by their yarn dealers' (Edwards 1967, p. 34). They had limited capital, spun on a commission and sent all of their yarn to a dealer, who kept them supplied with cotton and made cash advances. Since small spinners were at a disadvantage on foreign markets because of high transactions costs and unfavourable credit terms, they were often forced to sell on the less profitable home market.

Free trade extended this productive hierarchy to Ireland and the world-system beyond. Since Ireland's commercial ties were so underdeveloped, its cotton industry became dependent on the British re-export trade from the 1780s. The large English spinners increasingly subjugated Irish weaving through their dealers in Ireland, who regularly reduced their Irish prices to undercut local competition (Edwards 1967, p. 140). The pressure to sell yarn to Irish weavers increased as English spinning mills produced more and more during the 1790s. Eventually, the largest English spinners colluded

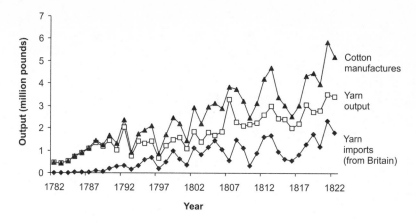

Figure 4.2 Irish cotton output (in weight) and its components, 1782–1822. Source of data: Irish Customs (various years).

to share out the Irish market at agreed minimum prices (Edwards 1967, p. 141).[11]

Irish weavers, even in Ulster, worked in homes and small weaving sheds long after power looms displaced hand looms in England (Green 1944; Mokyr 1983, pp. 176–7).[12] The persistence of hand looms was a rational response to the low price of Irish labour, which induced entrepreneurs to use a different factor mix than in England (Geary 1989, p. 262). But while it was rational to use cheap labour, given Ireland's exclusion from core innovations, the substitution of labour for machines was a semi-peripheral adaptive response that further constrained the region's long-term participation in capitalist industrialisation.

Figure 4.2 shows how this distinction affected the trajectories of the British and Irish cotton industries. Irish yarn output increased rapidly from 1782 to 1788, but was stagnant between 1788 and 1806 and rose slowly thereafter. On the other hand, British yarn exports to Ireland increased rapidly after 1790 and rose irregularly but steadily until the 1820s. British yarn was either woven into fabrics for the Irish market, or woven for British dealers who reimported the fabric for finishing and marketing around the world. O'Hearn (1994) estimates that Irish imports of English yarn rose annually by 5.3 per cent between 1790 and 1822, while Irish spinning expanded by less than 3.5 per cent. The Irish cotton industry became concentrated in weaving: Irish entrepreneurs bought cheap yarn from British spinners and dealers and, in a classic adaptive response, extended their exploitation of Irish weavers.

Although the Irish cotton industry became concentrated increasingly in weaving, there *were* efforts to broaden it. During the late eighteenth century, some merchants in Cork and Dublin invested in factories that finished cotton textiles (Dickson 1976, pp. 105–6). They made the short backward link into finishing cotton cloth to sell to their existing customers. But they had limited market access and depended on non-integrated supplies of cloth from unstable regional weaving industries. When the British spinners put out their yarn in Ireland in the early nineteenth century and, especially, when weaving was transferred outright to England in the 1820s, these finishers collapsed, regardless of their efficiency of operation.

The Irish 'cotton industry' was capable of periods of rapid expansion, but was highly dependent on British machines and materials. It had few of the innovative characteristics that made British cotton a leading sector. As core spinning concentrated in England, it increasingly became linked to semi-peripheral Irish weaving through flexible subcontracting relations that limited the possibilities for developing the Irish industry. The proportion of imports comprising total Irish cotton yarn consumption rose rapidly, from less than 1 per cent in 1782 to more than 30 per cent in 1795. After 1795, it fluctuated between 20 and 50 per cent, these fluctuations adding considerable instability to the Irish cotton trade. Irish capital's 'failure' to innovate more widely in cotton spinning was a rational reaction to a market that was periodically glutted by imports. Dislocations became particularly problematic under free trade after the union. Because its supply of yarn was unstable, Irish weaving was in a precarious position and Irish capital did not innovate. Without innovation, Irish weaving became vulnerable once technical changes and factory organisation swept the British weaving sector in the 1830s. Irish adaptive responses were successful for a time, but could not withstand a continually high rate of innovation by English competitors.

British supremacy and the collapse of Irish cotton

When the US imposed trade barriers against Britain in 1809, British manufacturers began dumping cloth as well as yarn in Ireland. Irish manufacturers could not respond by exporting their own cloth because they lacked a solid export infrastructure, the by-product of more than a century of restrictions on its trade with countries other than England. Irish attempts to export cloth to the US ended in disaster: Irish customs records show only a handful of small cotton textile shipments from Ireland to America after 1805.

The Irish cotton industry finally collapsed after England removed Irish tariffs on yarn in 1816 and cloth in 1824. Between 1825 and 1835, Irish yarn output fell from 3.6 million pounds (in weight) to 2.3 million pounds and cloth output fell from 6.3 million pounds to 2.9 million pounds (Irish Railway Commissioners 1837). As English weaving was mechanised, the Manchester manufacturers began to export finished cloth to Ireland rather than putting-out there. English cloth exports to Ireland averaged less than

80,000 yards before 1815, but reached 850,000 yards in 1822. British cloth exports rose to 5,000,000 yards in 1825 and 14,000,000 in 1835, while yarn exports fell from 3,000,000 pounds to 500,000 pounds.[13]

Belfast spinners started spinning flax when they could no longer compete in cotton. The number of cotton-spinning mills and imports of cotton wool into Belfast fell dramatically between the early 1820s and 1835 (Irish Customs 1823; Irish Railway Commissioners 1837, p. 73; Dickson 1976, p. 110). Dublin and Cork found no adaptive response. The recession of 1825–26 caused the greatest run of company failures in Dublin history to that time. The Cork industry entirely collapsed, causing emigration 'on a scale unique by pre-Famine standards' (Dickson 1976, p. 110). As Irish labour advantages decreased relative to English technical advantages, Irish weavers failed to remain competitive even in the coarser lines.

The overall nature, timing and depth of the peripheralisation of Irish textile manufactures between 1780 and 1835 are indicated by patterns of British penetration of Irish markets. Market penetration supported English innovations while it destabilised the Irish economy. At the same time, English market protection foreclosed reverse penetration. Irish (like Asian) textiles were prohibited from their most important export markets, England and the empire, when they were competitive. Meanwhile, the English industry established its own competitive advantages. England protected its imperial markets from Irish competition under the Navigation Acts while it established competitive advantages in export marketing and transport. Once Britain had established competitive advantages in spinning by the 1790s and in weaving by the 1830s, it enforced free trade throughout the empire, quickly penetrating its markets and making them unstable environments for innovation.

O'Hearn (1994) estimated import penetration into Irish cotton markets (yarn and cloth) from 1780 to 1822.[14] After an initial drop in import penetration due to Irish protection in the 1780s, there were two periods of rapid increase: 1790–1805 and 1816–35. The first phase of rapid import penetration was driven by English yarn exports, a result of the regional concentration of spinning in Lancashire and the peripheralisation of Irish weaving. Following Irish success in reducing English cloth imports, the share of yarn in import penetration rose rapidly, from 1–3 per cent in the early 1780s to 45 per cent in 1790 and more than 67 per cent in 1800. This helps explain the divergence of Irish growth rates in cotton before and after 1800. Overall, import penetration in cotton yarn and cloth ranged from 35 to 45 per cent during the early nineteenth century.

After 1816 another surge in cotton imports accompanied the end of Irish protection and the mechanisation of British weaving. Import penetration increased from a third in 1815 to more than 80 per cent in the mid-1830s. This came about because of a massive shift of British exports from yarn to cloth and clothing between 1825 and 1835. While British yarn accounted for 72 per cent of import penetration in 1825, cloth accounted for more than 80 per cent by 1835. This remarkable change represents the consolidation in England of the cotton industry as an integrated core activity, from transport through to spinning, weaving and finishing.

Ireland's modest export trade in cotton cloth for about a decade after 1816 did not reflect the industry's health. Irish cloth exports rose after 1816 because the British removed their own market protection. But these exports were the end product of putting-out, by Manchester during the 1820s and later by Scottish manufacturers trying to compete with mechanised English weaving. In time, Belfast weavers produced cloth rather than yarn for Glasgow rather than Manchester (Geary 1989, p. 27). This was an adaptive response by Scottish capital to the concentration of the English industry. Glasgow was peripheralised within the British industry, and Belfast subordinated to Glasgow until, finally, the subordinated Irish cotton cloth industry disappeared altogether.

One might conclude that Ireland's limited success in the cotton industry was enabled by its proximity to a supply of cotton wool and technology that would not have been available had Ireland not had access to English imports. On the other hand, Ireland became dependent on a supply system for cotton wool that was organised for the largest English spinners. It also became a consumer of second-hand English machinery rather than a producer and user of the latest technologies. The Irish cotton industry depended on England for its linked inputs, which further isolated weaving from the more innovative parts of the industry. Clustered innovating sectors like engineering and textile finishing were all concentrated in England. Not only was the Irish industry less mechanised than the British, but it relied on England for what machinery it had, as well as everyday supplies, from rollers and spindles to mill gearing. While Ireland had freer access to British machinery after the union, it had become dependent on British engineering and even the most advanced Irish producers remained a step or two behind the English industrial core.

Without guaranteed access to high-quality cotton, rational investors could hardly be expected to innovate by supplying the capital and technology that would allow Irish spinning to compete with its main British rivals. Erratic supply left spinning capacity underutilised and contributed to the failure of spinning mills, causing the regional sector as a whole to be more inefficient than better-supplied regions.

Ireland's dependence on unstable English channels of supply, however, was not simply a matter of geographical proximity. It was the result of Ireland's subordinate position in the Atlantic economy, built up over more than a century. Like other colonies and even non-colonies which were subject to British naval power, this prevented Ireland from establishing the commercial connections and naval capabilities that would enable access to raw materials from around the world. Once the subjugation of the Irish cotton industry caused its final collapse, the continuing needs of the Atlantic economy helped determine what would happen to the north-eastern Irish industrial regime. Once again, it was transformed into the production of linen, still a less profitable and less expansive 'peripheral' industry. But this time around linen was created with a difference: it was a more concentrated proletarian, factory-based industry.

Linen

The rise of a factory-based Irish linen industry in the nineteenth century masks the degree to which the industry remained semi-peripheral and sub-sidiary to the core sectors of the broad Atlantic project. Gill (1925, p. 41) emphasises the continuing domestic production of linen yarn as a major reason for the slow introduction of mechanised factory production in Ireland. The collapse of Irish cotton after 1824 finally brought Irish linen production into factories, rather than the characteristic English and Scottish pattern where dealers accumulated capital and concentrated textile produc-tion. Irish cotton production was more mechanised and centralised than linen, so when cotton capitalists moved into linen they brought their factory organisation with them. But the linen industry remained poorly developed in terms of its mechanisation and semi-peripheral in terms of its relatively low wages and stagnant markets, as well as its lack of linkages to other regional industrial sectors.

Mechanisation

Machine spinning of linen yarn was introduced first in England and Scotland, where it quickly made inroads into the remaining Irish linen yarn exports. But even in England, machine spinning spread much later in linen than in other textiles. The great drive to mechanise cotton spinning began in the 1780s with the introduction of the water frame and the mule. Some machine spinning of linen was introduced in England and Scotland in the 1790s and spread over the following thirty years. But this 'dry spinning' could not produce fine yarns because of the tendency of dry flax to break. Dry machine spinning was not introduced in Irish linen until twenty years after it was England, and then very slowly and only with subsidies from the Linen Board. Water-driven spindles in this early period were concentrated in the sail-making districts of Cork rather than around Belfast, spreading slowly to Ulster in the 1810s. Steam-powered spinning was introduced only forty years after it appeared in England (Takei 1994).

Even contemporary commentators remarked that the slow pace of mech-anisation in Ireland was caused by the low cost of spinning labour and the continuing agrarian base of the industry. Even though one person working a machine could spin ten times as much yarn as a hand spinner, one of Ireland's largest spinners noted that 'yarn spun by women is sold here much cheaper than the same article manufactured by machinery in England' (quoted in Gill 1925, p. 267).

When the wet spinning process enabled factories to spin finer yarns after the 1820s, the advantages of mechanised spinning increased. Wet spinning, which was introduced in Scotland in 1825, allowed linen yarns to be drawn finer because wet flax fibres did not break as easily. This was a necessary innovation if linen was to survive the competition from cotton. Its effect in Ireland, however, was not simply to give linen a new lease on life, but it also transformed linen into a more concentrated and proletarian industry. The mill production that had been introduced in cotton was now transformed for linen. Large mill owners used grants from the Linen Board and capital that was newly available with the introduction in 1824 of joint stock banking in Ulster to import wet-spinning machinery. Eventually, the economies of wet spinning were joined with steam power, following the example of a Belfast cotton spinner who transferred his business to linen. By 1838, there were forty spinning mills in Ireland; by 1853 there were eighty.

What followed in the mid-1800s was linen's concentration in the north-east of Ireland as British linen-producing areas moved into more profitable activities like jute (eastern Scotland) and making up clothing (Leeds and Scotland) (Coe 1969, p. 62). Where Ireland had about 40 per cent of the linen spindles working in the two islands in 1850, its share grew to 55 per cent by 1868 (Gill 1925, p. 319). This expansion, however, was still highly dependent on English and Scottish textiles. Cheap Irish labour in the now-routine spinning sector produced yarn for higher value-added linen weaving and making-up industries in England and Scotland. Irish yarn exports rose from four to four and a half million pounds (in weight) in the 1820s to nine million pounds in 1857 and twenty-eight million pounds in 1865 (Gill 1925, p. 319). Subsequently, as linen power weaving became routine, it began to decline in Britain and rise in Ireland.

As in other parts of the linen industry, mechanisation and factory organisation of weaving came much later and slower than in cotton. In Manchester, where the first steam loom was installed 1806, there were 2,000 power looms by 1818 and 10,000 by 1823. In Ireland, a few small weaving factories appeared in the 1820s, yet even this was mixed with domestic hand weaving.

Ironically, the demise of the Belfast cotton industry was the key step toward the final consolidation of factory production in linen. As Crawford (1988, pp. 48–9) and others have shown, Ulster linen weaving in the 1820s really comprised several distinct 'industries'. The finest linens were produced in the 'triangle' of Belfast and regions to the immediate south and west. Yet this industry was vulnerable because it had no tradition of making coarser, mass-produced goods that could compete with cotton. These coarser linens were concentrated in what is now the southern border region (Armagh, Monaghan, Cavan), although most of the better yarn produced here was exported to England, leaving the tow yarn for local weavers to make into the coarsest cloth, which brought a paltry return and reportedly left them near-destitute. A smaller industry in north Antrim consisted of part-time farmer-weavers who also made coarse cloths from tow yarn to supplement their farm incomes. Finally, the western area around Derry and Donegal produced shirt-quality linens that created the conditions for the area's transformation in later years into a shirt-making centre.

Belfast, initially the weakest linen region, survived longer. Its weavers were used to producing the finer cloths enabled by the introduction of wet spinning in the 1830s (Crawford 1988, p. 48). Cotton had produced a concentrated system of production there, with a small emerging capitalist class. As Belfast's cotton manufacturers found it harder to compete on the basis of cheap labour, the transition from factory cotton to factory linen proved both rational and necessary. Thus, Irish capitalist development in linen was not at all linear but rather a stop-and-go pattern, where the most 'proto-industrially' developed regions failed as factories rose in Belfast.

Weaving became concentrated in the middle of the nineteenth century when Belfast mill owners branched forward into weaving to complete the integration of production from spinning through bleaching and exporting. Weavers followed factory spinners into the towns. But weaving still relied on hand looms. Power looms were used in Scottish linen weaving as early as 1810 but were barely known in Ireland until after 1850 (Gill 1925, p. 268).

Not only was the Irish industry slow to mechanise, but even when it did its processes were older and more labour intensive. An Irish flax-spinning mill, for instance, required four times as many operatives per spindle as an English cotton-spinning mill (Gill 1925, p. 67). And the ratio of steam to water horsepower in the late 1920s was about 7.5:1 in Lancashire and 2:1 in Belfast (Geary 1989, p. 262). Geary (1989, p. 264) argues that the persistence of labour-intensive production was not an indicator of Irish inefficiency but simply a rational response to the cheapness of Irish labour, which induced entrepreneurs to use a different mix of factors of production than in England. But low capital:labour ratios also indicate peripherality.

Wages

Rather than competing intensively by economising through the use of machines, then, Irish capital continued to reduce wages and extend the use of hand labour even in factories. Irish piece-rates for weaving fell substantially between the 1820s and 1850s, including cuts of 69 per cent for cambric and 40 per cent for coarser cloths (Gill 1925, p. 327). While Irish wages had to fall for Irish linen to compete with British textiles, they were downwardly elastic because so many weavers were unemployed after the fall of Irish cotton and because of the continuing domestic nature of the Irish industry. Moreover, the use of power looms in England and Scotland drove down the piece-rates of hand-loom weavers throughout the islands.

Only the massive cuts in Irish labour supply due to starvation and emigration in the 1840s restored an upward push to wages, finally inducing mechanisation of linen weaving. The first power looms in Irish linen were installed in 1847 by an English engineer, who was followed by other English machine makers. According to one survey, the number of power looms in Irish linen manufacture rose from less than 100 in 1850 to more than 12,000 in 1868, 21,000 in 1881 and 32,000 in 1899 (Gill 1925, pp. 329, 332). Finally, half a century after the rise of steam-powered factory production in Lancashire, the Irish industry became a largely mechanised factory system, from scutching to spinning and weaving to bleaching.

The persistence of domestic and semi-proletarian production relations in Irish linen indicates its peripherality relative to largely proletarianised English industrial sectors (Wallerstein 1984, pp. 13–26). By comparing estimates of private and market sales, Gill (1925, p. 161) calculates a rise from 35 per cent of weavers working for a wage in 1770 to 40 per cent in 1784. Yet most of these were working for 'manufacturers' in the Irish sense, that is, they were semi-proletarians who generally worked part time in a small putting-out shed. Crawford (1988, pp. 32–53) disputes even these modest estimates of semi-proletarianisation and contends that the proportion of individual domestic workers was much higher. To the degree that wages were paid, however, they were always lower in Ireland's semi-peripheral industry than in Britain. This reflects lower productivity and lack of mechanisation relative to England or Scotland as well as the fact that lower profit rates left less for labour to demand through struggle.

Even after Ulster textiles became concentrated, the wage differential remained. Belfast spinning wages were about 72 per cent of Lancashire wages in 1833 and weavers' wages were substantially lower. The differential was even greater in terms of spending power, as Belfast's dependence on imports meant wage goods cost more there than in England. Irish wages were kept low by a large reserve army of labour and by the high proportion of female Irish urban labour. Women constituted consistently 70 per cent of Irish linen factory workers during the last half of the nineteenth century compared with 50 per cent in Lancashire textiles (Armstrong 1951, p. 241; Geary 1981, p. 44). Women, children and youths together consistently made up 80–90 per cent of factory linen workers (Boyle 1979, p. 148).

In Ireland, as elsewhere, linen workers made considerably less than those doing similar work in other textile industries. Plain-linen weavers made less than cotton weavers, reportedly subsisting at the barest minimum (Gill 1925, p. 158). Only a few weavers in the finest linen lines received higher wages. From the late 1700s until the 1810s, plain-linen weavers' wages were around 6*s* per week, while fine-linen weavers made 8–9*s*. By contrast, cotton weavers in 1800–11 received 9–15*s* and muslin weavers 18–21*s*. The same disparity held for spinning. Spinners of coarse linen made 1*s* 6*d* to 3*s* per week in 1800, while mill cotton spinners made as much as 16–30*s*.

The discrepancy between English textile and Irish linen wages continued after 1830. Average Manchester wages in 1832–33 were: cotton spinners 20–25*s* per week, dressers 28–30*s*, power-loom weavers 13–17*s*, mechanics 24–26*s*, machine makers 26–30*s* and iron founders 28–30*s* (Redford 1934, p. 80). By comparison, linen spinners in Belfast in 1855 received 4*s* 9*d*, roughers and sorters 13*s* to 16*s* 6*d* and weavers 9*s* (Armstrong 1951, p. 264). The relative wages for linen workers failed to improve and by 1913 the US Commerce Department found that linen had the lowest wages among 'UK' textiles while employing a far higher percentage of women (cited in Armstrong 1951, p. 265). Moreover, Irish weavers continued to be paid piece-rates, with a quality adjustment, throughout the nineteenth century, although spinners were paid a weekly wage because it was hard to measure individual output. Armstrong (1951, p. 266) even reports that whenever hours were shortened, Belfast factory owners responded by intensifying labour and squeezing wages.

Markets and demand

English cotton and its associated core sectors grew rapidly throughout the nineteenth century. Although demand was not *the* major propelling factor in English capitalist development, sufficiently expanding demand (including the capture of new markets) was necessary for core accumulation. Otherwise, rising productivity would have simply induced unemployment as fewer workers produced the existing level of product.

The differences between cotton and linen manufactures in this respect could hardly be more apparent. Figure 4.3 compares the output of English cotton cloth and Irish linen during the period of most rapid expansion of factory textile production, 1824–90 (data are not available for Irish linen production during 1826–50). While the production of cotton manufactures in England rose rapidly throughout the nineteenth century, Irish linen stagnated. A comparison of their rates of growth reveals the extent of the difference. While English cotton yarn and cloth output grew by 3.4 and 3.6 per cent per annum, respectively, Irish linen yarn output rose by only 0.27 per cent. Irish linen cloth output *fell* between 1824 and 1890 by 0.21 per cent per year.[15]

Despite a common current perception that Irish factory linen was the centre of a vibrant industrial sector in north-east Ireland, the global statistics reveal a different picture. Linen output actually stagnated during the nineteenth

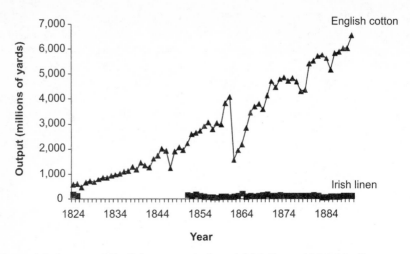

Figure 4.3 Output of English cotton cloth and Irish linen, 1824–90. (See note 15 for sources of data.)

century; the existing Ulster-wide level of output was simply concentrated in Belfast. Since the same level of output was produced with more productive mechanised factory labour, unemployment and underemployment rose in the countryside, along with a powerful impulse for migration to Belfast and emigration from Ireland altogether. Women hand spinners from the country-side often became machine weavers in Belfast, while the overwhelming proportion of urban men worked as general labourers. Those who remained in the countryside were generally consigned to chronic poverty and famine.

Linkages

Perhaps the most significant developmental characteristic of the British cotton industry was its linkages to other sectors. I have already mentioned cotton's linkages, including transport and distribution, as well as Murray's (1870) estimate that 154 ancillary industries supplied the cotton sector. In comparison, the linkage most commonly associated with Irish linen is Belfast's engineering industry. But even here the linkages were weaker than with other textiles. The initial scale and quality of Irish engineering were different from those in England, where a longer period of industrialisation and prosperity spanning both the wool and cotton economies created sufficient demand for highly specialised smiths. Irish smiths, to the contrary, never specialised. Nor did Irish ironmongers ever attempt to organise production like their English proto-industrial counterparts, but instead they simply became agents of British hardware makers, who competed with local suppliers (Coe 1969, p. 16).

The specialised industry around Belfast that was finally induced by textiles was very small. The first iron founders made boilers for bleachers as well as basic consumer items such as pots and pans. They all closed down within a few years. By 1800, there were only two foundries in Belfast, rising to eight in the 1830s and twenty in 1870, after which the numbers again fell off. The majority of foundries remained in Dublin until after 1850, when English competition became more severe. In the north, iron making never grew beyond textile and marine engineering and engineering firms owned all the large foundries. Steel or aluminium founding never took off in Belfast (Coe 1969, pp. 24–31).

Even in textile engineering, the possibilities for expansion were strictly limited to products that were either too costly to transport, so that they had to be made on the spot, or could not be adapted to linen. The former category included some steam engines and waterpower plant. Local firms largely carried out the erection and repair of waterwheels, for example. But as the vastly superior turbine technology took over in the second half of the nineteenth century, mills imported their turbines from Britain and elsewhere (Coe 1969, p. 37).

The first steam engines in Ireland came from Britain, but their basic technologies were easy to pirate and they were extremely expensive to transport. Irish founders thus enjoyed a competitive advantage over British companies for new machines. Yet Geary (1989, p. 262) cites evidence of a tendency to import used British steam machines. Moreover (as I have already pointed out), linen remained overwhelmingly dependent on waterpower, so that the demand for steam engineering remained small and machines were largely made by general foundries. Several Irish companies made steam engines during the last half of the nineteenth century, but by 1905 only one remained in business. The tenure of steam in the linen industry lasted for only a few years, as waterpower still dominated well past the 1850s and electric motors and internal combustion engines began to replace steam by 1875. The more specialised British engine makers had clear advantages in these technologies and again imports came to dominate Irish power plant.

The largest engineering sector that was tied to linen was textile machinery. Yet even this local industry was dominated by foreign firms for the production of linen machinery that could be adapted from disused cotton machinery. Flax breaking and scutching machinery, the oldest engineering sector in linen, was extremely basic and failed to improve much because better machinery required flax of a uniform quality, which was not available in Ireland. Even this basic trade declined in the second half of the nineteenth century. Neither carding nor hackling machines were made in Ulster before 1850 – the former were imported from Leeds while hackling continued to be done by hand. Some hackling machines were made in Ireland during the last half of the century, but never by more than three firms.

Nearly all early dry-spinning machinery was English, along with most early wet-spinning machines. An ordnance survey of 1838/39 identified a spinning mill near Belfast as the only one in Ireland that was wholly equipped with Irish machinery (Coe 1969, p. 63). While Belfast engineers probably made most flax-spinning machinery thereafter, the expansion of flax spinning lasted only until the late 1860s, after which a number of firms went out of business, leaving only three firms to make flax-preparing and spinning machinery by 1900.

I have already indicated that power weaving came especially late to Ireland. Power looms were introduced fairly rapidly in Belfast after 1850 but they were mostly English. Only the Jacquard loom for weaving damask was produced in Ireland, but this was a relatively minor part of the industry. Finally, finishing machinery before 1850 was crude. Beetling machines simply wrapped the cloth around a cylinder and beat it with wooden slats. Capital investments in bleaching works were concentrated in waterwheel mechanisms rather than other machinery. As English firms began to compete seriously in improved machinery for finishing, bleaching and dyeing after 1850, linen finishing became dependent once more on British imports. Machine printing was not introduced into Irish linen until the twentieth century, and then it relied entirely on British machine makers (Coe 1969, p. 73).

The engineering associated with linen never reached leading-sector proportions as engineering had in the English Midlands. Belfast engineering, like linen, was outstanding less in terms of its actual size than in its size relative to the largely non-industrial Irish countryside. The sector reached its heights much later than in England and competed in fewer products, and many lines were produced in Ireland for only a short time by a few producers.

But the contrasts between linkages in English cotton and Irish linen were greater still, as Murray's estimate of 154 English ancillary sectors indicates. Examination of the purchasing records of Belfast textile manufacturers indicates that a range of everyday supplies such as brushes, rollers, spindles and spare parts were supplied from Manchester. While engineering, because of its high-technology content, is often emphasised in studies of textile linkages, the production this array of everyday items probably employed more people than did the textile industry. The absence of their production from Irish industry constituted a severe limitation on the regional development effects of the linen economy.

North-eastern industrial concentration and general Irish peripheralisation

Since this study is mainly about how the Atlantic hegemonic project repeatedly affected Irish industry and Irish industrial transformation, its nineteenth-century focus is mainly on the concentrated industrial area of north-eastern Ireland. Yet the concentration of industry in the north-east obviously had effects on previously industrialised regions (even if they contained domestic industry). Moreover, the restrictions of the previous centuries had important limiting effects on industry throughout the island of Ireland. Therefore, it is important to show how production for the Atlantic economy affected economic activities outside the Belfast area, whether commerce was displaced, certain industries persisted, or agrarian production was transformed.

One result of the concentration of Irish linen production was a shift in commerce. Before 1800, Irish textiles were exported to England through Dublin. Around 1800, however, Dublin began to give way to direct trade between Belfast and England. The transport infrastructure around Belfast was improved, enabling the region's direct incorporation into the English-centred Atlantic economy instead of indirect incorporation through Dublin. North-eastern bleachers, who had long begrudged the interest rates and storage fees charged by Dublin factors, increased their direct trade with England. The number of factors in Dublin's linen hall fell from forty-six in 1808 to thirty in 1825 (Gill 1925, p. 190; Crawford 1972, p. 18). Despite these changes, Irish linen's dependence on English markets remained constant. Not only was a predominant and increasing amount of Irish linen exported, but Irish exports virtually all went to England, even if their final destination was a colonial market. Ninety-five per cent of Irish linen exports went to England in 1783, 93 per cent in 1802 and 96 per cent in 1825 (Gill 1925, p. 177).

As commerce stagnated or declined outside of the north-eastern linen region, only a limited number of industries survived. As a result, the urban population declined during the nineteenth century, even as it rose rapidly elsewhere in Europe. Outside Belfast and Dublin, the population of the 100 largest Irish towns fell from 694,000 in 1841 to 525,000 in 1926 (Crotty n.d.). The only notable industry that thrived outside Belfast was brewing (Bielenberg 1998).[16] Even here, there were parallels with linen, because the massive growth of Guinness during the century happened at the expense of the more than 200 small breweries that existed at the beginning of the century. The number of Irish breweries fell from 245 in 1835 to 115 in 1846 and just 39 at the end of the nineteenth century. By 1864, Guinness already made more than half the beer sold outside Dublin (Bielenberg 1998, pp. 109, 115, 116). Soon, it was the leading brewer in the islands of Ireland and Britain.

In a sense, Guinness is the exception that proves the rule when it comes to the limitations of dependent development in Ireland. The main reason for its success was the rapidly growing domestic market for beer: Irish consumption grew from less than four gallons per person in 1851 to more than twenty-six gallons in 1901. From the base of such healthy home demand, and building on economies of scale and the improved transport infrastructure between Ireland and England, Guinness became southern Ireland's only significant industrial exporter. This is precisely the kind of 'virtuous cycle' to industrial development that Senghaas (1985) identifies in other small European countries later in the century. But in Ireland, the single firm of Guinness was exceptional, as there was no generalised agrarian revolution or associated development of a local market that could have sustained more general industrialisation.

Instead, the concentration of industry in the north-east was paralleled by a progressive *underdevelopment* of the Irish countryside. The most obvious effect of the concentration of the linen and engineering industries around Belfast was that previously semi-industrial areas were deindustrialised while semi-proletarian families were thrown out of work. As a result, many families emigrated to Belfast, Britain or North America, while others faced subsistence crises because they could no longer supplement farming with spinning or weaving. On a wider scale, Irish agriculture was transformed. Crotty (1966, pp. 283, 356) shows that rising English urban demand raised beef prices by more than 300 per cent during 1816–1920, while the prices of butter and bacon were stagnant and wheat prices declined by a third. As a result, production shifted from tillage and dairying to dry cattle. This new rural economy did not need the large numbers of landless rural labourers who had come to dominate the countryside over the previous century. Thus, through famine, evictions and emigration, the Irish human population fell by two million during the last half of the nineteenth century, while the cattle population rose by about the same number (Crotty 1966, pp. 354–5). A new middle class of (mainly Irish Catholic) graziers also arose, according to Crotty (n.d., chapter 8), who bonded together in a moderate nationalist movement to try to extend throughout Ireland the rights of tenure that were enjoyed by northern settler farmers. Far from increasing the viability of the domestic Irish market, incomes from the new grazing economy were transferred into the hands of the landed classes. They spent or invested a large part of their incomes in England, either directly or indirectly through the joint stock banks that were established over the same period (Crotty n.d., chapter 8).

A revolution on the land did occur later in the century, when acts of the 1870s effectively transferred ownership of most Irish land to its occupiers. But this had little positive developmental effect, since the sector's dependence on the English urban market remained and tillage continued to decline.

Conclusions: the concentration and reperipheralisation of industry

The second industrial transformation of Ireland, like the first, was a subjugation of a potentially core industry (cotton) and its eventual replacement by semi-peripheral industry (linen), which had none of the former's advantages in terms of potential market expansion and linkages to other innovative activities. Because of these limitations, technical change in linen was slow while profit rates and wages remained relatively low.

On the other hand, this transformation was not meant strictly to impoverish Ireland. Like earlier policies, free trade and union with Britain were aimed at bringing Ireland under stricter political and economic control, so that it would provide goods and services that were important to nineteenth-century British hegemony, which was centred on the Atlantic economy. This contradictory process included, on the one hand, the concentration of industry around Belfast in factories and mills, where it had previously been scattered around the countryside in part-time domestic production. Such geographical concentration was also a concentration in strictly limited nodes of commodity chains, particularly linen spinning and weaving (not finishing) and semi-peripheral labour-intensive metal trades (boiler-making and rudimentary shipbuilding). This concentration gave the appearance of economic dynamism, which hid the reality of stagnation as Irish linen production actually fell during the nineteenth century. On the other hand, the countryside was peripheralised. Former textile regions were transformed into more strictly agrarian regions. Farming became concentrated and tenant farmers were pushed off the land. Ireland's population fell rapidly through starvation and emigration. Those who could not eke out a living on the land emigrated, either to Belfast or more often to Scotland, England and North America.

While this transformation had progressive aspects like proletarianisation and factory organisation of industry, it was also *under*developing insofar as it further limited Ireland's capability and options for further economic transformation in subsequent periods. As we shall see in the next chapter, Irish attempts to develop industry in the twentieth century continued to be limited by its underdeveloped trading infrastructure; its overdependence on livestock exports to England; the geographical overconcentration of its industry around Belfast and sectoral overconcentration in a few strictly defined economic activities; its infrastructural underdevelopment or mis-development; and the further weakening of indigenous capitalist classes. Native Irish commercial activity had already been quashed by the penal laws and the land settlement, while nineteenth-century settler farmers and landowners limited their activities more strictly than ever to farming after the Act of Union.

The subjugation of regions like Ireland and the semi-peripheral character of their few industrial activities are not simply an academic issue. The vulnerability of the Belfast region as a semi-peripheral industrial zone (and it was largely Belfast, rather than the whole of Ulster or even northern Ireland, that constituted the industrial zone after 1830) left it woefully exposed as its associated British core declined during the twentieth century. Lacking even the option of dependence on ascending core regions such as the US and Europe after the Second World War, the post-partition north-eastern economy declined rapidly to become one of the most depressed regions of the European periphery. England's gift of linen, although it outlasted the simultaneous gift of provisioning for a long time and went through several distinct phases, was a mixed blessing at best.

Notes

1   Deane (1968) estimates the size of the cotton industry much lower, at 5–6 per cent of GNP.

2   Cotton manufactures made up 52.8 per cent of the increase of value of British exports from 1785 to 1815, and 35 per cent from 1820 to 1850 (Farnie 1979, p. 10).

3   Manchester manufacturers consistently complained about the possibility of foreign mail missing the Saturday coach from London, which would put them two days behind their London competitors in dealing with foreign inquiries (Redford 1934, p. 189).

4   For a detailed explanation of techniques of estimating Irish and British cotton output and trade, see O'Hearn (1994). Irish data for 1764–1822 are from Irish Customs ledger books held in the National Library of Ireland. British data are from Baines (1835, p. 347) and use refinements by Blaug (1961, p. 377).

5   The exploratory technique of a running median identifies more precisely when growth rates shifted. There were clear breaks in the median rates of growth of Irish output in 1795–97 (when the median growth rate declined from 17.5–19.9 per cent to 9.6–17.5 per cent), in 1805–09 (when it declined to 9.4–9.6 per cent) and in 1816 (when it declined to 9.4 per cent). Unfortunately, Irish trade data are not available after 1822, but one would expect rather steady declines soon thereafter.

6   The distinction between the two industries in different time periods is even starker when we consider their earliest years. During 1782–95, output in the Irish industry grew at an estimated rate of more than 11 per cent per annum, while the English industry grew by 7 per cent. Thus, while the British industry maintained a rather even rate of growth through the 1790s, the Irish industry was already in decline.

7   Ironically, the English industrialists demanded free trade with France because they desired access to its markets and perceived no threat from the local industry (Redford 1934, p. 127).

8   In 1770 spinning was a bottleneck: six to eight people were required to spin enough yarn for one weaver. By 1785 the productivity of spinning labour increased so much that weaving had to expand for the yarn to be sold (Ellison 1886, p. 48).

9   Geary (1981, p. 41) estimates that coal was 2 per cent of total costs in the Irish 'cotton industry', while wages comprised 33 per cent. Belfast spinning wages were about 72 per cent of Lancashire wages in 1833 and weavers' wages were substantially lower.

10 In addition, a higher proportion of Irish urban labour was female than in Lancashire – a male:female ratio in Belfast of about 1:2 and in Lancashire of 1:1 – while women spinners earned less than one-third the wages of male spinners (Geary 1981, p. 44).

11 Even around Belfast, where there were some modern mills, the finer yarns continued to be imported from England. Ironically, skilled Ulster weavers were especially dependent on the British industry because Ulster's mills could not spin the fine yarns they needed to weave high-quality cloth (Geary 1981, p. 38). The dependent Ulster weavers were typically controlled by British spinners under the putting-out system.

12 There were 2,000 power looms in Manchester by 1818 and 10,000 by 1823, but Irish weaving was done almost entirely by hand as late as 1831 (Monaghan 1942, p. 10).

13 The remaining yarn exports came mainly from Scottish spinners, who were attempting to compete in an ever more difficult environment by their own adaptive response of putting-out in Ireland (Dickson 1976, p. 111).

14 Import penetration is defined by the ratios of Irish imports of cloth and yarn to apparent consumption, which is cloth imports and domestic cloth production minus cloth exports. In order to avoid double-counting, domestic production does not include cloth made from British yarn.

15 Output growth rates are estimated by ordinary least squares regressions of the logged output of each product on time in years. Neither of the growth coefficients for Irish output was statistically significant, indicating that they were practically zero. English yarn and cloth growth rates, on the other hand, were significant beyond the 0.01 level. Irish data are estimated from data on trade in flax and linen yarn, as well as acreage sown and yields of flax (see Boyle 1979, pp. 254–81). English data for 1824–26 are from Ellison (1886, table B) and for 1827–90 from Blaug (1961, pp. 358–81).

16 Smaller industries persisted in milling, rope-making, paper and glass. Concentration was also a feature of these industries during the nineteenth century (O'Malley 1989, p. 42).

Chapter 5

The third cycle of industrial transformation: import substitution to export-oriented industrialisation

Once the Irish are independent, necessity will turn them into protectionists.
Marx to Engels, 30 November 1867 (Marx and Engels 1971, p. 149)

If I were an Irishman I should find much to attract me in the economic outlook of your present government towards self-sufficiency ... let goods be homespun whenever it is reasonably and conveniently possible and, above all, let finance be primarily national.
J. M. Keynes, First Finlay Lecture, University College Dublin, 19 April 1933

The anti-systemic movements that thrived in Ireland from the time of its incorporation under English force continued to develop, culminating in the late-nineteenth-century to twentieth-century nationalist and republican movements for varied degrees of autonomy from English rule. An enduring aspect of Irish campaigns for autonomy was the desire to develop industrially and commercially, which was driven by the understanding that such development continued to be limited by English rule and the interests of English capital within the Atlantic economy. This desire to develop was originally concentrated among settler elites, but self-sufficient industrialisation had become a central plank of Irish nationalist movements by the late nineteenth century. Self-sufficiency was reflected in the very name of the political party that led Irish republicanism after it was founded in 1905: *Sinn Féin* ('We Ourselves'). Strongly influenced by protectionist economists like the German Friedrich List and Henry Carey in the US, the Sinn Féin leadership endorsed industrial protection as the cornerstone of its national economic development policy. Its first leader, Arthur Griffith, proclaimed, 'a nation cannot promote and further its civilisation, its prosperity and its social progress equally as well by exchanging agricultural products for manufactured goods as by establishing a manufacturing power of its own' (Griffith 1918).

While true, of course, this was also naïve economic strategy because it did not take into account the power and interests of other states within the Atlantic economy. This shortcoming should not be surprising. The US was only emerging as a world military and economic power, and its imperialistic military incursions in its Western hemispheric 'backyard' were matched by anti-colonial sentiments elsewhere. Moreover, the Fenian movement, a direct precursor of physical-force republicanism in the twentieth century, began and developed in the hothouse of the Irish-American community. Irish nationalists regarded the US as a 'counterbalance' to English power even though, despite the importance of the US population for raising arms and financial resources, the *special relationship* between the US and British states was never really threatened by popular US support for Irish nationalism. As the US began to displace British hegemony world-wide and, especially, in the Atlantic, Ireland continued to seek its support for the project of Irish self-determination. With few exceptions, there was little concern that US hegemonic interests might threaten Irish self-sufficiency as much as British imperialism.

Decolonisation and US hegemony

British hegemony was in decline after 1870, as the Irish land and independence movements gained in strength. By 1900, the US had surpassed Britain as the world's leading producer of iron, steel, coal and textiles. Mergers around the turn of the century made US industry the largest in the world. As McCormick (1989, p. 19) points out, this increase of US economic power was accompanied by an ideological shift away from protectionism to an informal imperialist programme of opening doors for US expansion. Beginning with the 1897 Dingley Tariff and the Open Door notes of 1899–1900, policy makers began to recognise that US supremacy was better served by freer global markets than by protected national and colonial markets. Since the US still lacked international commercial and financial structures, it was not yet ready to achieve hegemony, but for a time it sought joint world leadership with Britain.

After the First World War, Woodrow Wilson's administration extended US influence abroad. In his Fourteen Points statement of 1918, Wilson called for global free trade and an end to colonialism, a development that hardly escaped the attention of Irish republicans, who were on the verge of successfully achieving political independence for twenty-six of their thirty-two counties. Yet this perceived anti-colonialism was, as always, tempered by the special relationship: Wilson hoped to police the seas with a joint US-British naval force[1] and the US by and large 'deferred to Great Britain, the declining hegemon, on issues involving European security' (McCormick 1989, p. 27). Moreover, the Americans were hardly motivated by anti-colonial support for self-determination but hoped to substitute informal finance imperialism for formal political control.

During the 1920s and 1930s, the US made limited incursions against European control of colonial resources. American oil companies gained a foothold in the Middle East while the US stopped British plans to create a rubber cartel. Yet many US corporations still preferred to co-operate with European powers for access to their colonial resources instead of backing government policies to break down colonial control. This reflected a wider debate in US society between economic nationalists and 'internationalists'. Most small miners, farmers, ranchers and industrialists favoured a pro-tected US market. But large financial and industrial capitalists desired access to foreign materials and markets, especially as the world depression of the 1930s demonstrated that expanding accumulation required expand-ing markets and sources of supply.

With the election and repeated re-election of Franklin Roosevelt – and, especially, as the US gained predominant world power after the wartime devastation of Britain, Germany and Japan – the 'internationalists' gained the upper hand. Even before the US joined the Second World War it began to plan its post-war world leadership. In a series of secret *Studies of American Interests in the War and the Peace* organised by the Council on Foreign Relations (CFR), top academics, business people and political leaders set out blueprints for a post-war world economic order under the different scenarios of German victory and German defeat. These blueprints included an international monetary system (later established as the IMF), an international development bank (the International Bank for Reconstruction and Development, IBRD/World Bank) and agreements on international trade and the exploitation of minerals (Council on Foreign Relations 1946). After the war, CFR members dominated the executive agencies and post-war reconstruction bodies that would implement these programmes (Block 1977; Shoup and Minter 1977; Wexler 1983; Hogan 1987).

The post-war goal of US hegemony was to create a trading bloc, or *grand area*, in the interests of its major industries. Shifting US trade patterns, from primary to manufactured exports and from manufactured to primary imports, had already created problems for US producers. Peripheral exports of raw materials to the US were not rising as rapidly as US exports of finished goods (Upgren 1940c). This imbalance created inflationary pressures, threatening US industrial expansion (Upgren 1940a). And ravaged post-war European economies could hardly generate enough income to buy US products. Thus, lack of international demand, especially after the destruction of war, threatened US industrial expansion.

The grand area strategy was designed simultaneously to solve the prob-lems of resource supply and international demand. US capital exports would finance and organise European recovery and peripheral raw materials production. In a new Atlantic triangular trade, the US would sell its industrial products to Europeans, who would pay for them with colonial raw materials and with money earned from increased trade with their colonies (Upgren 1940b). Eventually, peripheral countries themselves might become important consumers of US products. This trading system would be regulated by foreign direct investment: while free trade opened the door to US capital exports and materials imports, direct control of peripheral mineral reserves by private US firms would ensure that such trade would increase over time.

The grand area strategy would integrate Asia and the European empires into the existing US–Western hemisphere bloc (Upgren 1940c, p. 18). The British empire – especially South Africa, India, Malaysia, Australia and New Zealand – contained most of the raw materials needed by US industry, while England was a massive importer of surplus Western grain, meat and dairy products. Europe as a whole was the key source of demand for US industrial exports. The bloc's remarkable self-sufficiency, especially if all of Europe and its empires were added, would enable rapid accumulation with stability. The principle of 'mutual self-interest' held that members would remain in the grand area if they were left with neither surplus exports nor unmet import demands (Upgren 1940b, 1941).

As Arrighi (1994, p. 239) argues following Chandler, this hegemonic strategy was powerful because US management of international trade was combined with managerial organisation of its highly developed multidivisional firms that *internalised transactions costs* (costs of moving intermediate inputs through the commodity chain from primary product to final consumption). The vertically integrated corporation could rapidly process intermediate products through different stages of production (*throughput*), thus lowering costs and increasing output per worker and machine. Central to obtaining these economies of speed, Chandler argues, were 'the development of new machinery, better raw materials, and intensified application of energy, followed by the creation of organizational design and procedures to coordinate and control the new high-volume flows through several processes of production' (1977, p. 244).

Initially, the new organisation of the multidimensional firm and its strategies of seeking economies of speed involved the integration of production throughout the North American continent. Once US companies completed their continent-wide integration, they began to move abroad in their search for materials and markets. As Hymer argues, 'in becoming national firms, US corporations learned how to become international' (1972, p. 121). As US managerial capitalism became transnational, however, it required open-door policies (rather than colonial control) throughout the world, to enable its subsidiaries to move primary and intermediate goods freely and quickly among themselves until they were assembled and marketed as final products throughout the world. With such open doors, as Staley had already emphasised before the war, a country needed raw materials and other inputs only 'within its trading area, not necessarily within its political boundaries' (1937, p. 58).

The key to US hegemony, then, was to change the meaning of post-war political boundaries to enable freer US investment and trade throughout the

European colonial empires. Then, giant integrated extracting–processing–fabricating transnational firms could step through the open doors to obtain cheap and assured access to materials, labour and markets. In other words, US policy in the post-war era aimed to break down European (especially British) control of colonial resources. Trade restrictions, land tenure regulations, the vesting of mineral rights in the crown, the control of foreign exchange and investment regulations were all strong barriers to the movement of US capital and, particularly, to US foreign direct investment (FDI). Slowly, through the process of tied lending under Marshall aid as well as more direct pressures, the US began to wrest control of colonial raw materials and open up investment opportunities (Bunker and O'Hearn 1993). Where Britain and the other European powers failed to introduce decolonisation processes from above, as in Jamaica, the US often encouraged but also tried to control liberation movements from below.

The obverse of the open door for transnational investors and traders was that the newly independent semi-peripheral states had to *give up their efforts at industrialisation through protection*. US economists, politicians and technical experts argued that such regions could modernise much quicker by specialising in export production for the world market, using the profits from specialisation to slowly establish more permanent although less ambitious industrial sectors. Moreover, transnational investors who entered through the open door would bring modern infrastructures and technologies, making such a route to modernisation more thoroughgoing. The economist Alvin Hansen, a leading adviser to US governments, argued that the 'legitimate goals' of peripheral and semi-peripheral industrialisation were limited to 'a moderate degree of industrialisation consistent with their resources, especially the manufacture of light consumer goods'. Other policy makers stressed the importance of countries concentrating on the economic use of resource-based activities in which they had comparative advantage (quoted in McCormick 1989, p. 52). Former colonies that hoped to industrialise through inward-looking policies were required to abandon their ambitions and instead embark on export-oriented development strategies.

Ironically, then, decolonisation simultaneously removed British colonial restrictions (thus raising peripheral hopes of self-determination and national development) *and* removed the most effective barrier to US economic penetration of former colonies (thus creating new threats to national self-determination). Southern Ireland, after partition, was an ambitious industrialising state with political and business elites who hoped to use political independence as a route to national economic development through industrialisation and agricultural progress. They partly succeeded but, in doing so, created conditions that enabled a third transition of Irish industry: from protected national industry to foreign-led dependent development. This story is not just another episode in the continuing history of *reiterative problem solving* between Ireland and the dominant Atlantic powers: it is also one example of many where twentieth-century decolonisation was followed by, indeed enabled, post-colonial *re*incorporation and *re*peripheralisation, under US influence.

Political independence and protection

After years of struggle, a section of the Irish nationalist movement signed a treaty with the British in 1921 that copperfastened partition on the island. The Irish Free State, 'southern Ireland', comprised twenty-six of the thirty-two counties on the island. 'Northern Ireland' contained just six of the nine historical counties of Ulster. This was the largest area that could be partitioned with a guaranteed in-built Protestant/unionist majority, as the other three counties were strongly Catholic. It also contained border regions that had Catholic/nationalist majorities but were important for strategic and economic reasons.

At partition, centuries of colonial limitations – commercial restrictions and two cycles of industrialisation followed by deindustrialisation and industrial transformation – left Ireland impoverished and industrially underdeveloped. Some recent economic historians have argued that Ireland was relatively wealthy at partition and became underdeveloped by its own poor performance thereafter (Lee 1989; Kennedy 1996). According to Maddison's estimates (1995, p. 93), Ireland's gross domestic product (GDP) per capita was a little less than half Britain's in 1913, although it was 73 per cent of French and 80 per cent of German GDP. By 1973, Irish GDP per capita had fallen to half the level of each of these three countries. The view that Ireland was relatively 'wealthy' at partition, however, is largely a mathematical misinterpretation: the denominator of Irish per capita income (population) had been drastically cut over the preceding seventy years by famine and emigration while the numerator (output) was stagnant. Lee (1973) estimates that Irish national income growth was the lowest in Europe between 1848 and 1914, at 0.5 per cent per annum; Mokyr (1983) puts it slightly higher, at 0.7 per cent (see also Ó Gráda 1994, p. 242). This does not denote 'development' or even efficiency in any meaningful sense. Rather, in European terms, southern Ireland at partition was a highly impoverished agrarian region with hardly any industry.

The 1921 treaty promoted continuity as much as change, dependence as much as independence. The 1922 constitution, a leading Irish historian observed, was 'a highly ingenious attempt … to reconcile the recent revolutionary past with the necessity of a continuing British connection' (Lyons 1973, p. 471). The new state remained in the British Commonwealth and the British retained right of access to designated 'treaty ports'.

The Free State's de facto economic bonds to England also continued. In 1923 agriculture made up about half of the Free State's domestic product and over 98 per cent of Irish exports went to Britain. As the Irish punt was tied to sterling, the country had no recourse to foreign exchange controls as an economic instrument, nor could it freely trade with non-sterling areas.

The main social change leading up to partition was the rise of a class of small owner-farmers, former tenants who won the right to purchase their land after the land wars. Where only 3 per cent of agrarian workers owned land in 1870, 64 per cent owned their farms by 1921. Three-quarters of farms were family-owned holdings of less than fifty acres. On the other hand, the total number of farm holdings exceeding one acre had fallen from about 570,000 in 1851 to 485,000 in 1911 and the number of farmers fell by even more (Ó Gráda 1994, p. 259). Most of the land (59.6 per cent) was in the hands of farmers who owned estates of more than 100 acres (Peillon 1982, p. 11).

Not that industrial employment made up for the falling numbers of farmers. What little manufacturing was left in the south at partition was mainly brewing, distilling and agricultural processing. Table 5.1 shows the size of southern manufacturing industries at the 1926 census of industrial production, the first after independence. Net output was heavily concentrated in a few drink and tobacco firms, with output in the rest of industry scattered over many very small firms. Only 130 companies employed more than 100 people. Moreover, factory returns from 1870 indicate that southern manufacturing had probably dwindled since the late 1800s.[2] Bielenberg (1998) finds that total Irish industrial output probably rose between 1840 and 1910, with increased output in textiles, shipbuilding, brewing and distilling slightly outweighing the decline of other sectors. Yet the most expansive industries were lost under partition and, while Irish industry was stagnant or declining between 1840 and 1910, British industry quadrupled (Ó Gráda 1994, p. 309).

Thus, the Irish industrial bourgeoisie was extremely weak at partition. Many of the larger firms, like Guinness and Player's tobacco, were subsidiaries

Table 5.1 Distribution of southern Irish manufacturing, 1926

Sector	Net output (£1,000s)	Employment	No. of firms	No. of proprietors
Food	4,064	19,422	923	550
Drink	5,928	7,000	113	74
Tobacco	1,129	2,096	16	11
Other	5,286	29,250	1,412	801
Total	16,407	57,768	2,464	1,436

Source of data: Department of Industry and Commerce (1933).

of British-based conglomerates. The Irish stock exchange in 1933 listed only twenty-five companies, with share capital of IR£14.3 million. Five were brewers or distillers, with share capital of IR£11 million. A single company, Guinness, accounted for exactly two-thirds of Irish share capital (Beddy 1943–44). These large concerns made up the most cohesive section of the bourgeoisie through informal social ties and membership of British trade associations but their nationality reduced their political power.

Smaller capitalists were not so well organised. They had no major employers' organisations or federations. Local chambers of commerce represented merchant interests rather than industrialists. Although some industries were concentrated in Dublin, key sectors such as flour milling and creameries were scattered throughout the country. But most 'manufacturers' were just artisans such as smiths and small millers. More than half of those employed in Irish industry in the 1920s were in establishments with fewer than ten workers (Department of Industry and Commerce 1933, p. ix).

The division of Irish industry into large and small concerns corresponds roughly to capitalist divisions over the major issue facing industry: free trade versus protection. Ninety per cent of Irish manufactured exports were concentrated in food and drink, produced mainly by a few large firms. More than 80 per cent of the output of other sectors, dominated by small producers, was sold at home.[3] Obviously, exporting industrialists wanted to continue free trade because they profited from Ireland's dependence on Britain. But owners of small and medium-sized firms favoured protection, since competing imports of shoes, clothing and grain threatened their business. Some were *potential* large industrialists who hoped protection would bring new opportunities for profitable investment. Several coach-builders, for example, lobbied the government for restrictions on car imports so that they could assemble cars themselves (Jacobson 1977).

The greatest pressures for protection, however, came from the popular classes. This is an important distinction from the two earlier cycles of industrialisation, in cotton and wool, where disaffected settlers and landowners initiated demands on England to allow local industrialisation. The 1926 census found 150,000 'industrial workers', even though there were fewer than 20,000 factory workers. Some were self-employed artisans but the majority were in transport and services rather than manufacturing. Worker solidarity had grown following the establishment of the Irish Trades Union Congress (ITUC) in 1894 and the ITUC had 189,000 members at partition (Meenan 1970, p. 156). The Irish labour movement was heavily nationalist and republican and was unified in support of industrial development through protection and the creation of state industry.

Thus, popular pressure mounted for a more nationalist economic and political regime. Moderate elements of the nationalist opposition, led by Eamon De Valera, formed the Fianna Fáil political party in 1926. In 1932, they were voted into office on a platform that promised a vigorous programme for economic self-sufficiency and the erection of indigenous industry behind protective barriers.

There was already some development of protection even before 1932. When the customs and excise system of the Free State was created in 1923, revenue duties imposed by Britain were continued. A few tariffs were added over the next seven years: to boots and shoes, soap and candles, sugar confectionery, cocoa preparations and glass bottles in 1924; to some personal clothing items, blankets and rugs, furniture and bedsteads in 1925; and to oatmeal in 1926 (Revenue Commissioners of Ireland, various years). A 1926 tariff commission examined the case for establishing new tariffs but its chair, Finance Secretary James McElligott, was extremely conservative and argued that protection would only create inefficient industry and invite British retaliation. He blocked further extension of tariffs (Fanning 1978, pp. 204–6).

Besides protection, the minister for industry and commerce was pressing for a programme of comprehensive state planning. He argued that break-downs of the price system created limitations to growth and that, through planning, the agricultural surplus could provide capital for import-substituting industry. Such radicalism did not get very far, although the minister also wanted to create free trade zones for US manufacturers, who were, he claimed, 'anxious to place their products in the European markets at prices based on European costs'.[4] The time was not yet right for such an outward-oriented strategy, however, and the most important local forces supported self-sufficiency and indigenous industrialisation.

Two months after taking office in 1932, the nationalist Fianna Fáil government introduced forty-three new tariffs. Newly elected Fianna Fáil dail deputies also refused to pledge allegiance to the British crown and the government announced it would not pay annuities to Britain for Irish purchases of colonial lands.[5] When the British reacted by imposing unilateral duties on Irish agricultural exports, the Irish government gave the minister of industry and commerce greatly increased powers to impose customs duties.

The new measures transformed Irish economic strategy. The list of tariffs grew from sixty-eight articles in 1931 to 281 in 1936. With the addition of import quotas, 1,947 articles were protected by 1938. One observer wrote that 'the last surviving example of a predominantly free trading state left in the world' had become 'one of the most heavily tariffed countries that could be found' (Meenan 1970, p. 142). Ryan (1948–49) found that the tariff level rose from 9 per cent in 1931 to 45 per cent in 1935. As a result, tariff revenues nearly doubled as a percentage of imports from 1930 to 1935 but a severe drop in imports following Britain's trade restrictions moderated their rise.

Although the new Irish tariffs were high compared with those in the period before 1932, they were still moderate by world standards. A 1942 study of relative tariff levels in twenty major countries ranked Ireland tenth in processed foods, fifteenth in building materials, twelfth in chemicals and twelfth in household goods. Ireland ranked eighteenth in metals and metal products, ahead of only Sweden and the Netherlands (American Tariff League 1942, p. 14). Industrial protection was moderated by two factors. First, the government never attempted to restrict imported industrial raw materials or capital goods. Domestic production of these goods was never encouraged, so new manufacturers had to import many factors of production that could have been produced locally. *Capital deepening* was thus a problem, although the government never perceived it as such. Second, most tariffs were implemented at the request of Irish industrialists rather than for systematic developmental goals. Protection was political patronage rather than a coherent industrialisation strategy. Since imports were available when local products were not, Irish protectionism never created a Hirschman-ian scenario, where imbalanced industrial growth creates *needs* for other products, inducing new producers to step in and fill the gaps (Hirschman 1958).

Nor did state industry step in much where private industry was unwilling. Only five state companies had been established by 1945[6] and even these were opposed by powerful sections of the bureaucracy (Fanning 1978). Even during severe stagnation in 1945, the Department of Industry and Commerce insisted that 'the industrial structure of this country has been erected on a basis of private enterprise and ... the government feels that in general the continued expansion and development of industry may be safely entrusted to private individuals and groups'.[7]

Irish protectionism, then, became dominated by a coalition between the state and its fledgling bourgeoisie, on whom it pinned its hopes for industrial-isation. As a result, class conflict brewed within the nationalist coalition whenever the regime sided with domestic capital on issues of public spending and wage moderation.

The government complemented tariffs and quotas with supporting legislation and limited industrial finance. The Control of Manufactures Acts in 1932 and 1933 limited foreigners to minority participation in new industry, although loopholes allowed some British investors to supply the Irish market. The Industrial Credit Company was established in 1933 to underwrite new industrial projects and expansions.

The regime immediately encountered hostile external conditions. Ironically, though Irish nationalists sought industrialisation to reduce economic dependence on England, cattle exports to England were the primary source of foreign exchange for industrial inputs while export earnings gave farmers discretionary income to buy domestic manufactures. Thus, English recessions threatened Irish expansion since England would then buy fewer Irish farm exports. An even more damaging development was Britain's hostile economic war against Ireland's infant development regime. Between July 1932 and March 1935, Britain collected £10.7 million of unilateral duties

on Irish agricultural exports against 'defaulted' Irish land annuities of
£14.5 million (Lyons 1973, p. 611). Unilateral duties on industrial exports
took another £1 million. Following English import quotas, Irish agricultural exports plummeted from more than IR£33 million to less than
IR£12 million in 1934; total exports fell from IR£45 million to IR£18
million (Department of Industry and Commerce 1935).

The Anglo-Irish trade agreement of 1938 restored trade relations with
Britain but then the Second World War caused Britain once again to restrict
its imports from Ireland. War also created scarcities of important industrial
inputs and Irish imports fell from £46.8 million in 1940 to £26.4 million in
1943 (Central Statistics Office 1980, p. 187). This severely restricted Irish
industrial development.

Given these difficulties, it is surprising that Ireland developed any industry
at all. Yet manufacturing output grew by 7.3 per cent annually between 1932
and 1939, and manufacturing employment rose from 62,608 to 101,004.
Expansion was particularly rapid in metals, chemicals, clay and cement,
clothing and footwear, paper and leather (see table 5.2). Although some
new investments might have occurred without protection (Fitzgerald 1959,
p. 146), Irish industrial expansion in the 1930s is impressive considering

Table 5.2 Growth of employment and output in selected industries under
import substitution, 1931–39

Sector	Employment			Net output (£1,000s)		
	1931	1939	1939/1931	1931	1939	1939/1931
Grain	3,215	4,566	1.42	1,135	1,902	1.68
Sugar	2,798	4,917	1.76	528	1,670	3.16
Clay/cement	732	2,570	3.51	124	725	5.85
Timber	2,338	3,689	1.58	417	733	1.76
Metals	1,729	4,591	2.66	286	968	3.38
Vehicles	969	3,500	3.61	595	898	1.51
Engineering	1,086	2,987	2.75	195	659	3.38
Textiles	1,593	3,563	2.24	122	535	4.39
Woollen	2,458	3,098	1.26	314	578	1.84
Clothing	6,073	12,613	2.08	661	1,610	2.44
Boot/shoe	1,125	5,644	5.02	200	938	4.69
Hosiery	1,210	3,981	3.29	124	650	5.24
Leather	285	1,301	4.56	45	334	7.42
Paper	802	2,363	2.95	105	536	5.10
Printing	5,743	6,917	1.20	1,421	1,925	1.35
Chemicals	560	1,836	3.28	177	702	3.97

Source: author's calculations from the *Census of Industrial Production* (Department of
Commerce and Industry, various years).

the hostile conditions under which import-substitution industrialisation (ISI) was attempted.

Yet ISI ultimately met chronic structural problems. Dependence on imported factors of production caused balance-of-payments problems as well as bottlenecks when supply was short. Thus, the *Census of Industrial Production* (Department of Commerce and Industry, various years) shows that southern Irish industrial growth slowed considerably in the war years 1939–45: output fell in grain milling (14.4 per cent), vehicles (41.1 per cent) and metal products (8.2 per cent). The regime was also unable to induce domestic capitalists to reinvest. After they exhausted the few highly profitable local possibilities, Irish industrialists reinvested their profits in British financial markets.

Successes of the 1930s were thus related to a phase of 'easy industrialis-ation', when protection enabled profit taking in basic goods. Once the war in Europe ended and the US began to extend its hegemonic control throughout Europe, Irish ISI faced the inevitable test: could it expand beyond the easy stage, or would it collapse under the pressures of internal contradictions and external forces?

Forces for change

Irish industry did not expand as quickly after the Second World War as it had before the war. There is little evidence that the local market was 'exhausted'. In 1949, the Department of Industry and Commerce identified IR£60 million worth of imported products that could have been made in Ireland, creating 45,000 jobs.[8] In 1951, it compiled a long list of locally demanded products that had never been made in Ireland, from ceramic and paper products, to plastics and steel pipes, to washing machines and vacuum cleaners. But local industry simply seemed unwilling to invest in these lines. Instead, Irish assets held abroad rose dramatically, from £250 million in 1939 to £400 million in 1949. Irish commercial banks more than doubled their British holdings (Whitaker 1948–49). A leading Irish econ-omist claimed that the Irish invested more capital abroad per person than any other nation in the world (Geary 1951, p. 399). But, despite the Department of Industry and Commerce holding 'more than a suspicion that manufacturers are content to concentrate upon a limited field which will give them the best return with the minimum of effort',[9] the state insisted that industry must be 'erected on a basis of private enterprise'[10] and refused to control this outflow.

Meanwhile, Irish imports from North America grew from $28 million in 1940 to $68 million in 1948 and $95 million in 1949, creating massive dollar trade deficits.[11] US officials did not hesitate to remind the Irish government that only $2 million of its $25–30 million annual income came from exports, the rest coming from tourism ($11 million) and emigrant remittances ($12 million).[12] Moreover, 90 per cent of Irish exports continued to flow to Britain, earning sterling, which was not convertible to dollars (Central Statistics Office 1947).

The changing Irish class structure was also raising demands for industrial employment. The number of small farmers (those with less than fifteen acres) halved between 1926 and 1951. The number of medium-sized farms fell by a third, as did that of hired agricultural labourers. In all, farm employment fell from 53 to 40 per cent of total employment (Central Statistics Office 1928, pp. 4–5; Central Statistics Office 1954, pp. 4–5). Farmers who moved to towns and cities became a crucial swing vote, a considerable electoral threat that could turn on any Irish regime that could not supply adequate work.

Although the numbers of protected manufacturing firms had grown by 35 per cent between 1931 and 1947 (table 5.3), the domestic bourgeoisie was still a relatively young class with limited political power or even a broad political programme to counter rising popular discontent. Most new corporate owners concentrated on their individual interests rather than their class interests. They might establish industrial branch associations to petition the government about tariffs or other policies, but rather than drawing capital together these associations competed among each other: 'Dublin vs. Cork, city vs. country, large vs. small, producers vs. suppliers, etc.' ('66 Business Conference 1967, p. 48). By the 1960s, their average membership was just twenty to thirty companies each and many, like the flour milling industry, simply functioned as cartels whose main function was to limit entry and to control production and prices. On the other hand, local chambers of commerce continued to support free trade instead of protection. The leading Irish industrial journal dismissed the large Dublin chamber, which was established under Cromwell, as 'middlemen and agents for foreign goods'.[13]

The closest thing to 'class-wide' capitalist organisation was the Federation of Irish Manufacturers (FIM), set up in 1932. FIM stood for 'the protection of Irish industry in furtherance of our industrial self-sufficiency and productive ability'. Its main object was to ensure that 'industrial development shall be retained in the hands of Saorstat [Free State] nationals' (O'Hagan and Foley 1982, p. 15) and membership was restricted to Irish-owned firms. Its primary activity was pressing the state to plug loopholes that allowed foreign companies to circumvent the Control of Manufactures Acts. The FIM's political power was reflected in its ability to get legislation enacted, from the Control of Manufactures Acts to anti-worker employment provisions. During the 1930s and 1940s, all major ministers attended the FIM's annual conferences and dinners and a liaison group from the Department of Industry and Commerce attended all its meetings.[14] As ISI stagnated in the 1950s, however, the FIM's membership dwindled and

Table 5.3 Numbers of industrial establishments in Ireland, 1931–58

Sector	1931	1938	1947	1958
Food				
All firms	904	908	959	972
> 10 employees	404	473	489	523
> 100 employees	30	44	45	71
Drink				
All	130	122	117	136
> 10	60	54	70	98
> 100	12	11	16	16
Textiles				
All	101	167	155	199
> 10	67	114	124	165
> 100	20	33	41	52
Clothing				
All	138	311	316	377
> 10	123	255	281	328
> 100	24	52	59	52
Wood				
All	244	359	341	363
> 10	124	166	182	182
> 100	5	12	15	10
Paper				
All	161	244	243	237
> 10	105	142	150	163
> 100	13	24	26	28
Clay				
All	74	148	112	120
> 10	16	53	41	60
> 100	1	9	10	12
Chemicals				
All	38	141	133	138
> 10	24	68	89	92
> 100	5	7	7	9
Metal industries				
All	198	418	366	354
> 10	87	202	210	231
> 100	5	25	28	44
Miscellaneous industries				
All	221	282	274	210
> 10	83	95	150	103
> 100	6	7	16	10
Totals				
All	2,209	3,151	2,986	3,106
>10	1,093	1,622	1,786	1,945
>100	121	224	263	304

Source: *Census of Industrial Production* (Department of Commerce and Industry, various years).

attendance at its annual meetings fell from hundreds to dozens.[15] Members began to complain that the government did not pay 'sufficient regard' to its suggestions.[16]

Irish capital, then, was hardly a united front acting in its recognised class interests. It tended toward collective action only in defensive situations, when industry was threatened, for example, by state attempts to control business. It was highly divided by size, region and industrial sector. Its divisions could boil over into destructive intra-class spats, such as a years-long court battle in the 1940s between the FIM and the smaller National Agricultural and Industrial Development Association. If there was an 'inner circle' of large corporate powers, as proposed by Useem (1984), it was still comprised of foreign companies that identified with free trade instead of protection.

Meanwhile, the industrial working class had grown with protected industry. Industrial workers rose from 13.4 per cent of employees in 1926 to 21.8 per cent in 1951. Trade union membership quadrupled in the same period, although the unions became less militant (McCarthy 1977). Industrial workers supported protectionism, yet their consistent pressure for higher wages and social programmes continually brought them into conflict with the state. Popular support for protectionism remained into the 1950s, when class discontent over economic stagnation began to rise.

Regime proposals for change

As ISI floundered, leading sections of the southern Irish state proposed changes to the system of industrial promotion. An intra-state conflict emerged between fiscal conservatives and those who favoured industrial expansion. Expansionists were centred in the Departments of Industry and Commerce and External Affairs, and later in semi-state bodies like the Industrial Development Authority (IDA). Opposition to expansionism centred in the Department of Finance, which emphasised its inflationary consequences. The Central Bank and other fiscal conservatives supported that department. This 'deflationary coalition' contended that the country's problems could be solved only by reducing government spending.

If there was a point of agreement, it was that *inefficiency* was the main reason for economic stagnation. Expansionists argued that protection prevented the price mechanism from ensuring the efficient distribution of resources. They proposed two options for change: (1) industrial regulation and (2) attracting new export-oriented projects. The Department of Finance opposed both policies as state-centred and inflationary. Domestic capital aligned with the conservatives against government regulation, leaving the attraction of export-oriented industry as the only remaining option. This is ironic, as we shall see, because emergent US hegemony and US corporate expansionism in Europe linked export orientation to free trade and, thereby, to the eventual destruction of the very industrialists who most resisted government controls.

In 1947 the Department of Industry and Commerce attempted to create an 'industrial efficiency bureau' to combat excess profit taking and restrictive trade practices. In the first instance, the bureau was to be a 'friendly adviser' with limited price-controlling powers. Companies that did not respond adequately would face a court of inquiry, supplied with powers to subpoena corporate documents. If companies did not follow the bureau's subsequent directives on efficiency, the state could impound excess profits, fix prices and remove tariffs and quotas. If essential goods or substantial employment was involved, the minister could seize a company's assets and run it as a state concern.[17]

Reactions to these proposals were immediate and hostile, from the conservative bureaucrats to Irish capital. The FIM claimed that the proposed legislation would do away with the right of private enterprise. It requested a meeting with the taoiseach to discuss 'a tendency' among ministers to imply that manufacturers had generally 'possessed themselves of unreasonable and excessive profits at the expense of the buying public' (Federation of Irish Manufacturers 1949). In the face of such hostile mobilisation, the government dropped the proposals and replaced them with weaker legislation enabling tariff reviews.[18] Any doubts that direct state regulation was unacceptable were expelled two years later when efforts to break up a cartel in the flour milling industry were defeated in spite of considerable popular support.

A 1948 proposal to establish the IDA for government control of industry shows how the defeat of government regulation was turned into success for programmes to attract new industry. Struggle over this proposal also marked the return of a missing actor, hegemonic power and its Atlantic interests, to a dominant role in Irish economic decision making. This time the hegemonic power was not Britain but the US.

The draft bill on the IDA envisaged that it would initiate schemes to attract industry *and* investigate the (mis)operation of industrial protection. The IDA was to have power to summon witnesses and documents from private industry. But conservatives strongly opposed such a body as 'a very dangerous machine for the exercise of corruption' and a possible 'gang of crack-pot socialistic planners'. To avoid this, the Department of Finance insisted that board members must be drawn solely from the bourgeoisie because 'to be judicial in relation to private enterprise, one must be free from jealousy and envy – one is only free from these when one has reached a reasonable success in life and members should only be selected from the latter class'.[19]

Irish capital, the FIM *and* the Chambers of Commerce solidly opposed granting the IDA powers of subpoena to investigate business. The Drapers

Chamber of Trade called such powers 'an unjust interference with the liberty of the individual'.[20] *The Irish Times* wrote that IDA investigations would create resentment by those who 'regard their business as their own business'.[21]

These complaints strongly influenced the final nature of the IDA. Its five directors were prominent company directors and representatives from the FIM and the Federated Union of Employers. But the regime also exploited splits within Irish capital, and those who sat on the IDA were among the most expansionist and outwardly oriented business people. The IDA that was finally created was not the policeman that industrialists feared. Rather, it was to become the single most important institution charged with attracting new industry to Ireland.[22]

The opposition of capital and powerful bureaucrats can satisfactorily explain the IDA's exclusion from a regulatory role. But they cannot explain why proposals to set up the IDA as an agent to attract new foreign investors succeeded despite opposition from many of the same sources. To understand this shift we must return to the analysis of hegemony. Here, one sees how the southern Irish economy, which had withdrawn from British domination, was *re*incorporated into a new US-centred Atlantic economy. In the process, like wool and cotton before, a semi-autonomous indigenous industry was transformed into a newly dependent one based on the interests of the dominant core power. This time the dominant interest was US capital's desire to gain entry into European markets, the Atlantic part of its global *grand area* strategy.

Enter the world economy

> The Marshall Plan is an act of unparalleled generosity from one nation to other nations.
>
> Eamon DeValera, 12 January 1948

> Mr. Marshall was telling the Senate Foreign Relations Committee how the money allocated for the purchase of European countries would be paid. Each state, apparently, will be bought separately, by private treaty.... The government in each case will be administered by a Grey Eminence ... and the cabinet will be answerable to him on the usual democratic basis, namely 'or else...'.
>
> Myles na Gopaleen, *Cruiskeen Lawn*

Between the wars, protectionism insulated the south of Ireland from some of the forces that had restricted its economic activities under British rule. Yet the country that emerged from the Second World War increasingly depended on imports from beyond the sterling area. Ireland was reincorporated in the global economy, but this time into an Atlantic economy whose axes and centre of activity had moved from England to the US.

Post-war Europe provided the US with its opportunity to consolidate its grand area. Officials from the Economic Cooperation Administration (ECA), the administrative organ of the Marshall Plan, let the European colonial powers know that the US wanted to exchange aid for access to their markets.[23] Even a reconstructed Europe could never afford all the US imports they required, however, so the shortfall would be made up with colonial raw materials.[24] Despite the fears of European capitalists that US plans would threaten their protected domestic and colonial markets, most Western European states simply needed dollars and were willing to let the US into their colonies to get them.

European colonial powers generally gave the US access to their colonies in return for reconstruction aid. The British sounded hollow when they complained of 'imperializm [*sic*] in the efforts made by the Americans to assert their ascendancy in international organizations such as the [World] Bank and the [International Monetary] Fund'.[25] Even their own Treasury reckoned it could reconstruct Britain with US aid and let the colonies pay with their raw materials, which were the 'quid for the quo'.[26] Ascendancy was exactly what the US asserted as it implemented its grand area strategy of regional trading blocs in Europe and the Third World, regulated through military force and through the trading infrastructures of Bretton Woods, the IMF and the World Bank.

Shortly before a new Irish coalition government with its own ideas about expansion took office in 1948, US Secretary of State George Marshall announced his famous plan for European economic recovery. According to leading Marshall planner Paul Nitze, 'we had [projected] a balance of payments aggregate surplus of $20 to $25 billion over five years. There was the probability of a bankrupt world; thus we had to give priority to an aid program' (quoted in Wexler 1983, p. 14). In the words of Ernest Gross, 'so long as Europe remained as it was, the U.S. economy would suffer. Our export market was obviously in an exposed and unsatisfactory position'.[27] Soon, an internal Irish debate about development policy became embroiled in the US's new Atlantic plans.

Although Ireland had been officially neutral during the war, the ECA offered it assistance in 1948. The Irish Finance Department opposed receiving aid but the Americans were making Irish politicians an offer they could not refuse. Marshall aid was a way to deliver election promises. The new minister for external affairs, the radical Sean MacBride, hoped European Recovery Program (ERP) funds would help him increase the state's role in investment. Without aid, he argued, 'Ireland will find herself practically unable to obtain most of the requirements she needs from the dollar areas'.[28] Marshall aid was particularly attractive because it emphasised increased industrial production. As the ECA chief and Studebaker president Paul Hoffman said in his nomination hearings, 'the administrator and his staff should keep their eyes on one goal, and that is increased production' (Wexler 1983, p. 57).

The Irish also hoped that closer economic and political ties with the US and Europe would insulate them from British interference. The ERP was Ireland's first opportunity to participate in a major European organisation independently of Britain. The terms of the ERP convention, said an External Affairs Department memo, 'coupled with the power of Ireland as a member of the Council and the influence of Ireland in America, will afford us considerable protection against harsh economic dealings directed against us by Britain or any of the other participating countries'.[29] Such naïve optimism proved unfounded even in the short term, when members of a mid-1948 Irish delegation to the US found 'obvious' ECA favouritism to England over Ireland.[30]

But Irish hopes to use European and US associations as a shield against Britain were understandable. Britain was experiencing severe difficulties in its dollar trade and urged Ireland to reduce its dollar imports, which reached $141 million in 1946. The resulting trade deficit meant that Ireland had to draw heavily on the sterling area's *dollar pool*. Since Britain still held over 95 per cent of Ireland's foreign trade, its central bank exercised strong influence on the Irish financial community. Thus, the Department of Finance and the Irish Central Bank supported British pressure to restrict dollar imports. The US, however, encouraged Irish export expansion to pay for dollar imports. Thus, the export-promotion policies that the new Irish government and expansionary bureaucrats favoured agreed with US designs in Europe. Sean MacBride led the Irish negotiations over Marshall aid, and his expansionary thinking placed him alongside the Irish Department of Industry and Commerce and against the Department of Finance.

Before the Americans committed funds, the conditions of aid were negotiated.[31] The US Congress insisted on tying Marshall funds to European trade liberalisation, which threatened Irish protection. Aid recipients had to join the newly formed Organisation for European Economic Cooperation (OEEC) in 1948. Despite Finance Department objections that Irish interests were 'obviously closer to those of Great Britain because of the direction of our foreign trade and our position as a large sterling creditor',[32] Ireland signed the Convention for European Economic Cooperation in Paris on 16 April 1948.

The Department of External Affairs controlled the Irish delegation to the OEEC and handled Ireland's negotiations with the US. The Department of Finance, left high and dry, reacted sourly: 'we cannot expect any measure of salvation from the so-called Marshall Plan' (quoted in Fanning 1978, p. 411). For their part, the Americans made it clear how they expected the Irish to use their aid. They insisted that the Irish draw up acceptable spending plans and informed MacBride that aid should be 'used for national development purposes of a productive nature and would not be invested in British and other securities'.[33]

This statement was aimed directly at the Department of Finance, which wanted to use the aid to redeem government debt (Fanning 1978, p. 419).

Finance Secretary McElligott argued that 'it is no business of the Americans what we do with the loan counterpart' and that loans were preferable to grants because 'you are subject to less snooping by Americans'.[34] While this showed more than a little naïveté about the possibility of receiving any form of US aid without strings, the Department of Finance realised that Marshall aid funds would someday run out and, then, 'a serious scarcity of dollars will overtake us'.[35]

The US soon escalated its demands. The chief of the ECA mission to Ireland wrote to MacBride in late 1949 of his 'great concern' that 'next year Ireland will begin to need dollars from some source not now in sight, or she will be obliged to reduce dollar purchases drastically'. He found in talks with Irish officials a 'lightness of concern' with dollar earnings and an attitude that 'it is not Ireland's problem'. He continued, 'I have reluctantly come to the conclusion that Ireland is not facing up to this problem'. The ECA chief said that Ireland should have progressed beyond the stage of plans and schemes. In a direct intervention in Irish economic affairs, he suggested that Ireland should set up an export corporation and give US corporations access to Irish natural resources 'directly or indirectly' to raise the country's dollar earnings.[36]

US pressures to gain free entry to Ireland for its corporations came at the same time as a new ECA programme for US corporations that guaranteed their investments in Europe and assured them that they could transfer any profits they repatriated into dollars. While only thirty-eight US companies took advantage of the programme at the time, it presaged the massive post-war rise in US corporate investments in Europe and other areas (Wexler 1983, p. 88).

The US also applied more subtle pressure on Ireland. The chairman of the board of National City Bank in New York told T. K. Whitaker, then a principal officer in the Department of Finance, that Britain would probably get no more aid because Americans considered their nationalisation pro-gramme and welfare state 'obnoxious'. US taxpayers, he claimed, were 'very much averse to being taxed to further socialist policies in Britain'. The banker continued that Britain regulated foreign capital too much and that 'American investors would wish to have control over enterprises in which their capital was invested'. Moreover, high corporate taxation in Britain made investments 'virtually impossible'.[37] The message to Ireland was crystal clear, perhaps too clear: when the US gave Ireland a loan instead of a grant, a State Department official told MacBride that his case 'suffered from the absence of a Communist movement in Ireland'.[38]

Also in late 1949, the US Congress was pressuring the ECA to increase its requirements that aid recipients liberalise their trade. In a lecture to the Irish Institute of Bankers, an American journalist noted that Marshall aid was now 'granted not on a basis of need, but on a basis of merit'. Aid now depended on efforts to make currency convertible, liberalise trade and

integrate the European economy. The US demanded 'universal nondiscrim-
inatory free trade' in Europe.[39]

In October 1949, Paul Hoffman addressed the OEEC council, calling for
'the formation of a single large market within which quantitative restriction on the movement of goods, monetary barriers to the flow of payments
and, eventually, all tariffs are swept away'. He expected the OEEC to
present a programme for European economic integration within months
(quoted in Wexler 1983, p. 156). Two days later, the OEEC agreed to 50
per cent trade liberalisation within forty-five days. In February 1950,
Hoffman asked Congress to let him earmark $600 million of the 1950/51
aid appropriation 'to encourage the aggressive pursuit of a program of
liberalized trade and payments'. He promised Congress that 'after we hold
out these funds ... we will have a payments union within 90 days' (Wexler
1983, pp. 169–70). In response, the OEEC proposed a plan to create a
European payments union to establish and maintain free trade after Marshall
aid ended.

The expansionary coalition in Ireland used US pressure to push its public
investment programme past objections by fiscal conservatives. MacBride
secured his pet programmes for reforestation and purchases of raw materials
and capital goods.[40] He openly admitted using US pressure to win support
for his department's spending programmes over Department of Finance
objections.[41] The Irish government also established the IDA and the Exports
Board, as 'suggested' in the letter from the US ECA chief.[42] A system of
grants to industrial enterprises for building new factories and buying
machinery, originally suggested by the ECA as a way of using Marshall
funds, became the Underdeveloped Areas Act of 1951 and was extended
throughout Ireland in 1956.[43] The creation of new export-oriented industrialisation policies was the price the Irish had to pay for US support in their
internal fight against fiscal conservatism.

Yet the Irish worried that free trade would decimate key domestic
industries like footwear, clothing and textiles (Committee on Industrial
Organisation 1965). They were not convinced that the new system of
grants and incentives could replace protection as the main instrument of
industrialisation. The existing record of foreign investment in Europe gave
little hope that TNCs could replace the domestic jobs that would be lost to
free trade. In short, the government worried that industrial collapse could
ultimately threaten the state's legitimacy.

Despite Irish resistance, the OEEC drew the country further into free
trade than it wanted. Under US pressure at the end of 1949, OEEC
members had to remove quotas from at least 50 per cent of their imports in
three categories: agricultural products, raw materials and manufactured
goods. The obligation was raised to 60 per cent in September 1950 and 75
per cent in February 1951. Ireland reluctantly acceded because it would
lose Marshall funds if it refused to comply.[44]

When liberalisation obligations were raised to 90 per cent in 1955, the Irish regime was in a quandary. It had pleaded since 1951 that its position was special because its industry was underdeveloped and because it already had free access to its most important export market under the Anglo-Irish trade agreements. Ireland had little to gain from trade liberalisation and much to lose. Expansionists had wrested control of Irish development strategy from the fiscally conservative Finance coalition, but *it* was already losing control to US hegemonic policy.

The Department of Industry and Commerce worried, first, that if it agreed to 90 per cent liberalisation, a further demand would inevitably follow. Second, once a product or group of products was liberalised it could not be reprotected even if conditions changed. Third, and most worrying, was the fear that the OEEC would soon move from quota controls to tariff reduction, which would threaten Irish industry's main source of protection. 'It should be noted', warned the Department of Industry and Commerce, 'that the OEEC have already appointed a special committee to study the question of tariffs as distinct from quotas ... an all-out attack on high tariffs will be launched shortly'.[45]

Nothing less than the future direction of Irish economic development was at stake. Either the country could try to expand its exports through incentives and efficiency measures, while securing indigenous industry through *selective* protection; or it would have to withdraw protection completely, in favour of free trade, relying on foreign investment for industrial expansion. 'Whether we like it or not', the regime privately recognised, 'it is clear that industrial development in Ireland is not likely to continue without the assistance of tariffs at rates which, by comparison with those in vogue in many other European countries, must be called high. Wishful thinking will not alter this situation, which rises from our proximity to and contacts with Britain and our late start in the industrial field'.[46]

In summarising the threat of European integration, the Department of Industry and Commerce concluded, 'broadly speaking, our recent industrial development has been achieved largely from the "obvious" and "easy" sectors (e.g., textiles, footwear) ... from now on the problem of expansion is going to be more and more difficult. We may, therefore, be sacrificing the right to afford protection by way of quota at the very point when it is likely to be most needed.... *This leads to the question whether there is any point at which we shall be forced to choose between European cooperation on the one hand and the development of our own country on the other*'[47] (my emphasis).

Internal pressures against free trade were considerable. Irish manufacturers had already criticised the Anglo-Irish trade agreements on the grounds that they surrendered the government's right (and duty) to protect Irish industry. Accepting OEEC obligations surrendered sovereignty even more, and without apparent advantages to Irish industry. Yet Irish industry was divided and weakened by a decade of economic stagnation. And powerful sections of industry in Ireland were still more interested in the British market than in protection.

In the end, however, it was international pressures that proved too strong for protectionism. The southern Irish government was forced to accede to the OEEC because of 'wider considerations of European co-operation and national prestige'.[48] Non-compliance would have brought Ireland's expulsion from the OEEC, leading the US to withdraw support and future aid.[49] In early 1955, seven years after an expansionary government first tried to use US aid to finance its development schemes, US and European pressure forced it to move from protection to free trade.

The significance of crisis

US hegemony had no specific interests yet in 1950s Ireland. Foreign direct investments had not yet gained momentum and Ireland's tiny market was insignificant to US exporters. The State Department felt that Ireland's contribution to European recovery was 'primarily to provide additional food'.[50] Broader interests in a stable, non-communist, integrated, free-trading Europe drove US post-war expansion in the Atlantic.

External pressures laid the foundations of the transition from ISI to foreign-dominated export-led industrialisation (ELI) by the mid-1950s. Specific policies like the IDA, Exports Board and the industrial grants scheme were all results of the pressures and opportunities of Marshall aid. Sections of the Irish government happily obliged because these policies and the aid that accompanied them enabled them to introduce their own pet programmes. But Ireland's integration into Europe and its introduction of ELI were not automatic. There was still considerable opposition from parts of the state and most of Irish capital.

Fiscal conservatives tenaciously advocated public austerity measures. In 1949, senior Finance official T. K. Whitaker wrote a scathing attack on the dangers of using Marshall aid to fund new spending programmes. He divided state expenditure into 'productive' and 'social' components, and claimed that social spending was excessive. Whitaker also insisted that high taxes discouraged private investment.[51] The government responded that his analysis was too restrictive and 'gloomy' and that all sides should be 'discussing a dynamic economy not a static one!'[52]

As Marshall funds ran out in 1951 and Ireland's balance-of-payments deficit grew, the Department of Finance gained support for its austerity policies. The Central Bank reported that the government was 'spending more than the nation can afford' (Central Bank 1951, pp. 9–17). Expansionary measures were replaced by policies that reduced exports and employment. From 1952, austerity budgets abolished food subsidies and cut social services.

The Department of Finance drew up strictly balanced budgets and spear-headed an all-out campaign against wage demands. Just-deposed taoiseach John Costello claimed that the Department of Finance had 'triumphed over progress'.[53] An analyst later called these 'the years of stagnation in which the increasing struggle against inflation displaced economic growth as an attainable object of policy' (Lynch 1969, p. 199). Not surprisingly, workers and farmers rejected the restrictive policies and supported change, even if it meant foreign-dominated industry and free trade.

Austerity programmes continued through 1955, when the Department of Finance added an intensive campaign for higher interest rates to 'encourage saving' and 'put a brake on new borrowing'.[54] Despite deepening recession, Whitaker insisted that 'it is only within the four walls of solvency that we can build up production and employment'.[55] The Central Bank refused to cover the government's borrowing needs and the secretary of finance wrote to the taoiseach that the governor of the Central Bank had lost confidence in the government. He added, 'we just cannot go on in this way'.[56]

But four years of austerity policies had taken cruel effect. In 1955/56, industrial production fell by 3 per cent; agricultural production by 7 per cent; GNP by 1.3 per cent; and employment by nearly 2 per cent (4 per cent in the following year) (Central Statistics Office, various years). During five years of Finance-imposed recession, employment fell by nearly 10 per cent. When census results revealed a 2.11 per cent decline of population between 1951 and 1956, deep recession turned into a legitimation crisis for the government. Change was necessary, but the option of expanding indigenous investment had already been cut off by the defeat of state regulation and by European trade liberalisation. Once deflationary monetarist policies were discredited by economic crisis, liberal outward-looking policies were the sole remaining alternative.

The government wasted no time in launching an attack on the fiscal conservatives. The parliamentary secretary to the government charged the Department of Finance and banks with exaggerating the monetary side of the crisis and lying about the reserves of sterling held by Irish banks in Britain. Furthermore, foreign exchange deficits were not so great if Marshall aid and invisible exports were included. The secretary accused the Department of 'conditioning' government to follow policies that were 'contrary to the good of the community'.[57]

In late 1956, the taoiseach announced a series of industrial grants, tax breaks for exporters and other incentives to industry which became the hallmark of a new regime of foreign-led industrialisation. The Industrial Grants Act of 1956 extended capital grants for new manufacturing projects throughout the country. Finance Acts of 1956, 1957 and 1958 gave 100 per cent profits tax relief to exporters.[58] The taoiseach still promised to 'favour home investment rather than foreign investment'[59] but the new regime was a tacit admission that domestic industrialisation was dead. This was the end product of a new policy direction that irrevocably began when the IDA, an Exports Board and an Industrial Grants Board were set up in the early 1950s at the suggestion of the US administration, to be followed by OEEC-imposed trade liberalisation.

Ireland joined the IMF and World Bank in 1957. It also removed the Control of Manufactures Acts that restricted foreign investments, the last barriers to export-oriented development. Deep recession and rising despair about indigenous capital's willingness to expand had overturned the regime's attitude toward foreign investment. Already in 1951, the Department of Industry and Commerce had insisted that 'if manufacturers are either unwilling or unable to undertake this further expansion, the Minister will then try to induce new groups, *either within or without the country* to undertake the task' (my emphasis).[60] This became official policy when the Industrial Development (Encouragement of External Investment) Act of 1958 removed restrictions on foreign investment and gave the IDA extended powers to seek out and encourage foreign investment.

The new ELI regime was firmly in place. Yet one more piece of the transition bears explaining. An indigenous capitalist class was created during the 1930s as the engine of southern Irish economic change. It never became a 'ruling class' in any real sense, yet it held power within the Irish social structure. How was opposition from this class suppressed? The answer is important if we are seriously to maintain that incorporation is a contradictory and contingent process, rather than the determinant one that some critical development approaches are accused of promoting.

The crisis and Irish capital

Domestic capital's legitimacy as an engine of Irish industrialisation was fatally damaged during the 1950s and resistance to foreign investment was eliminated. Future taoiseach and economist Garret Fitzgerald claimed that: 'the sense of failure of past economic policies predisposed Irish people almost overnight to favour new departures; and this mood of rejection extended to the policy of protection ... so rapidly were public attitudes on this issue reversed that those who had an interest in maintaining industrial protection and who had hitherto secured the support of public opinion on this issue found it impossible to resist this movement of opinion' (1968, pp. 54–5).

Conflict between domestic capital and the state began when the Department of Industry and Commerce attempted to control industrial efficiency in 1947. By the 1950s, things had become so bad that the FIM sometimes asked representatives from Industry and Commerce not to attend its meetings because they 'would be embarrassed by the discussions'.[61] As economic crisis deepened in 1957, the FIM complained that Irish firms were not being consulted about new legislation.[62] The regime could exclude domestic capital in this way because local industry was split over issues of foreign investment and free trade and discredited by its failure to expand. The government exploited this split by recruiting outward-oriented industrialists on to important bodies like the IDA.

The split within Irish capital over foreign investment and free trade deepened during 1956–57. Some local industrialists resented the regime's new programmes to encourage foreign investment. Resentment grew following the widely publicised case of a German timber company, one of the first large-scale foreign projects in Ireland, which financed 75 per cent of its investment from an Irish government grant, 15 per cent from local subscriptions and only 10 per cent from its own sources.[63] At the start of 1959, the journal *Irish Industry* wrote: 'Today our Irish Government is favouring the foreign investor more than ever before. Huge free grants of the Irish people's money are being given to those coming in here to establish industries, a good portion of such free grants being from monies received in taxation from Irish manufacturers. We regret that the Federation of Irish Manufacturers is almost completely silent on this matter.'[64]

At the FIM's annual meetings some members spoke against government incentives to foreign industry, but others argued that local industrialists should expand, themselves, instead of opposing foreign industry.[65]

The split widened when the OEEC proposed in 1956 the creation of a European Free Trade Area (FTA). From the beginning, most experts felt it was a foregone conclusion that the FTA would succeed. The FIM's president opposed the FTA, and suggested that bilateral trade agreements would be better for Irish industry.[66] But his members were split on the issue. One FIM council member insisted that 'small industrialists down the country are unanimously of the belief that if you go into this free trade area you can shut down shop'. Other delegates argued that past experience of free trade was 'no criterion of what will happen in the new Free Trade area'.[67]

Irish Industry expressed the fear that 'the country is being allowed the option to commit economic suicide'.[68] But Irish capital could not unite against free trade. At a symposium on the proposed FTA in early 1957, manufacturers expressed fears of international economic retaliation if Ireland did not join the scheme.[69] The president of the Cork Regional Group of the FIM predicted that Ireland would have to join the area because it would be 'economic suicide to stay out'.[70]

Put succinctly, the Irish bourgeoisie was powerless to stop free trade. In a second symposium on free trade in 1958, delegates expressed complete resignation to its inevitability. Instead of opposing free trade, they argued about obtaining government assistance to prepare for foreign competition.[71] The FIM president said the only course of action was to pressure the regime to give Irish companies grants to modernise.[72] Other speakers called for lower wages and lower taxes to help them survive free trade.

Resignation about the inevitability of free trade split Irish capital even further. Those who felt that they could survive had little incentive to unite with those who were likely to fail. Vocational bodies were formed within industrial sectors to help industries 'adapt to free trade', but in practice they further disunited Irish capital.

Irish free trade with Europe was postponed when Britain refused to join the FTA (now the European Union, EU) and formed the rival European Free Trade Association (EFTA). Ireland then withdrew its own application from the FTA because it still feared losing access to the British beef market. Ireland unilaterally liberalised its trade for the next decade in preparation for its inescapable entry into the European Economic Community (EEC), along with Britain, in 1973.

Conclusions: shifting hegemony and short-lived self-sufficiency

Ireland's third historical attempt to industrialise was part of a phase of the struggle for national self-determination, which developed into a full-scale national liberation movement in the twentieth century, culminating in the partition of Ireland in 1920 and the victory of the nationalist Fianna Fáil party in the south of Ireland in 1932. Like earlier attempts to industrialise in wool and cotton, this attempt accompanied a movement for political independence from England. Unlike earlier phases, however, self-sufficient industrialisation was a nationalist economic programme rather than a demand by propertied settlers that they be allowed to undertake in Ireland the same activities they would have been free to pursue in England. This time, it was a popular programme that encompassed the Irish working and middle classes.

Ireland attempted industrialisation and political independence during a period of English difficulty, as it lost hegemonic status and endured recession and war. This time, the US rather than England directed Ireland's reincorporation in a new Atlantic regime. The Irish Free State's earlier success in disincorporating from British rule made it easier for the US to reincorporate and reperipheralise it because there was no need to displace British rule. In places like Jamaica or Malaysia, the US had to deal with British resistance before it gained access to local materials and markets. On the other hand, Irish independence and industrial self-sufficiency placed different obstacles in the way of US hegemonic control. Not only had Irish classes achieved a measure of independent national identity, but new classes had material interests in maintaining protection. These interests had to be compromised before export-oriented, export-dependent industrialisation could replace ISI. Economic crisis and emigration discredited the existing development regime, moving popular classes to place their hopes in US promises of modernity and weakening domestic capital's opposition to the emergent regime.

Unlike the previous two industrial transformations, the Irish economy was not transformed back into an agrarian peripheral zone with a small concentrated zone of semi-peripheral industry. Rather, the new dependent industrial zone spanned most of the island, concentrating in the south rather than in the still-occupied and troubled north. The nineteenth-century transformation from a semi-independent industrialising state to a dependent agrarian state involved the destruction of the leading industry, cotton, and the concentration of factory linen production around Belfast. On the island as a whole, industry declined, but linen's concentration around Belfast gave the appearance of regional industrial ascent. The twentieth-century transformation from an internally industrialising state to a dependent site for foreign industry involved the replacement of indigenous industry by a foreign industrial sector. This gave the appearance an emergent modern economy involved in leading core sectors like electronics and pharmaceuticals. Chapter 6 analyses the results of this transformation.

Notes

1   Wilson told a leading British politician, 'We should between us do the whole of the marine policing of the world.... Together, we should have vastly preponderating navies over any forces that could possibly be brought against us' (quoted in McCormick 1989, p. 22).

2   A crude estimate of southern manufacturing employment in 1870 is possible using data from the 1870 factory returns and an estimate of southern proportions of Irish factory workers in each sector taken from censuses of industrial production for 1907 and 1912. This indicates slightly more than 21,000 factory workers in the twenty-six counties in 1870 (estimated from data in Ó Gráda 1994, pp. 310, 312).

3   Department of Industry and Commerce (1926). The June 1923 Fiscal Inquiry Committee identified the 'anti-protection' industrial sectors as malting, brewing and distilling; jute; biscuits; and agricultural industry. 'Pro-protection' sectors were identified as grain milling, confectionery, woollen piece goods, clothing, fellmongery and tanning, boots and shoes, cycles, agricultural machinery, galvanised hollow-ware, furniture and wood, brushes, paper and printing, fertilisers, glass bottles and pottery. See Geary (1951, pp. 399–418).

4   Memorandum by Gordon Campbell, 'Industrial development' (19 July 1927), P35b/10; Department of Industry and Commerce memorandum, 'Preliminary notes on planned economies' (1927), P35b/10.

5   The land annuities were annual repayments made by tenants in respect of money advanced by the colonial government for the purchase of their holdings under the Land Purchase Acts. Until 1932, the annuities were collected from small farmers by the Irish government and transferred to the British commissioners of the national debt. In 1932, most annuities still had over thirty-five years to run. On the republican movement in opposition to the annuities, see O'Donnell (1963).

6   These dealt in industrial alcohol (Ceimici Teoranta, established 1938), sugar (Comhlucht Siuicre Eireann, 1933), electricity (Electricity Supply Board, 1927), air transport (Aer Lingus, 1936) and shipping (Irish Shipping Ltd, 1941).

7   Department of Industry and Commerce, 'Memorandum of industrial development for An Taoiseach' (October 1945), S11987B.

8   'Openings for industry', *The Irish Times* (10 March 1950), p. 5.

9   Department of Industry and Commerce, 'Memorandum for submission to the government on Paragraph 7 (Industrial Development) of Statement of Government Policy' (22 October 1951), S11987B. An earlier list was compiled in 1945 – see Department of Industry and Commerce, 'Memorandum on industrial development for An Taoiseach' (October 1945), S11987B.

10 Department of Industry and Commerce, 'Memorandum on industrial development for An Taoiseach' (October 1945), S11987B.

11 Department of Finance (T. K. Whitaker) memorandum, 'Financial policy' (26 November 1949), P35c/47.

12 Letter from J. E. Corrigan, chief of ECA mission to Ireland, to minister for external affairs Sean MacBride (7 December 1949), P35c/47.

13 'The imminence of the free trade area', *Irish Industry*, 25:11 (November 1957), p. 3.

14 'Management talks with Kevin McCourt', *Management*, 25:3 (March 1978), p. 30.

15 'Will you come into my parlour?' *Irish Industry*, 25:2 (February 1957), p. 3.

16 'Management talks with Kevin McCourt', *Management*, 25:3 (March 1978), p. 30.

17 Department of Industry and Commerce explanatory memorandum, 'On proposed legislation to establish an industrial efficiency bureau and to amend the Control of Prices Acts in certain respects' (1946), S11987.

18 Department of Industry and Commerce, 'Proposals to enact legislation for the better control of wholesale and retail prices of goods and services and for the promotion of efficiency in certain industrial undertakings' (15 January 1947), S11987B.

19 Department of Finance holograph, 'Memorandum on proposed Industrial Development Board' (1949), P35b/75.

20 Drapers Chamber of Trade, letter to minister of industry and commerce (April 1950), S14474A. See also letter to minister of industry and commerce from the Association of Chambers of Commerce (27 March 1950), S14474A, and from the Federation of Irish Manufacturers (24 March 1950), S14474A.

21 'Openings for industry', *The Irish Times* (10 March 1950), p. 5.

22 If consultations with Irish capital were selective, the working class was excluded from decisions about the creation and staffing of the IDA. In early 1949 the secretary of the Congress of Irish Trade Unions wrote to the minister for industry and commerce to protest about the composition of the IDA and the lack of consultation with labour about its creation. When a delegation from the Congress later met the taoiseach to complain that they had not been consulted about the IDA, he curtly informed them of the 'dangers' he saw in trade union proposals for consultation and participation in decision making. Correspondence between L. Crawford, secretary of the

Congress of Irish Unions, and minister for industry and commerce Daniel Morrisey (March 1949), S14474A. Department of the Taoiseach memorandum, 'Deputation received by taoiseach from Irish Trade Union Congress' (23 May 1949), S14474A.

23 Letter from minister of state to secretary of state Caine (26 July 1947), CO 852/877/1 #4.
24 Notes on #15 by Glover (31 October 1947) and T. W. Davies (4 November 1947), CO 852/877/1 #16.
25 Letter from Oliver Franks (British Ambassador to US) to Foreign Office (31 December 1949), FO 371/82937.
26 Letter from Gorell-Barnes to T. L. Rowan (Treasury) (5 August 1948), FO 371/71822.
27 Ibid., p. 14.
28 Department of External Affairs, 'Submission to the government concerning interdepartmental and staff organisation required for the administration of the European Recovery Plan' (28 April 1948), S14299.
29 Ibid.
30 Joint report of delegation to the U.S.A. 18–28th May, 1948 (minister for external affairs Sean McBride, secretary of finance James McElligott, secretary of external affairs F. H. Boland, Department of Finance officer G. P. S. Hogan), S14106C.
31 Some Irish analysts have argued that Marshall aid carried no strings. Hederman, for example, states 'there is no sign in the "Marshall Plan" of a policy of "divide and rule", nor any strings, other than an anti-Communist bias' (1983, p. 19).
32 Internal Department of Finance memorandum (19 August 1947); quoted in Fanning (1978, p. 411).
33 Sean MacBride, letter to the government attached to Department of External Affairs' 'Memorandum for the government' (16 December 1948), P35c/2.
34 Secretary of finance James McElligott, letter to minister of finance Patrick McGilligan (17 December 1948), P35c/2.
35 Department of Finance (T. K. Whitaker) memorandum, 'Financial policy' (26 November 1949), P35c/47.
36 Letter from J. E. Corrigan, chief of ECA mission to Ireland, to minister for external affairs Sean MacBride (7 December 1949), P35b/52.
37 T. K. Whitaker, letter to minister of finance Patrick McGilligan (24 August 1949), P35c/8.
38 Joint report of delegation to the U.S.A. 18–28th May, 1948 (minister for external affairs Sean McBride, secretary of finance James McElligott, secretary of external affairs F. H. Boland, Department of Finance officer G. P. S. Hogan), S14106C.
39 Minister of finance Patrick McGilligan's notes on a lecture by Paul Bureau, assistant city editor, *News Chronicle*, to Irish Institute of Bankers, Dublin (28 October 1948), P35c/11.
40 Department of External Affairs, 'Memorandum to government on proposal for establishment of a Land Development Authority' (16 February 1949), P35c/42.
41 Interdepartmental ERP committee meeting (minutes) (7 September 1951), S14106H.

42 It was common knowledge among Irish bureaucrats that the IDA and Exports Board were direct results of ECA pressure. See M. Breathnach (principal officer, Department of Finance), 'On memorandum of foreign affairs' (4 May 1950), P35b/52. See also internal Department of Finance memorandum to T. K. Whitaker (later sent to minister of finance), 'IDA report on export corporation' (6 October 1949), P35b/52. According to this memorandum, 'it would be imprudent to agree to the [exports board] scheme solely to satisfy the ECA authorities or to avoid the possibility of a reduction in grant aid'.

43 See minister for external affairs Sean MacBride's memorandum, 'Irish currency counterpart of ECA loans' (30 December 1948), P35b/75. See also Department of Industry and Commerce comments on Department of External Affairs, 'Memorandum for the government' (16 December 1949), P35c/2.

44 Department of Industry and Commerce, 'Memorandum for cabinet committee: OEEC liberalization of trade' (4 March 1955), P35b/57.

45 Ibid., p. 4.

46 Ibid., p. 9.

47 Ibid., pp. 8, 10.

48 Department of Agriculture, 'Memorandum for cabinet committee: liberalisation of trade' (22 February 1955), P35b/57.

49 Department of External Affairs, 'Memorandum for cabinet committee: extension and stabilisation of liberalisation of trade' (22 February 1955), P35b/57.

50 US State Department, *The European Recovery Programme. Country Studies, Chapter 8: Ireland* (1948), S14106, p. 23.

51 Department of Finance (T. K. Whitaker) memorandum, 'Financial policy' (26 November 1949), P35c/47.

52 Letter from taoiseach John Costello to minister of finance Patrick McGilligan concerning T. K. Whitaker's memorandum 'Financial policy' (26 November 1949), P35c/47.

53 *Dail Debates*, vol. 129 (January–March 1955), column 1955.

54 Department of Finance, 'most confidential' memorandum, 'The economic situation' (9 December 1955), P35c/117.

55 T. K. Whitaker, 'secret' memorandum to the minister of finance (10 October 1956), P35c/117.

56 Secretary of finance James McElligott's letter to taoiseach John Costello (10 September 1956), P35c/117.

57 General correspondence between parliamentary secretary to the government John O'Donovan and minister of finance Gerald Sweetman (January 1956), P35c/117.

58 Exports profits tax relief had a difficult and contradictory passage to enactment. The IDA suggested it in 1949 on the grounds that indigenous investors gave no hope of appreciably increasing their exports. It was again supported by an ad hoc Dollar Exports Advisory Committee, commissioned by the Department of Industry and Commerce in 1950. But opposition from the Department of Finance, the Central Bank and the Revenue Commissioners (the Irish taxing authority) held up passage until 1956–58.

59 Toiseach John Costello, speech, 'The policy for production' (5 October 1956), P35c/117.

60 Department of Industry and Commerce, 'Memorandum for submission to the

government on Paragraph 7 (Industrial Development) of Statement of Government Policy' (22 October 1951), S11987B.

61 'Management talks with Kevin McCourt', *Management*, 25:3 (March 1978), p. 30.

62 'Federation of Irish Manufacturers: annual general meeting', *Irish Industry*, 25:2 (February 1957), p. 43.

63 'Ireland for the – foreigner', *Irish Industry*, 26:11 (November 1958), p. 1.

64 'The Federation of Irish Manufacturers', *Irish Industry*, 27:1 (January 1959), pp. 3–4.

65 'The Federation of Irish Industries: annual general meeting', *Irish Industry*, 27:2 (February 1959), pp. 15–40.

66 'Federation of Irish Manufacturers: annual general meeting', *Irish Industry*, 25:2 (February 1957), p. 31.

67 Ibid., pp. 39–45.

68 'Will you come into my parlour?', *Irish Industry*, 25:2 (February 1957), p. 3.

69 'Symposium on proposed Free Trade Area', *Irish Industry*, 25:3 (March 1957), pp. 65–88.

70 'Annual meeting of Cork Regional Group of Federation of Irish Manufacturers', *Irish Industry*, 25:6 (June 1957), p. 25.

71 'Discussion on free trade proposals', *Irish Industry*, 26:3 (March 1958), pp. 49–65.

72 '24th annual meeting: Federation of Irish Manufacturers', *Irish Industry*, 26:3 (March 1958), pp. 24–5.

Chapter 6

The transformed industry: foreign investment

'Suppose the people just don't like sago, like me?'
A very low, unmusical laugh escaped from McPherson.
'If they prefer starvation they are welcome.'
'Well, how will you get this sago plantation going?'
'Sago trees will grow anywhere, and two freighters loaded with shoots will arrive shortly. A simple bill in your parliament expropriating the small farmers and peasants can be passed quickly, with a guarantee that there will be no evictions, or at least very few. You are a young man Hartigan. You will probably live to see your land covered with pathless sago forests, a glorious sight and itself a guarantee of American health, liberty and social cleanliness.'

Flann O'Brien, *Slattery's Sago Saga*

Maturing US hegemony: outward movement of capital

The hegemonic processes that led to the Marshall Plan and the US 'open door' policy and that provided the context for European integration took time to mature. While US policy makers were urging and, in some cases, forcing nations to enact policies that were friendly to US private investors, it took some time for these private investments to become prominent in many regions of the world. In some places, the door was opened but US capital hardly entered. Where there were critical raw material deposits, as in Jamaica, US capital jumped in as soon as possible with the aid and sponsorship of the US government to dislodge remaining colonial barriers to entry (Bunker and O'Hearn 1993). The outward movement of manufacturing was more uneven. It depended on specific corporate interests in market access (as in Brazilian subsidiaries of car manufacturers), access to cheap labour (textiles and the so-called 'new international division of labour') and other factors. It also depended on moves by trade unions and local forces in the US to retain manufacturing at home, especially after the great industrial regions began to be transformed into 'rust belts' by the late 1960s and 1970s.

The uneven nature of outward movement of US capital was also affected by specificities of prospective host regions. European integration was not a smooth process, especially where Britain and Ireland were concerned. Ireland was generally ready to join the EEC in the late 1950s, with all the major political parties willing to trade some Irish neutrality in the hope of reducing economic dependence on the British market and seeking out new sources of economic growth. Yet Britain's membership application (along with those of Ireland, Denmark and Norway) was rejected in 1962 as a result of disputes with France, and Britain instead joined a parallel grouping, the EFTA. Although the south of Ireland had achieved a degree of economic autonomy from Britain since independence, and was now more responsive in many ways to US economic interests than to British, it was still too dependent on British trade relations to join what was now the European Community (EC) on its own. As a result, large-scale movements of US capital into the now outward-oriented Irish economy were delayed until after Ireland entered the EC along with Britain in 1973.

The kinds of industrial projects the Irish state could now attract had changed since the late 1950s and 1960s. Some US 'sunset industries' like textiles and basic manufactures were interested in better access to the European market in an effort to stave off the effects of increased foreign competition. But the best hopes of attracting TNC investments were the 'sunrise industries' like computers, pharmaceuticals and fibre optics.[1] This was a period when 'the American economy produced less but consumed more, while the rest of the world-system produced more but consumed less' (McCormick 1989, p. 193). Core regions like Germany were expanding their production of high-tech manufactures, while many semi-peripheral regions were hosts to foreign-owned factories producing less high-tech parts or performing routine assembly operations of the same products. Cars, computers and scientific instruments were becoming 'world products' only in the sense that the multiple production processes of their commodity chains were sited throughout the world. Their parent companies remained distinctly North American, European or Japanese. A partial exception was the East Asian tigers, whose own companies had limited success in technical upgrading into high-tech production lines and production processes.

Within this context, the Irish state and, especially, the Irish IDA embarked on one of the most ambitious efforts world-wide to become a key semi-peripheral site where large numbers of TNCs, particularly from the US, would locate off-shore production facilities. In order to get free access to the European market, these firms had to produce a significant amount of value-added in the European market. Ireland, with its tax-free incentives, its huge grants, its lack of regulations and its cheap English-speaking labour force, was in a distinctly favourable position to attract US producers of computers, drugs, medical equipment and soft drinks. In doing so, it again became an *intermediating periphery* between the two great core regions of the Atlantic economy, this time with the US TNCs producing manufactures and regions of the EC consuming them.

Foreign investment and Irish industry

The orthodoxy that foreign penetration would cause prosperity by trans-
ferring capital, modern technology and jobs to the host country was widely
accepted in Ireland by the mid-1950s. An early proponent of foreign-led
industrialisation claimed, 'by far the most hopeful means of getting good
management, technical knowledge and capital all at once is from subsidiaries of large foreign companies ... a plant which is paid for by foreign
capital is a great deal better than one which has to be paid for from the
scanty savings of the Republic' (Carter 1957, p. 140). Supporters embraced
the new orthodoxy that exports were an engine of growth and foreign
investors, by exporting their products, would earn foreign exchange that
could be turned to broader economic development.

Yet there was no conception of turning foreign investments into domestic
development, for example through Hirschmanian linkages. If anything, the
experience of recession had made Irish policy makers somewhat cynical
about domestic industrial expansion. Rather, the fact that the Americans
were driving regional economic change, combined with a sort of blind faith
that foreign investments and exports could bring prosperity, translated into
extreme liberal policies that reduced constraints on foreign firms that came
to Ireland. These included tax holidays, tariff-free importation of inputs
and export of products, tax-free repatriation of profits and other unearned
incomes, the absence of linkage requirements and so on. The other side of
this avoidance of regulation was policies to attract TNCs by *abrogating*
free market principles: special subsidised interest rates and grants that
covered 30–40 per cent of capital investments by potential exporters. This
ensemble of policies paralleled the *unstrategic* protectionism of the 1930s
insofar as general incentives were extended to attract a class of investors,
without much attention to controlling or channelling their actual activities
toward any long-term developmental purpose.

Because of this lack of strategic vision, the foreign sector remained
outside the weak 'economic planning' structures that were applied to the
rest of the economy beginning in the 1960s. Exports were the residual in
the new five-year economic 'programmes' (really only forecasts) that began
in 1958. Little information was collected on the size or impact of TNCs
until the IDA began employment surveys in 1973 and surveys of cost
components in manufacturing in 1983. Meanwhile, foreign companies
began to dominate the southern Irish economy.

A few TNC subsidiaries arrived each year during the late 1950s and
1960s, but after accession to the EC in 1973 the numbers increased to
major proportions (O'Hearn 1987). TNC investments grew steadily from a
tenth to a third of total fixed capital investments during the 1960s and then
jumped rapidly at the beginning of the 1970s as Ireland prepared to join the
EC along with Britain. After a short pause during the first oil crisis, foreign

capital investments grew rapidly and consistently during 1974–81 (over 27 per cent per annum at current prices). US-owned electronics, pharmaceutical and health-care firms led this expansion. Ireland was becoming a key export platform for US TNCs which desired duty-free access to the large and growing EC market. This was part of the US vision of hegemony beginning with the Marshall Plan and the US 'open door' policy of the 1950s, but it became a widespread reality in Ireland only in the 1970s.

The degree and changing nature of foreign penetration are indicated by employment in TNC subsidiaries. TNCs in basic industries like metal manufactures had become significant employers by 1960, when new foreign industry accounted for half the annual increases in manufacturing employment. Early TNC projects were in basic manufactures from cranes and hardware to pencils and plastic goods. Significantly, they were predominantly European rather than US owned. By the mid-1960s, the majority of new manufacturing jobs were in TNC subsidiaries, but still with only a smattering of high-tech projects like electronics. US firms began to locate in Ireland in larger numbers after Ireland joined the EC in 1973 because it gave them a foothold from which they could export freely to the European market. Whereas there were only about a quarter as many employees in US firms as in non-US TNCs in 1973, by 1990 employment in US companies had almost tripled and was virtually equal to that of other TNCs (table 6.1). During that period, employment in subsidiaries of US companies rose from about one in every fourteen manufacturing employees to nearly one in four. Typically, US computer and pharmaceutical companies located relatively unskilled links of their commodity chains in Ireland, mostly final assemblies of products for re-export to the continent. Changes in the profile of foreign investments reflected changing regional economic structures, particularly changing US designs on European markets. But they were also associated with intensive and quite successful marketing campaigns by the IDA, which quickly identified the growth potential of US manufacturers.

From the beginning of ELI, new foreign industry was of a much larger scale than domestic Irish industry. In 1960, the average new TNC subsidiary employed fifty workers. This grew to 114 in 1973. During the 1970s, however, the average employment of foreign projects began to shrink, primarily because targeted electronics and pharmaceutical firms tended to employ fewer people. In 1980, the average TNC employed 111 persons; by 1985, only ninety-one. While many new subsidiaries of the 1960s were larger projects (fourteen employed over 500 and four employed over 1,000), few of the new high-tech subsidiaries of the 1970s and 1980s employed more than 200. Among foreign manufacturers of computer equipment, average firm size fell from 509 in 1973 to 156 in 1986. New electronics firms included fewer global giants like Digital or IBM and more of the new wave of small 'yuppie' firms.

The Irish financial press was always quick to credit openness to foreign capital as the main reason for Irish economic recoveries and expansions.

ufacturing employment by nationality of firm,
-91[a]

	US TNCs	Other TNCs	Irish	Total
	16,791	58,382	153,852	229,025
1974	16,668	59,516	152,803	228,987
1975	18,742	56,726	146,405	221,873
1976	21,790	58,156	147,037	226,983
1977	25,672	58,693	149,074	233,439
1978	28,751	59,856	152,641	241,248
1979	33,191	61,499	156,855	251,545
1980	34,639	60,662	149,343	244,644
1981	35,735	58,397	147,438	241,570
1982	37,159	55,813	141,877	234,849
1983	38,160	51,103	134,143	223,406
1984	37,827	49,290	128,577	215,694
1985	36,893	45,247	124,697	209,837
1986	37,798	47,432	120,728	205,958
1987	37,742	46,581	117,007	201,330
1988	40,568	46,760	117,311	204,639
1989	43,693	47,715	119,860	211,268
1990	46,062	47,246	120,555	213,863
1991	47,015	47,262	119,412	213,689

[a]Surveys for 1982–91 taken in November; surveys for 1972–81 taken in January of following year.
Source of data: unpublished IDA employment surveys.

After economic growth resurged and emigration halted in the early 1960s, there was widespread feeling that this 'miracle' was caused by opening up the Irish economy to foreign industrial investments. Kennedy and Dowling (1975), however, argue convincingly that the economic upturn was due to Keynesian fiscal policies rather than foreign investments. The small numbers and size of new foreign investments support this conclusion, as they were hardly adequate to sustain a medium-term economic recovery. Nonetheless, public illusion is often more important than reality in providing legitimacy to economic regimes. A second Irish 'miracle' occurred with the upturn in numbers of new projects after 1972, which gave the illusion that EC membership was the key to Irish development hopes. Prominent public announcements of new foreign investments and 'job approvals' by the IDA,[2] accompanied by a world-wide 'invest in Ireland' advertising campaign, were the flip side of a disastrous but quiet collapse of indigenous industry due to the same EC free trade policies that attracted the foreign investments.

Table 6.2 Change in industrial employment during year by nationality of ownership, 1974–91

Year	US TNCs	Other TNCs	Irish	Total
1974	−123	1,134	−1,049	−38
1975	2,074	−2,790	−6,398	−7,114
1976	3,048	1,430	632	5,110
1977	3,882	537	2,037	6,456
1978	3,079	1,163	3,567	7,809
1979	4,440	1,643	4,214	10,297
1980	1,448	−837	−7,512	−6,901
1981	1,096	−2,265	−1,905	−3,074
1982	1,424	−2,584	−5,561	−6,721
1983	1,001	−4,710	−7,734	−11,443
1984	−333	−1,813	−5,566	−7,712
1985	−934	−4,043	−3,880	−5,857
1986	905	2,185	−3,969	−3,879
1987	−56	−851	−3,721	−4,628
1988	2,826	179	304	3,309
1989	3,125	955	2,549	6,629
1990	2,369	−469	695	2,595
1991	953	16	−1,143	−174

Source of data: unpublished IDA employment surveys.

Once again, Ireland was transformed from an economy that was attempting autonomous development into an intermediating periphery within the Atlantic economy. Its developmental path was largely subject to its ability to exploit or 'hook on' to outward movements of capital by the leading Atlantic power, this time the US rather than England. The driving cause of changing foreign direct investment was the changing global economy. The late 1960s and 1970s were a period of rapidly increasing world-wide direct investment in high-tech sectors such as electronics. This shift in the structure of the international division of labour coincided with Ireland's accession to the EC. Free imports of intermediate goods into Ireland and re-exports of final products into Europe were a powerful incentive for US-based electronics and pharmaceutical firms to locate in Ireland.

Yet dependence on US investments was an unsure bet, subject to bust as well as boom. Growing Irish dependence on more narrowly defined foreign sectors was apparent by the late 1970s, when government spokespersons announced their intentions to 'target' TNCs in microchip technologies. Rising US investment initially offset a fall of domestic industrial employment after 1973. The managing director of the IDA claimed in 1979 that the foreign electronics sector was 'recession-resistant' and that electronics employment would grow to 25,000–30,000 by 1985, with more than a third of its workers (11,500) in highly skilled job categories (Killeen 1979, p. 14). But he was quickly proven wrong. Real fixed TNC investments fell by about 10 per cent annually during the global economic restructuring of the 1980s and TNC employment began to fall (table 6.2), precipitating a severe economic crisis that will be discussed at some length below. In 1985, according to IDA employment surveys, fewer than 19,000 people were employed in electronics and less than a quarter of those were in highly skilled categories. Employment in US-owned firms fell to a level in the early 1980s that could not compensate rapidly falling employment in Irish-owned companies and non-American TNCs. Then, employment in US subsidiaries, including electronics, began to fall in 1984 and did not recover until the late 1980s and 1990s, when rapidly rising TNC investments caused rapid economic growth that defined the so-called 'Celtic tiger', which will be discussed in chapter 7.

Foreign penetration also created instability in Ireland owing to its effects on existing industry, especially Irish-owned industry. Two aspects of the new TNC-led industrialisation regime had a major impact on domestic Irish industry. These were the structure of industrial incentives and the removal of protection under European free trade. Incentives were biased toward new, exporting foreign industry, which received grants totalling about 40 per cent of investment costs, while local firms received 'retooling' grants of 25 per cent, if anything. The owner of a local engineering company protested typically that the IDA 'would break their necks if they found a German coming in, but they weren't interested in anyone of their own and couldn't care less' (Fogarty 1973, p. 33).

A more important factor, however, was free trade, which opened the Irish market to competing imports. In the two decades between 1960 and 1980, imports took over Irish markets for virtually every category of manufactured goods. A country that had virtually clothed and shod itself in 1960 imported more than 77 per cent of its clothing in 1980. Imports jumped spectacularly in textiles, leather, chemicals, metals and machinery and miscellaneous manufactures. The share of imports in non-electric machinery rose from 55 per cent to more than 98 per cent, an indication that the Irish regime had little interest in building domestic industry through capital deepening.

The effects of such a large-scale influx of manufactured imports on domestic industry were predictable. Three-quarters of Irish clothing firms, two-thirds of textile firms and half of metals/engineering firms failed within thirteen years after Ireland joined the EC. By 1980, employment in indigenous firms fell by over 80 per cent in textiles and clothing, and by more than half in chemicals, metal products and miscellaneous manufactures. Indigenous firms that received grants to 'adapt' to free trade failed at the same rate. Only non-traded sectors like clay/cement survived free trade. Since free trade was necessary for the attraction of TNCs, which was considered to be the 'engine' of export-oriented growth after 1960, the destruction of Irish indigenous industry is best viewed as an *external diseconomy* of foreign penetration.

Job losses in older, protected firms were just about balanced by employment in new indigenous industry until 1980, and then employment in indigenous firms fell rapidly. New jobs in domestic firms amounted to less than 45 per cent of jobs lost in ISI-oriented companies between 1973 and 1987. Those years saw a net loss of 35,000 jobs in indigenous industry, nearly a quarter of total indigenous industrial employment in 1972. Job losses were particularly large in the food, textile and clothing sectors. As a result, the structure of indigenous industry changed following EC accession. The most striking change was a rapid fall in average firm size, from thirty-nine employees in 1973 to eighteen in 1986. Extremely small firms replaced large ones that closed. Nearly two-thirds of new indigenous firms after 1973 employed fewer than ten employees. The modal new domestic 'firm' was someone with their own tools who serviced domestic homeowners. One survey of new Irish companies concluded that 'the biggest major external catalyst for these entrepreneurs was the domestic house market, through the products that went into houses rather than construction work' (Rothery 1977, p. 56).

The rapid decline of large Irish firms contributed to a basic change in the ownership composition of manufacturing. In 1963, 28 per cent of manufacturing firms employing over 500 people were foreign owned. This proportion grew to 48 per cent in 1973 and 57 per cent in 1986. Ten per cent of those employing 20–499 people were foreign in 1963, 19.5 per cent in 1973 and 25.5 per cent in 1980. Foreign industry came to dominate the largest-scale manufacturing in Ireland while indigenous industry became dominated by the tiny firm.

These structural changes in domestic industry affected the Irish class structure. Older Irish firms were predominantly family owned and family run. A few Irish families controlled the largest firms in interlocking directorships, along with an 'outer circle' of small- to medium-scale capitalists. This changed after the 1970s. If the Irish industrial bourgeoisie of the 1940s and 1950s consisted of 'prominent identifiable extended families' (Kelleher 1987) the new post-1970s Irish entrepreneur was a young 'frustrated employee' with some vocational or shop-floor training and 'welding gear in his back yard' (Rothery 1977, p. 58). Few of these petty industrialists reached significant size, at least before the 1990s.

Besides indigenous firms, there were also TNCs in Ireland before the 1960s, mainly British companies that supplied the Irish market. The majority were established before the 1920s but 299 foreign companies were issued licences to manufacture in Ireland during 1932–58.[3] For a time, these companies withstood free trade more successfully than their Irish counterparts. Some received IDA grants to retool and several even built new factories with IDA money. In 1973, seventy-one British firms had received grants to retool; they employed an average of 190 workers, compared with thirty-nine in domestic Irish industry. Total employment in British-owned companies at the time of EC accession was more than 33,000, but this had fallen below 15,000 by 1990. During this period, employment in British-owned firms fell in every year except 1979. Outside the food sector, total employment in older TNCs fell from 11,933 in 1973 to 3,531 in 1986; the number of companies fell from sixty-eight to thirty-seven. Larger companies fared better: eight of the eleven largest companies survived into the 1990s.

By the 1980s, the engine of Irish economic change was again the foreign sector, this time US TNCs that sought access to the European market. Boom and bust were primarily dependent on the movement of US capital, and the major economic effort of the Irish state was to increase the ability of its development agency, the IDA, to attract more foreign projects by targeting key economic sectors.

In what respects was US hegemonic domination new, different from British domination? Was the new phase a basis for meaningful, if dependent, development or was it another phase of semi-peripheral industrialisation that again limited Ireland's ability to participate in more highly skilled and profitable *core* activities, although in a new Europe rather than the old British empire? As we shall see, one set of rather bleak answers began to emerge in the 1970s and, especially, in the 1980s. A remarkably different and more optimistic one emerged in the 1990s. To see the differences, and whether the 1990s really marked a break from earlier phases of dependent development, it is important to carefully trace the transformation of industry in Ireland after the transition to free trade, export orientation and EC/EU membership.

The transformed industry: engine of modernity or another peripheralisation?

The third Irish industrial transformation, in the southern three-quarters of the island, from self-sufficient ISI to foreign-dominated ELI, arrived in Ireland with the promise that it was different from previous, British-led transformations. Even those who viewed previous, British-led transformations as underdeveloping hoped that this new engine would finally propel Ireland into modernity, to take its place among its advanced European neighbours. This attitude reflected the modernisationist ethos that dominated the social sciences and popular discourses of the time. It also accepted US anti-colonial posturing at face value, creating the hope that US power would balance the detrimental effects of the British connection – so recently experienced in the economic war of the 1930s – giving Ireland space to develop. In the popular phrase of the day, a thriving foreign sector would be the 'rising tide that lifts all boats'.

But where would these broader developmental effects arise? How, if at all, would foreign projects in Ireland, no matter how innovative in themselves, relate to other local activities? While the TNC activities that were coming to dominate the southern Irish economy had to articulate *somewhere*, the question is whether they could create the clusters of high-profit activities, the articulated 'virtuous cycles' that, according to Senghaas (1985), could enable local economies to escape from the condition of peripherality.

The answer to this question has several components. First, where did TNC profits accrue? Were they reinvested locally to promote economic growth? Or were they repatriated elsewhere, thereby wasting this multiplier? Second, did transnational activities induce local activities in links of the commodity chain that surrounded them? Here, Hirschman's (1958) question of whether an activity *links* to related activities is central. Finally, there is the question of their broader external economies or diseconomies. In the Irish case, we are particularly concerned about whether the economic regime that attracts TNCs encourages or discourages activities in local sectors.

Profitability and capital transfers

The IDA's main marketing campaign in the early 1970s boasted that profits of US companies operating in Ireland were twice their EC average. From 1983, comprehensive IDA surveys of cost components revealed stark differences in profit levels between firms of different nationality (table 6.3).

Table 6.3 Profit rates for Irish firms and TNCs (profits as a percentage of sales), 1983–90

Year	Irish	TNCs	US TNCs			TNC share of total profits
			Computers	Pharma-ceuticals	Total	
1983	−0.27	19.03	25.51	36.57	24.17	101.87
1984	1.75	21.73	29.72	47.10	30.82	91.47
1985	1.42	20.27	27.14	48.25	29.27	93.00
1986	2.50	19.73	25.97	48.68	29.17	87.03
1987	3.06	22.58	29.26	42.86	29.54	87.96
1988	4.27	22.62	31.41	40.96	30.28	84.93
1989	5.13	22.10	23.46	49.45	28.97	85.05
1990	3.88	23.48	32.40	49.38	32.18	86.61

Source of data: unpublished IDA survey data.

Table 6.4 Profits received and repatriated by TNC subsidiaries in the south of Ireland, 1983–90

Year	(1) Profits in US-owned leading sectors[a]	(2) TNC profits	(3) Repatriated profits	(1) / (2)	(3) / (2)
1983	678	936	659	0.724	0.704
1984	1,070	1,372	940	0.780	0.685
1985	1,097	1,405	1,321	0.781	0.940
1986	947	1,291	1,358	0.734	1.052
1987	1,108	1,712	1,442	0.647	0.842
1988	1,331	1,958	2,093	0.680	1.069
1989	1,281	2,114	2,564	0.606	1.213
1990	1,609	2,297	2,507	0.700	1.091
1983–90	9,121	13,085	12,884	0.697	0.985

[a]US metals/engineering and chemicals sectors. These sectors are dominated by computers and pharmaceuticals, respectively.
Source: unpublished data provided by the Central Statistics Office and IDA.

Irish-owned firms averaged profit rates (profits as a proportion of sales) of just 2.7 per cent, while TNCs averaged 21.4 per cent. Profit rates of US-owned companies were even greater: US subsidiaries averaged 29.3 per cent and US pharmaceuticals subsidiaries 45.4 per cent. Although partly due to transfer pricing, these disparities indicated vastly different expansionary potentials of foreign and domestic industry.

Whether these potentials were realised in Ireland depended on whether TNCs reinvested or repatriated their profits. During 1983–90, nearly all TNC profits (98.5 per cent) were repatriated from Ireland (table 6.4). These foreign profit repatriations comprised an increasing share of total corporate profits received in Ireland. In the early 1970s, TNCs repatriated a fifth of the total corporate profits (including non-industrial profits) received in Ireland, but by the late 1980s half of the profits received in Ireland were repatriated, rising to 55 per cent in the 1990s (table 6.5). Thus, not only did repatriated profits comprise more than a tenth of Irish GDP, which was lost to local developmental purposes, but more than half of the capital available for accumulation was lost to other regions of the world economy. Of the remaining 45 per cent, most came from services, commerce and real estate, and little was reinvested in industry.

Thus, the investment impact of TNCs was restricted mainly to their original projects. The high proportion of unprofitable local economic activities and their distorted *sectoral* distribution exemplifies the *vicious cycles of development* to which Mjoset (1992) refers, following Senghaas

Table 6.5 Repatriated profits as a proportion of total corporate profits received in Ireland, 1970–95

Year	(1) Repatriated TNC profits	(2) Total company profits	(1) / (2)
1970	26	130	0.2000
1971	28	143	0.1958
1972	24	192	0.1250
1973	36	270	0.1333
1974	45	290	0.1552
1975	47	274	0.1715
1976	89	537	0.1657
1977	128	722	0.1773
1978	206	866	0.2379
1979	219	1,008	0.2173
1980	258	974	0.2649
1981	362	1,370	0.2642
1982	499	1,521	0.3281
1983	659	1,821	0.3619
1984	940	2,360	0.3983
1985	1,321	2,798	0.4721
1986	1,358	3,379	0.4019
1987	1,442	3,762	0.3833
1988	2,093	4,163	0.5028
1989	2,564	4,874	0.5261
1990	2,507	4,940	0.5075
1991	2,377	5,270	0.4510
1992	2,735	5,572	0.4908
1993	3,652	6,546	0.5579
1994	4,001	7,278	0.5497
1995	4,680	8,307[a]	0.5634

[a]Preliminary estimate.
Source: unpublished data provided by the Central Statistics Office.

(1985) and Amin (1975). The development of an articulated industrial structure is impeded because industrial reinvestments are blocked by the diversion of TNC resources to operations abroad, due to corporate development strategies that have no relation to local or regional priorities. Meanwhile, the resources that remain in the local economy are concentrated in service and commercial sectors. Ironically, this skews the local economy into a 'service orientation' that looks superficially like Bell's (1974) *post-industrial society*. But the *disarticulated* service society lacks the linkages between services and high-tech industry or the relatively high material standards of living that Bell described.

Linkages

In the 1970s and 1980s, the local developmental effects of TNCS were reduced by their high rates of profit repatriations. But another possible source of TNC-led development is linkages to multiple other activities, which aggregate regionally. TNCs that located in Ireland after the 1950s have been extremely profitable and often utilise high-tech production techniques to produce high-tech products. Although their profitability is largely unconnected to the local economy because of profit repatriations, TNCs could still encourage innovation in the local economy if they induced profitable and expansive clusters of activities around them. Thus, do TNCs create *linkages* with other firms which either supply them with intermediate goods and services (backward linkages) or which process their products further (forward linkages)? I have already shown that the textile sectors of Lancashire and Ireland in the eighteenth and nineteenth centuries differed in this respect. The former induced whole systems of linked activities while the latter depended on outside sources for many of its material and technical inputs.

The IDA 'discovered' linkages in the early 1980s after a highly publicised 1982 report by a US consultancy firm (Telesis Consultancy Group 1982). The IDA launched a *national linkages programme* in 1985 and began collecting systematic data on where companies bought their material and service inputs. The linkages programme aspired to tie specific US electronics subsidiaries to existing domestic suppliers, with five- to seven-year targets for increasing local purchases. It did not attempt to follow Hirschman's original prescription that the linkages should induce *new* activities, to produce an expanding range of products. Nor, because of EC regulations about free trade, could the Irish state protect its capital or cajole it, East Asian-style, to enter new activities.[4]

Three early surveys estimated the backward linkages of manufacturing firms, in 1966, 1971 and 1974 (Survey Team 1967; O hUiginn 1972; McAleese 1977). A fourth survey measured linkages in a region of western Ireland (Stewart 1976a, 1976b). Since 1983, the IDA has taken an annual census of manufacturing firms that employ more than thirty people, collecting data on where they buy their material and service imports, what proportion of their product they export and their profit rates.[5]

The early studies reached contradictory conclusions because they differed in coverage, definitions and interpretations of results. Using data from 1971, Buckley found that TNCs purchased only 31.5 per cent of their material inputs from local sources while Irish firms purchased 68.3 per cent. He showed the difference to be statistically significant, yet he argued that it was mainly due to the concentration of foreign firms in low-linkage sectors (Buckley 1974, p. 319). McAleese and McDonald analysed the 1966 and 1974 surveys of grant-aided firms and found that TNCs in non-food sectors purchased 11.2 per cent of their inputs from local sources, while new domestic firms purchased 22.2 per cent from local sources. Although domestic firms bought twice as much of their inputs locally as TNCs, the authors concluded that backward linkages were 'not significantly different' between indigenous and foreign firms and that 'the picture of foreign enterprises forming a distinct enclave is seriously flawed' (McAleese and MacDonald 1978, pp. 334–5). They provided no statistical tests for this conclusion while they minimised the rather significant finding that only 11 per cent of TNCs' material purchases were from local sources. They interpreted the absence of linkages to new domestic firms as the absence of duality between TNC and indigenous corporate performance (a 'good') rather than a domestic failure to induce linkages.

A more comprehensive measure of TNC linkages comes from unpublished IDA (later Forfás) surveys of 'Irish economy expenditures'. The survey results for backward material linkages (local purchases of materials) during 1983–90 are reported in table 6.6.[6] The rationale for concentrating on material linkages is that they encourage new *manufacturing* activities, which are more likely to be core-like or innovative than locally purchased services.

The survey results strongly support theses of duality and low backward linkages by TNCs. TNC subsidiaries in all sectors except paper/printing consistently bought fewer inputs locally than Irish firms. During the 1980s, local material purchases by Irish firms averaged about 44 per cent of their output, almost four times the average for TNCs (12 per cent). Linkages were especially low among US subsidiaries in the leading sectors of computers (6.7 per cent) and pharmaceuticals (3.25 per cent), which later came to dominate the miracle recovery of the so-called 'Celtic tiger' economy in the 1990s. TNC backward linkages in Ireland were also low relative to other TNC-penetrated regions around the world, like Mexico or Brazil.[7]

Backward linkages could be so low in TNC subsidiaries because they purchase their material inputs from foreign rather than domestic sources *or* because their material purchases are smaller relative to their overall costs. This is an important issue. If TNCs purchase their inputs from foreign instead of local sources, they could be considered inferior to local firms in developmental terms because they induce less extra local manufacturing through their purchases. This might be expected where 'purchases' are simply internal transfers from one TNC subsidiary to another. On the other hand, if TNCs use fewer material inputs than local firms, perhaps because they are especially efficient, the whole idea that participating in 'leading sectors' could induce generalised industrial development may be called into question.

Local linkages (here specifically material purchases as a proportion of company revenues) can be analysed as the product of three components: (1) the proportion of local material purchases to total material purchases,

Table 6.6 Irish-sourced material purchases as a percentage of sales, by industrial sector and nationality of ownership, 1983–90

Sector	1983	1984	1985	1986	1987	1988	1989	1990
Food								
Irish	67.78	66.20	65.13	63.67	62.88	60.26	61.57	61.38
TNC	44.13	43.55	35.00	34.39	36.02	37.27	39.18	39.60
Drink/tobacco								
Irish	25.33	19.36	17.30	14.05	18.62	20.82	22.86	22.57
TNC	16.56	17.82	18.36	10.93	16.84	17.82	19.92	17.68
Textiles								
Irish	8.42	7.47	8.55	9.92	26.14	25.37	10.61	7.45
TNC	4.49	3.86	8.45	7.84	9.25	9.52	6.45	5.38
Clothing								
Irish	18.75	10.25	11.88	25.20	24.35	10.41	8.32	8.45
TNC	9.70	6.85	5.46	4.20	5.18	7.13	6.77	5.80
Wood/furniture								
Irish	36.68	42.98	28.73	30.62	28.53	31.15	24.65	23.23
TNC	13.37	7.05	29.66	24.59	21.82	19.54	19.37	20.64
Paper/printing								
Irish	8.59	9.10	6.49	6.98	7.85	8.57	13.01	13.08
TNC	7.54	7.06	9.36	7.28	15.11	17.49	24.27	25.10
Clay/cement								
Irish	6.57	7.78	6.69	9.68	9.58	6.21	15.58	14.99
TNC	7.09	5.56	2.89	8.48	8.17	8.87	8.59	9.27
Chemicals								
Irish	24.94	17.98	17.39	19.12	20.57	33.43	37.40	31.11
TNC	6.91	4.83	6.42	5.63	5.50	5.88	5.96	6.35
of which US	8.67	6.12	6.23	4.53	4.76	5.42	6.52	6.95
Metals/engineering								
Irish	12.69	11.37	20.36	17.35	14.80	15.43	16.87	15.07
TNC	5.40	4.97	4.71	5.15	5.52	6.08	6.60	6.85
of which US	4.59	4.45	4.35	4.93	4.90	5.15	5.85	5.74
Miscellaneous								
Irish	13.50	9.85	10.28	10.90	6.27	7.92	7.33	7.62
TNC	6.98	9.70	9.87	8.45	8.97	9.53	9.85	8.79
All manufacturing								
Irish	47.96	42.31	44.63	44.54	44.78	40.72	41.94	41.97
TNC	13.30	12.43	11.15	11.23	12.09	12.63	11.66	12.02
of which US	6.53	5.04	5.17	5.59	5.44	6.49	7.52	7.58

Source: author's calculations from survey data supplied by the IDA.

(2) the proportion of material purchases to total costs and (3) the proportion of costs to sales. This indicates three possible sources of difference between Irish firms and TNCs: (1) TNCs import a larger proportion of their material inputs, (2) TNCs buy fewer material inputs relative to their total costs of production and (3) TNCs have lower costs relative to sales because their profit rates are higher. Once this decomposition is made using IDA survey results, it is clear that TNCs have lower linkages predominantly because they import more of their material inputs. Foreign purchasing accounts for two-thirds of the difference in linkage performance between Irish firms and TNCs. There is no substantial difference between the cost structures of domestic and foreign companies as both buy material inputs in roughly the same proportion to total costs. The remaining difference in linkages results from the fact that TNCs make so much more profit than Irish firms, and thus their costs of production are a much smaller proportion of sales.

These differences are particularly stark in the US-owned leading sectors. US-owned chemicals subsidiaries not only purchase a smaller proportion of materials in Ireland than other chemical companies, but their profit rate of nearly 50 per cent means that their lower costs as a percentage of sales accounts for nearly half of the differential between their linkages and those of domestic companies. Overall, two-thirds of the lower linkage performance of US subsidiaries in Ireland is explained by foreign sourcing of intermediate goods. A fifth is explained by their high rates of profit. If these profits were reinvested locally it would constitute an *investment linkage*, inducing new activities in the firm itself if not in clusters of suppliers. But I have already shown that the predominant share of TNC profits is repatriated abroad.

The IDA survey data also indicated a general decline in backward linkages during the 1980s because US-owned pharmaceutical and computer subsidiaries bought so few material inputs in Ireland, while their share of total manufacturing rose during the same period.

This failure to improve significantly after more than a decade of IDA linkage programmes indicates that host countries such as Ireland have limited ability to induce foreign subsidiaries to increase their local material linkages. This seemed to contradict the IDA's repeated referrals to computer projects as high-linkage investments that would eventually encompass all stages of production, from research and development to end-user products. As I will show in chapter 7, however, this claim would arise again in the 1990s, when a US-led exports boom brought historically high economic growth rates to the south of Ireland.

The IDA surveys did suggest that TNCs were more likely to purchase locally provided services than materials and components. In 1990, local purchases of services represented 14.5 per cent of TNCs' sales revenues, compared with 13 per cent of Irish companies' sales revenues. While Irish firms bought 85 per cent of their services in Ireland, TNCs bought 80 per cent of their services in Ireland (US computer and pharmaceutical firms bought 77.5 per cent and 65.8 per cent, respectively, in Ireland). This indicated that TNCs were buying a large proportion of their services in Ireland, although many of these 'local purchases' were from other TNC subsidiaries operating in Ireland rather than from indigenous firms.

The fact that TNCs encourage local service firms but not local manufacturers raises another important point about dependent export platforms like Ireland. This pattern of economic change suggests that globalisation creates oversized domestic service sectors alongside TNC-dominated manufacturing sectors. To the degree that services are relatively low-wage and low-profit activities, their predominance in the indigenous economy increases the duality between foreign manufacturers and local sectors.

Finally, it is important to distinguish the extent to which TNCs have low linkages because they are concentrated in sectors (such as electronics and chemicals) that have low linkages relative to the sectors where domestic firms are concentrated (such as food). O'Hearn (1988, chapter 12) tested this by calculating the log odds of backward linkages arising from foreign-owned and Irish-owned operations, and then distinguishing between intra-sectoral and sector-distributional causes of TNCs' low backward linkages. These tests indicated that both industrial sector *and* foreign ownership have highly significant effects on the likelihood that a firm will buy local material inputs. Controlling for industrial sector, foreign firms were still significantly less likely to use local inputs.

The evidence from the 1980s clearly indicates that, although TNC subsidiaries in the south of Ireland were concentrated in 'core' sectors with especially high profit rates, little of their economic dynamic was transferred to the indigenous economy. Profits were repatriated abroad while TNCs did not link either among themselves or with Irish producers.

One need hardly dwell on the question of forward linkages in the south of Ireland. The raison d'être of its development strategy was to encourage TNCs to export their output. As an *intermediating periphery* between the US and Europe, Ireland attracted US companies that sought to export into EU markets.

The IDA surveys confirm this. In each year between 1983 and 1990, TNCs exported more than 90 per cent of their products. US firms in computers and pharmaceuticals exported more than 98 per cent of their products while all US companies exported 96 per cent of their product. O'Hearn (1988) found that, unlike backward linkages, foreign ownership was the only significant predictor of export performance, regardless of the industrial sector in which the TNCs were located.

Company start-ups by people who were formerly employed by TNCs are an indirect linkage. The Irish government cited spin-offs as a particular reason for concentrating on electronics investments during the late 1970s and 1980s (Killeen 1979). Rothery's (1977) survey of twenty-five successful Irish businesses identified spin-offs as an important way of spawning new businesses. Of thirty-eight 'emerging entrepreneurs' who were interviewed, all but one cited frustration as an employee as the major reason for starting their new business. Of the eighteen new businesses that produced a product, sixteen copied existing products. The greatest single source of technical information was the entrepreneur's last employer.

But closer inspection of Rothery's findings shows that TNCs had little to do with these spin-offs. Only one of the twenty-five surveyed firms used grant-aided foreign firms as its initial market. There were no examples of product innovation, licence or joint venture. The new firms did not produce technically advanced goods, or even products related to innovative TNC-dominated sectors, but mostly goods such as bath tubs and heating systems for domestic construction.

Colgan and Onyemadum (1981) identified just thirty-five domestic firms in electronics, the sector most likely to provide spin-offs from TNCs. Only six were spin-offs. Four were started directly after their promoters left an 'incubator' firm, while the other two promoters worked in non-related firms before starting their businesses. Four of the incubator firms were US owned, one was British and one Irish. The average age of the spin-offs was about four years and the average workforce numbered twenty-four. None of them innovated in their product, but instead copied existing low-technology products. Other studies also show that foreign electronics subsidiaries produced few spin-offs before the 1990s (O'Brien 1985; Eolas 1989).

Export orientation and industrialisation

Irish development strategy after 1960 was deceptively simple: attract as much foreign industry as possible, increase exports as much as possible, and economic development will follow.[8] Even before the Irish economic boom of the 1990s, most Irish academics, bureaucrats and financial experts insisted that the regime was successful. In terms of foreign investments and exports, it was hard to disagree. On the other hand, these target policy variables did not positively affect developmental variables like economic growth, employment and general material well-being.

Exports grew in real terms at an annual rate of more than 8 per cent from 1960 to 1986 and more than 9 per cent from 1986 to 1994. Manufactured exports grew even more rapidly, at an annual rate of more than 10 per cent during 1960–94. Exports of pharmaceuticals and computers by TNCs grew most rapidly after the 1970s.

Foreign direct investment, the underlying engine of export growth, also grew rapidly from the 1960s to the 1980s. From 1960 to 1980, the annual rate of increase of TNC fixed capital investments was about 15 per cent in real terms. Although this rate of increase fell during the 1970s, foreign investment flows were still quite high, particularly compared with stagnant domestic investment levels. But by the 1970s the Irish regime was finding it more difficult to maintain high inflows of foreign investment. In the 1980s, foreign investments began to fall rapidly and did not recover until the 1990s. To revive investment rates, the IDA first targeted US-based electronics firms and then pharmaceuticals and health-related TNCs. More recently, it concentrated on attracting TNCs in financial and industrial services.

The unevenness of foreign investment flows shows the dangers inherent in overdependence on TNCs in a few sectors and largely from a single country. US companies came to Ireland in the 1970s to gain access to EC markets. When recession turned to restructuring in the 1980s, many US subsidiaries either cut back their operations or left Ireland altogether. The effectiveness of TNC-led growth was also questioned by the lack of connection between policy variables like export growth or TNC investment growth and ultimate policy objectives like employment creation and rising standards of living. During the first fifteen years after Ireland joined the EC, industrial exports and foreign investments both boomed, by about 10–11 per cent annually. Yet manufacturing employment fell by nearly 0.5 per cent annually, total employment was stagnant and per capita GNP rose by less than 1 per cent per year. Irish successes in achieving policy targets like exports and investment growth were not matched by similar results in the ultimate developmental goals of high growth rates and job creation. From 1980 to 1986, the south of Ireland experienced an economic stagnation that was unprecedented since the beginning of ISI in 1932, unmatched even by the recession of the mid-1950s. During the early 1980s, per capita GNP never grew by even 1 per cent in any year and in three years it declined.

O'Hearn (1990) examined the relationships between foreign investment flows, foreign penetration and economic growth during 1960–83. While he found clear evidence that TNC investment flows were positively associated with economic growth, TNC *penetration* (the size of the stock of foreign assets) was negatively associated with economic growth. On the other hand, while foreign penetration had a significant negative effect on capital investment, which was in turn associated with slower economic growth, other factors associated with foreign penetration were even more important to economic growth. Specifically, import penetration, which accompanied TNC penetration, had a highly significant negative relationship with both investment growth and income growth. Thus, the most important cause of economic stagnation was Ireland's radical policy of free trade, encouraged by the US since the 1940s and enforced first by the OEEC and later by the EC/EU. Free trade reduced economic growth both by reducing investment growth and by causing the decline of Irish industry. O'Malley (1989) and Mjoset (1992) advanced similar arguments about the failures of the 1970s and 1980s.

Free trade and foreign investment transformed Irish industry but transferred many of its 'developmental' effects outward. This not only brought slower economic growth overall, but it also had differential effects on different economic sectors. Net output in most sectors slowed considerably after the 1960s, especially after Ireland joined the EC. Textiles and clothing declined after 1973, while food, drink, wood, paper and clay experienced near-zero growth rates. Only the foreign-dominated sectors like electronics and chemicals experienced annual growth rates of more than 5 per cent after Ireland entered the EC.

While the foreign penetration of Irish industry was associated with slow growth rates, the regime's success in creating employment, its ultimate target variable, was dismal. TNC operations were considerably less labour intensive than the activities they replaced and they did not replace them in adequate numbers to counteract their low labour intensity. Thus, employment grew at an even slower rate than GNP. As growth rates turned negative in the 1980s, employment deteriorated rapidly. Different measures of employment and unemployment in Ireland vary widely, and official unemployment rates were adjusted several times in ways that reduced reported unemployment. Even so, official unemployment rates rose from 5–6 per cent in the early 1970s, to 8–9 per cent in the late 1970s, to nearly 20 per cent in 1985. The Organisation for Economic Cooperation and Development (OECD 1993) reported an Irish unemployment rate of 21 per cent for 1992. The actual rate was even higher if one counts unemployed people who were on temporary training schemes (about 40,000 in 1992, with estimates of unemployed that ranged from 300,000 to 195,000). And all of this was happening during a time when people were emigrating from the south of Ireland in high numbers: some 472,300 between 1982 and 1993 (Courtney 1995, p. 68).

Another problem is that during the 1980s Irish unemployment changed from being predominantly short term to predominantly long term. While 36.9 per cent of the unemployed were out of work for more than one year in 1983, one of the lowest proportions in Europe, 67.2 per cent were long-term unemployed by 1990 (OECD 1992).[9] This was easily the highest rate in the EC.

The other Irish economy: northern decline

Meanwhile, deindustrialisation and *un*development in the north of Ireland were even more rapid and chronic than in the south, although some of the worst social effects were eased by British social welfare programmes. Since it was not disincorporated from dependence on the British economy because of partition, the north did not follow the same development path as the south. The demise of the British maritime economy was particularly disastrous for the north and its core industries, linen textiles and shipbuilding, went into decline even as southern ISI was being built up. The north had a short respite when demand rose during the Second World War but the linen industry collapsed in the 1950s after the introduction of synthetic fibres (Isles and Cuthbert 1957; Rowthorn and Wayne 1988). Unlike the south, which faced its crisis of the 1950s by turning to a broad-based programme of attracting foreign investments from Europe and North America, the north turned to English companies in synthetic textiles and other basic industrial products. Northern governments regularly went to Westminster to ask for the power to introduce similar programmes to those being introduced in the south, particularly tax breaks and grants. But they were refused special consideration until the 1970s, on the basis that Britain had many areas that were deindustrialised and were in need of new industrial investments. While the south built up a culture of attracting foreign companies, and the IDA became one of the leading investment-attraction bodies in the world, the north had no such experience. Its Industrial Development Board was not even set up until 1982.

Three English firms – Cortaulds, ICI and British Enkalon – dominated the northern synthetic textile sector for little more than a decade. Employment in the sector grew from 1,500 in the 1950s to 9,000 in 1973 (Northern Ireland Economic Council 1983, p. 38).

But producing in the north of Ireland was an adaptive response of wage saving for these declining English firms and they soon moved to cheaper locations of the global South or collapsed altogether. Between 1972 and 1982, when foreign-based electronics employment was expanding in the south of Ireland, nearly 8,000 jobs were lost in the northern textiles sector. Foreign investments were already declining in the north in the early 1960s, so there was little new investment to replace the English firms as they left (O'Hearn 1998b, p. 61). As war made the north an unattractive site for investments and as the south of Ireland, Scotland, Wales and English regions all increased their abilities to attract foreign capital, the north went into severe economic decline. New jobs created in non-British foreign companies fell to less than 150 per year in the mid-1970s. Thus, where non-British TNCs employed over 80,000 people in the south in 1990, they employed barely 10,000 in the north.

By the 1990s, manufacturing had fallen to less than 18 per cent of northern Irish employment, while services expanded to 74 per cent. There were both chronic unemployment and chronic underemployment, although the social effects of economic marginalisation were muted for the loyalist Protestant population by sectarian inequality. Catholic men were consistently unemployed at two and a half times the rates of Protestant men. Part of the difference was due to traditional patterns of employment and part was due to the high proportion of security jobs in total employment, the vast majority of which went to Protestants.

At the macro-level, the northern economy was simply unable to sustain itself. Not only was it dependent on government-sponsored jobs, but its revenues were so low that half of state expenditures were funded by subsidy from London. Rowthorn (1987, pp. 117–18) described the northern Irish economy as a 'vast workhouse in which most of the inmates are engaged in servicing and controlling each other'. Ironically, unionists used this high subvention to support their case for continuing the tie with Britain. Surely, the southern government, which was so heavily in debt and was managing an economy in deep recession, could hardly afford to keep the north at the level of social welfare to which it was accustomed. This, however, all began to change with the emergence of the 'Celtic tiger' in the 1990s.

Conclusions: again on innovation and industrial transformation

The transformation from indigenous to foreign-led industrialisation in post-partition southern Ireland brought increasing dependence on investments by US-owned TNCs. These investments were increasingly concentrated in a few sectors that constituted the 'dynamic' part of the Irish economy. They drove periods of growth when investment flows were rapid, but also periods of decline when they were too moderate to offset indigenous contraction. The latter included the period of deep recession and despondency in the 1980s, when southern Irish unemployment reached historically high levels.

But how did the new dependency affect Irish economic change in general, not just in terms of wealth and employment but also in terms of encouraging processes leading to national systems of innovation?

Compared with Irish firms, leading US subsidiaries looked good in terms of their output, productivity and profitability, which are common indicators of innovation. US-owned computer and pharmaceuticals firms accounted for 16 per cent of industrial output in the south of Ireland in 1990, with just 9 per cent of industrial workers. They accumulated a vastly larger share of profits than their shares of investment, sales or employment. They received 43.5 per cent of the industrial profits accumulated in the south of Ireland – three times their share of output (US TNCs overall received more than three-quarters of industrial profits) – but paid less than a tenth of industrial wages.

But innovative activities cluster. In more recent terminology, they agglomerate. Not only do they expand in and of themselves, but they also induce other self-expanding activities through linkages, spin-offs and other multipliers. Core firms buy inputs from other core suppliers, including their own corporate relations. They reinvest and expand. They buy considerable amounts of high-waged labour power even though most of their activities are relatively capital intensive.

This core dynamism did not reach into indigenous parts of the southern Irish economy. US-owned computer and pharmaceuticals firms accounted for only 3 per cent of local material purchases by industrial companies (table 6.7). Their share of backward material linkages was only a *fifth* of their share of output. Although they purchased more services than materials in Ireland, they bought very little from Irish *industrial* firms. Likewise, forward linkages from US computer and pharmaceuticals subsidiaries hardly existed, since they exported more than 98 per cent of their product. US firms overall accounted for two-thirds of Ireland's non-food exports, although they produced only a third of industrial output. And while they spent little on local products, either directly through linkages or indirectly through wages, they repatriated their super-profits rather than reinvesting them. Thus, the leading TNC subsidiaries 'clustered' outward, to their parent companies, to their operations in other regions and to other producers of their material input needs outside Ireland. The combination of low wages and high profits meant that these subsidiaries contributed significantly to increased class inequality. Yet, even here, profits accrued mainly to an international capitalist class outside Ireland, so TNCs contributed less to inequality *within* Ireland than to global inequality between Ireland and other regions.

How do these characteristics compare with previous industrial transformations under British colonialism? Unlike earlier British transformations, the twentieth-century transformation was more balanced: US capital entered where protected Irish industry declined, so there was more of a *transformation* of industry than a *deindustrialisation*. New industries replaced old in the earlier transformations from wool and cotton, as well, but widespread deindustrialisation was the result for most regions of Ireland. While US capital was unable to fully replace the jobs that were lost to free trade, and while it was disarticulated from the rest of the economy, it did not peripheralise the countryside. This freed the Irish from their previous experience of persistent subsistence crises, but it also induced substantial depopulation of the countryside through urbanisation and emigration. Where the children of Irish tenants of earlier centuries left the land to emigrate or perhaps to starve, the late-twentieth-century farmer's children either emigrated or moved to Dublin. Once there, a new form of subsistence crisis emerged in the forms of unemployment, the dole and low-waged service work.

Where British-dependent nineteenth-century industrialisation concentrated around Belfast, US-dependent industrialisation spread more widely throughout the southern economy, although it concentrated in certain areas like Dublin, Cork and Shannon. But the most crucial difference between British-dependent industry and US-dependent industry is their dominant activities. US-owned firms in Ireland concentrated in high-tech core sectors like computers and pharmaceuticals, even though they articulated with external regions rather than the semi-peripheral host economy. Industrial firms under British rule concentrated in semi-peripheral industrial pursuits like linen and shipbuilding, relatively low-profit and low-wage industries whose possibilities for expansion were severely limited. Industrial expansion in

Table 6.7 Contributions of leading US-owned sectors to Irish industrial categories, 1990

Sector	Percentage of output	Percentage of exports	Percentage of profits	Percentage of total Irish purchases	Percentage of Irish material purchases	Percentage of Irish service purchases	Percentage of wages paid
Computers	10.44	16.92	24.17	5.05	1.38	11.71	4.44
Pharmaceuticals	5.47	9.07	19.28	2.23	1.65	3.29	4.52
Computers and pharmaceuticals	15.91	25.99	43.45	7.28	3.03	15.00	8.96
All US TNCs	33.22	51.83	76.36	18.37	10.06	33.43	25.24

Source: author's calculations from survey data supplied by the IDA.

century was limited by the global strategies of the multi-
NC, in the context of cycles of world economic activity and
ditions of competition between the US and hegemonic aspirants.
ansion in earlier periods was limited by direct colonial policies
against Irish textile trades and commerce, and by limited supplies of raw
materials, limited market demand and the development of close substitutes.

The early linen industry, transformed from the wool industry, was
relatively well integrated, with strong linkages to suppliers. But its technical
requirements were low and its relations of production were both domestic
and semi-subsidiary to agricultural activities. The later linen industry, on
the other hand, had external technological linkages, mainly to Lancashire,
with its raw material partly local and partly imported. US-dominated
export industry has had the fewest linkages of any of these transformed
industrial stages. Although far more high tech than any form of linen
production, the high technologies and semi-fabricates used by US subsidiaries were mainly supplied from outside Ireland.

Finally, southern Ireland in the late twentieth century played a much
different role relative to dominant hegemonic strategies than did the island
of Ireland in earlier centuries. Under British domination, the Irish economy
was subordinate. Activities that were useful to empire while not competitive with leading British sectors were encouraged in Ireland, as a way of
bringing production within empire, supporting the naval effort and shifting
the centre of the world economy from the Baltic to the Atlantic. Whether
industrial or agricultural, Irish production was crucial to British hegemony.

Twentieth-century southern Ireland, however, was simply a geographical
space to the US. It was an important space because it allowed leading US
corporations to gain freer access to European markets. But Ireland was far
more marginal to US hegemonic strategies than it had been to Britain's,
since increasing numbers of other spaces in the European periphery and
even the European core could serve the same functions, if not quite as
profitably. Moreover, while Britain played a central role in Irish economic
and political affairs, the US had little interest in what Ireland did with the
rest of its economy so long as it remained attractive as a trade conduit to
Europe. Ireland's dependence on British markets for its cattle and dairy
products continued, only to be reduced in the latter part of the twentieth
century by the rise of Middle Eastern sources of demand for beef. The
transformation of the domestic Irish economy, especially the decline of
domestic industry, was less a matter of direct policy than an externality of
free trade policies that were intended for entirely different purposes.

In the 1980s, Ireland appeared to confirm the thesis that extreme dependent
industrialisation policies were likely to be underdeveloping (see O'Hearn
1989, 1990). While developmental states like the four East Asian tigers
were highly successful in many developmental respects, Ireland was a case
where free trade and foreign investment penetration seemed to create

stagnation, fiscal crisis and rampant unemployment. Looking back on the experience of the 1960s up to the 1980s, a leading Irish economist remarked that 'the foreign led industrial growth strategy developed into, at best, a zero-sum game' (Bradley 1990, p. 140). Moreover, despite deep recession, the Irish state was locked into its dependent development strategy, not just because of its relationship with the US but also because of the rules of EC membership. An even more appalling spectre loomed if the country pursued a more autocentric development strategy, which would have involved leaving or being expelled from the EC.

Yet, in a few short years, things turned around dramatically. After a few years more, the southern Irish economy was climbing up the ranks of EU members in terms of per capita national income. As the new century arrived, the economy had apparently transformed from being Europe's 'sick man' to its outstanding success story. Had Ireland successfully managed to break out of several centuries of path-dependent underdevelopment, by taking a *switching point* to a new developmental trajectory? Had policies that once led to stagnation now become the right strategy for the 1990s? Or was the economy now in another upward swing of the same dependent cycle, albeit a rather spectacular one, with its long-term developmental prospects still in question? I will pursue these questions in chapter 7.

Notes

1 Unlike the south of Ireland, the northern economy remained dependent on foreign investments in textiles, especially from Britain. This and the outbreak of conflict were the main reasons for the subsequent rapid economic decline of the area (see O'Hearn 1998b).

2 In order to maximise the positive publicity from new investments, the government always announced projects along with a figure for 'approved jobs'. In practice, TNCs on average created only about half as many jobs as the initial figure of 'approvals'. It was in the interests of both parties to inflate these figures – the IDA and Irish government, in order to create the impression that they were creating more employment than was actually true, and the TNCs in order to justify larger grants from the IDA.

3 *Dáil Debates*, 168 (May 1958), p. 274.

4 For more description of the national linkages programme, see Kennedy (1991).

5 Complete results of the 1983 survey and partial results of the 1984–90 surveys were made available to the author by the IDA.

6 It is important to analyse sectoral-level data as well as general linkage levels in manufacturing because local purchases have different meanings in different sectors. While local purchases by a new computer or chemical firm may rightly be regarded as a backward linkage, for example, local purchases by food processors are more accurately conceptualised as *forward* linkages from agriculture (because the agricultural activities would exist without the processors,

but not vice versa). This and other clarifications of the concept of linkages in an Irish context are made by Kennedy (1991).

7 Connor (1977), for example, finds that US subsidiaries in Brazil and Mexico purchased 76 and 69 per cent, respectively, of their material inputs locally in 1972. This compares with an average of about 6 per cent in Ireland during the 1980s. US chemicals subsidiaries in Brazil bought 45 per cent of their material inputs locally and those in Mexico bought 55 per cent locally. This compares with about 6 per cent in Ireland. The same differences apply to different degrees in every industrial sector, including high-linkage sectors such as food products.

8 For a review of Irish thinking on the relationship between exports and growth, see Kennedy and Dowling (1975, part II, especially chapter 4).

9 In the north, 50 per cent were long-term unemployed in 1992 (Borooah 1993, pp. 6, 15).

Chapter 7

Riding the new economy:
from green donkey to Celtic tiger

I have seen the new economy – an economy driven by information, research, knowledge, and technology. A new economy that values the productive capacity of people above all else. A new economy linked to a global marketplace that zaps dollars, deutschemarks, and data around the world at the speed of light. A new economy that brings the promise of a better life for all Americans.

I have discovered many things on my journey, and have as many questions as I have answers, but one thing's for sure: this is not your father's economy. The new economy is workers who learn throughout a lifetime, not those with a single skill. It is entrepreneurs who take risks, not managers who take a pass. It is economic growth because of environmental protection – not in spite of it. The new economy is networked, not hierarchical. Distributed, not top-down. Creative, not complacent. Multicolored, not single-hued. It thrives on reinvention, not bureaucracy. It focusses on results, not red-tape. It is customized, not standardized. It is bits, more than brawn. Wits, more than widgets. Wired, not tired. Partnership, not confrontation. The new economy is hyperlinked, hyper-speed, hypertext, and at times just plain hyper.

Al Gore, 9 July 1997[1]

At the end of the 1980s the future of the southern Irish economy did not look good. Economic growth was stagnant, unemployment was at a historic high and exceeded anywhere in the EU except possibly Spain, and the state was one of the most indebted in the world. Socially, things appeared to be going from bad to worse because the state was compounding the economic miseries with an austerity programme that shut down or cut back many facilities for the poorest sections of the population. Among the few bright spots were the continued high levels of EU fiscal transfers, which enabled significant infrastructural projects, and the high numbers of technical graduates, who were a potential resource if only they could be kept at home. Economic strategy was generally a continuation of the past liberal policies, except for the higher commitment to fiscal and wage restraint and new corporatist 'social partnership' programmes that aimed to enforce restraint by bringing the representatives of labour and capital into the consultative process. Liberalisation was being intensified with EU programmes for a single European market and eventually for monetary integration, along with deregulation and privatisation. The Irish state tinkered a bit with the structures of its industrial promotion agencies and it intensified its efforts to provide information and advice to local entrepreneurs. But the engine of growth was still foreign investments and any future recovery depended on a turnaround from disinvestment to heavy investment by US capital.

At the global level, in response to crises and recession, transnational capital began to change patterns of investment and states changed their developmental and social welfare policies. By the late 1980s, a discussion of *restructuring* dominated the academic discourse. This entailed a change in the patterns of global investment by TNCs, including general retrenchment and disinvestment from commitments made during the 1980s. Economic power appeared to be shifting eastward, with a Japan-centred Pacific economy challenging the Atlantic economy as the leading productive region. The newly industrialised countries (NICs) of East Asia combined with Japan in a regional division of labour that was highly productive, and pioneered many of the new technologies like robotics and information technology (IT). These were often integrated into existing products like cars, consumer durables and capital equipment. As the Cold War ended, it was unclear whether US politico-military power would be as central to hegemony as it had been in years past. Some analysts began to speculate that Japan might challenge the US as global hegemon. Others, like Fred Bergsten of the US Council for Foreign Relations, asked whether Japan could achieve hegemony without military significance and a leading geopolitical presence, or whether the US could reclaim hegemony as the world's leading debtor state. Bergsten suggested that a new system of *bigemonie* might be emerging, with Japan and the US jointly at the centre (Bergsten 1987; Chase-Dunn 1989, p. 184; McCormick 1989, pp. 236–43; Arrighi 1994, pp. 325–56).

Answers to these questions began to emerge only in the mid- to late 1990s, after the US entered its longest period of peacetime economic growth as world leader in the so-called 'new economy'. Its corporations reclaimed economic leadership in the new IT technologies and IT-connected services, which experienced a boom in business and consumer demand.[2] The US state reasserted its muscle as the political consequences of the end of the Cold War became clearer. With the Asian economic crisis of the mid-1990s and political attention turning to the Gulf War and the realignment of the former Soviet bloc, the Atlantic economy again became more central. Investment and marketing efforts, too, returned to Europe after the EU created a 'big market' in 1992. US capital, after its retrenchment in the 1980s, returned to Europe in a big way during the 1990s.

The resurgence of US investments, however, took a decidedly different form from earlier decades. Corporate organisation and strategies shifted from standardised mass production to *flexible production*. Production was co-ordinated more by IT, enabling companies to respond more flexibly to the customised demands of their consumers. Products were made in smaller batches, inventories reduced and new technologies used to enable alterations of product design and specifications. Most importantly, production was divided into smaller discrete processes or components, with new technologies enabling greater co-ordination of different production sites so that final assembly or production could be located closer to the consumer, making the producer more responsive to changing consumer requirements or demands. Decentralised production sites required fewer workers for a vastly increased value-added.

The development of flexible production brought two important global trends. One was a decentralisation of production so that transnational investment grew rapidly. The second was that many of the new investments agglomerated close to each other in foreign investment *complexes*. TNCs were relatively footloose in the 1970s, choosing production sites mainly by the degree to which local packages of incentives and labour resources suited their internal profitability strategies. But under flexible production it was important not only that a firm was closer to final markets but also that its suppliers and the other firms it supplied were also close by. Amin (1992) argues that producers of many traditional products continued to locate according to previous principles. Yet the producers of leading products like IT and biotechnologies, which created the global investment surge of the 1990s, clearly preferred to agglomerate in a few key locations.

The other element of restructuring happened at state levels. Countries that had been plagued by debts and economic stagnation were persuaded and cajoled to change their economic structures and strategies. Many indebted states signed up to World Bank and IMF *structural adjustment programmes*, where they agreed to broad trade liberalisation policies in return for loans to finance their debts. These policies included privatisation of public functions, cutbacks of social programmes and the application of free market principles to wages, prices and trade. In addition, scores of countries signed up to the GATT and, following the conclusion of the Uruguay Round of negotiations in 1994, had to abide by the free trade and investment principles of the World Trade Organization (George 1992). McMichael (1996) even argues that this new phase of *globalisation* differed from the earlier phase of *developmentalism* insofar as states no longer expected to follow the earlier Western path of industrial development but rather readjusted their developmental goals toward maximum participation in the world market.

Restructuring, the 'new economy' and Irish recovery

An extraordinary economic boom began in the US in the 1990s. The Dow Jones Industrial Average rose from 3,000 points in 1991 to more than 10,000 in 1999. GDP grew annually by more than 3 per cent in the first half of the 1990s and 4 per cent in the last half. Unemployment fell to 4.25 per cent in 1999 and below 2 per cent in some regions. The world's largest budget deficit in 1990 was turned into a surplus by 1997. All of this was done in the context of low inflation and low interest rates. Much of the economic activity and, particularly, the paper profits and shares held by corporate managers and even many workers were of questionable value. Most of the new jobs were in services like retail trade, where median earnings were only about 40 per cent of those in manufacturing. Job security was notoriously low (Persuad and Lusane 2000, p. 26). Throughout the 1990s and into the new century, experts spoke of the US expansion as an economic bubble that was waiting to burst. Warning signs came from occasional plunges in vastly overvalued shares, especially in the new 'dot.com' firms that sprang up at the end of the 1990s.[3] Further indications of impending recession appeared at the start of George W. Bush's presidency.

Yet there was another side to this often-puzzling US expansion. This was the reassertion of US leadership in high-tech sectors, particularly in computers and all the products that surrounded them. US producers regained market leadership in products from semiconductors to software at a time when business spending on IT-based equipment boomed and when consumers bought new IT products like personal computers as well as traditional consumer durables that incorporated IT components. US companies met this booming demand by doubling the rate of productivity growth over the previous twenty-five years. This, together with a labour force that was neutralised by job insecurity, enabled them to raise the annual 'speed limit' of US economic growth (the top rate at which the economy can grow without meeting labour shortages and invoking wage rises and inflation) to more than 4 per cent (Tyson 1999, p. 8).

The expansion of IT production and the ever-increasing search for new markets caused a revival of foreign direct investment by US TNCs. When they began to invest again in Europe, it was unclear what the effects would be on the EU periphery. If investment was indeed agglomerating, it was likely to be restricted to a few zones, possibly core zones where the final consumers were located and where the largest numbers of skilled workers resided. Wage savings were not particularly important since the new production processes used very little labour and were highly profitable. Foreign investors were often willing to offer relatively high wages and benefits. England, in particular, seemed to be in an advantageous position as its earlier phase of deindustrialisation left substantial numbers of highly educated and English-speaking surplus workers seeking employment. Moreover, its physical and financial infrastructures and established trading relations with continental markets gave it clear advantages. Regions like Spain and Portugal seemed less attractive since their advantages in cheaper labour and even state incentives were outweighed by these other factors.

Ireland was in between. It had, over two decades, educated large numbers of technicians with the skills that were required by firms producing the new technologies. Yet most of these people had left Ireland years previously because there was no work. Would they ever return from their good jobs in California's Silicon Valley and elsewhere? The vast majority of available workers were unskilled or semi-skilled, unemployed often for the long term and dispirited. The country was still plagued by bad transport and communications infrastructure, although this had improved substantially through projects that were funded by the EU. But the IDA was one of the best industrial attraction agencies in the world, good not only at identifying and attracting foreign projects but also at supporting them once they came to Ireland. Its job was considerably eased by the lack of government regulations, Ireland being probably the most pro-business location in the EU.

Moreover, the business environment was rapidly improving with the reintroduction of a corporatist industrial relations system, now known as *social partnership*, which delivered wage restraint and labour quiescence. The numbers of strikes each year had fallen from a high of nearly 200 in 1984 to less than fifty in 1989, where they remained throughout the 1990s (Labour Relations Commission, various years). Trade unions – severely weakened by the 1980s recession, by the anti-union stance of the high-tech TNCs and by the job insecurity of the 1990s – traded wage restraint and flexibility for other benefits to workers, such as tax cuts. But social partnership went beyond its earlier tripartite forms to include farming organisations and a 'social pillar' that represented socially excluded groups from outside the trade unions. The social partners negotiated a series of national agreements whose main aim was to ensure wage restraint and agreement around fiscal restraint.[4]

Social partnership has been credited with enabling the Irish regime to maintain a macro-economic environment that was favourable to growth (IMF 2000). In addition to pay restraint, the state corrected its severe debt problem with an austerity policy during 1987–89 and fiscal restraint thereafter. Cutbacks were enabled by securing agreement through social partnership and the fiscal turnaround was helped by a doubling of EU structural payments to Ireland and favourable foreign exchange movements. The 'favourable macro-economic environment' also included moves toward deregulation and privatisation. Inflation, exchange rates and interest rates were removed from political and industrial relations arenas in the run-up to European economic and monetary union (this also meant that they were no longer instruments of Irish economic policy). All of this created an environment that was even more pro-business than in the 1970s and 1980s. Social consensus was managed in this context by the recent memory of recession and rampant unemployment. It could be expected to continue as long as economic growth created new jobs and inflation remained sufficiently low to keep workers and those on state support satisfied with very modest increases in their incomes.

most attractive aspect of Ireland to the TNCs, however, was its tax Where other European regions taxed corporate profits at rates of 30– cent and more, Ireland had by far the lowest profits taxes for manufacturers and providers of traded services, at 10 per cent. Even this rate was forced on the state by the EU, which considered its earlier dual tax regime – zero rates for (mainly foreign) exporters and higher rates for (mainly indigenous) producers for the local market – to be illegally discriminatory. In response, the Irish state simply introduced an across-the-board 10 per cent tax rate for all manufacturers.[5] If tax holidays were a key attraction to foreign investors in the 1970s, they were even more of an attraction in the 'new economy' of the 1990s, characterised as it was by massive paper profits and a huge increase in profits-per-worker in certain sectors.

In the end, the attractions of southern Ireland, especially the tax regime and pro-business atmosphere, were decisive. It became one of the few locations of agglomerated foreign investments in computers and associated products like software and computer services. In 1990, at a historically high cost to the IDA and the Irish state, Intel chose a location at Leixlip near Dublin as its European site for the production of computer chips. Intel moved into Ireland in two stages – in 1991 and 1995 – investing IR£1 billion in the first stage, of which nearly IR£70 million was paid directly by grants from the Irish government. Moreover, Intel financed its investments through tax loopholes that cost the state an additional IR£140 million by the end of 1996. A similar package was negotiated for Intel's second stage of expansion. The cost per job was huge: in terms of direct grants, more than IR£30,000 compared with an average of IR£12,000 per job in other IDA-sponsored projects during the 1990s (close to the average annual wage of the jobs it attracted). Once tax loopholes are considered, the cost to the state was possibly double the amount of grants.

But the IDA was not just buying Intel. Nearly every major player in the computer industry followed Intel to Ireland. Within a few years, the TNC sector in Ireland included practically every major IT firm: Gateway, Dell, AST, Apple, Hewlett-Packard and Siemens-Nixdorff in PCs; Intel, Fujitsu, Xilinx and Analog Devices in integrated circuits; Seagate and Quantum in disk drives; Microsoft, Lotus and Oracle in software. Moreover, the country became the major centre for telesales and teleservicing for Dell, Gateway, IBM, Digital and many others. Along with these leading firms came hundreds of less well known producers of boards, power supplies, cables, connectors, data storage, printers, networking and everything else that goes into or around computers, as well as services that are connected to or use computers. Southern Ireland's share of foreign investment inflows into the EU tripled between 1991 and 1994. According to the IDA, it attracted 40 per cent of US electronics investments in Europe. A similar but smaller agglomeration of foreign chemical (pharmaceutical) companies also located in Ireland, including Pfizer, whose resounding market success with Viagra (produced

Table 7.1 Fixed industrial investments in southern Ireland by country of ownership (IR£millions at constant 1990 prices), 1983–98

Year	US TNCs	Other TNCs	Irish firms	US share of total	Irish share of total
1983	136.6	114.2	131.8	0.357	0.345
1984	138.7	88.9	112.3	0.408	0.331
1985	117.1	103.2	99.5	0.366	0.311
1986	96.6	117.8	78.7	0.330	0.269
1987	98.3	143.7	93.5	0.293	0.279
1988	84.4	83.8	105.7	0.308	0.386
1989	84.0	54.1	88.3	0.371	0.390
1990	68.4	52.0	90.0	0.325	0.427
1991	109.8	114.6	71.6	0.371	0.242
1992	126.7	81.6	60.5	0.471	0.225
1993	175.5	62.2	49.1	0.612	0.171
1994	137.1	48.3	52.8	0.576	0.222
1995	157.9	44.2	56.7	0.610	0.219
1996	252.8	49.9	97.1	0.632	0.243
1997	259.0	51.6	70.3	0.680	0.185
1998	256.0	71.3	62.2	0.657	0.160

Source: data supplied to author by the Central Statistics Office.

in Cork) helped cause Irish output of organic chemical products to rise by 70 per cent when it was first introduced on the market in the late 1990s. In the first half of 2000, exports of organic chemicals rose by 112 per cent, leading experts to predict Ireland's growth rate for the year could be several percentage points higher than the 10 per cent forecasts of the Irish Central Bank. Again, this surge in exports was dominated by the single product Viagra. An additional surge in computer exports back to the US was dominated by a few new IT multinationals (Keena 2000).

The shift in US investments and their effect on total fixed investment in manufacturing is seen in table 7.1. Fixed investments by US firms fell rapidly during the 1980s, from IR£104 million in 1983 to IR£68 million in 1990. Yet they rose dramatically in the 1990s, by nearly 400 per cent, while investments by other TNCs and Irish firms declined significantly. As a result, the share of US-based firms in total fixed industrial investment rose from just under a third in 1990 to two-thirds in 1997–98. Since indigenous industrial investments were falling in real terms, their share of total industrial investments fell to 16 per cent, less than half their share during the 1980s. The moderate rise of total industrial fixed investments that underlay the coming of the Celtic tiger, therefore, masked two distinct stories, of rising investments by US TNCs and falling investments by indigenous firms and other TNCs.

Economic growth rates

As one would expect, such a high inflow of US-based TNC investments, directed at shifting US products in the 'new' sectors into European markets, had a significant impact on economic growth. After a few years of moderate growth while the new US investments got up and running, the southern Irish economy began to boom in 1994. GDP growth rates rose from 5.8 per cent in 1994, remaining at least as high through the rest of the decade and culminating in the country's first ever rate of more than 10 per cent, in 1997 (table 7.2). GNP growth was slower, mainly because of the large outflow of TNC profits, which are included in GDP but not in GNP.

These rates of growth were so high, at least by EU standards, that a 1994 article in Morgan Stanley's Euroletter asked, only partly tongue in cheek, whether Ireland was now a Celtic tiger, after the high-growth economies of East Asia (Gardiner 1994). This seemed somewhat premature at the time but as Irish growth rates rose further in the later years of the 1990s the name stuck. It came to signify a successful economic model that other peripheral European countries might want to emulate.

The nature of that model – including the relative contributions of foreign and domestic firms, and the importance of different state policies – is still debated (see, for example, O'Hearn 2000; Ó Riain 2000). Yet economic growth was clearly dominated by the effects of TNCs. During 1990–95, southern Irish GDP grew by IR£11,448 million while TNC value-added (profits, taxes and wages) grew by IR£5,098 million. In other words, TNCs were directly responsible for 45 per cent of Irish economic growth during the first half of the 1990s, and were indirectly responsible for an unknown additional amount of growth in sectors like construction and services. Moreover, the impact of TNCs was rising fast. Between 1995

Table 7.2 Southern Irish real economic growth rates in the 1990s (%)

Year	GDP	GNP
1991	1.9	2.3
1992	3.3	2.3
1993	2.7	3.4
1994	5.8	6.3
1995	9.7	8.2
1996	7.7	7.4
1997	10.7	9.3
1998	8.6	7.8
1999	9.8	7.8

Source: national income and expenditure data provided to the author by the Central Statistics Office.

and 1999, GDP grew by IR£27,643 million, while TNC value-added
by about IR£24,000 million (TNC profits alone grew by IR£14,529 m
over the same period). Thus, in the second half of the 1990s, TNCs di
accounted for 85 per cent of economic growth in terms of their value-
added, and their profits alone accounted for 53 per cent of economic
growth! Where TNCs' value-added was equivalent to 14 per cent of GDP
in 1990, it rose above 50 per cent in 1999.

The effect of TNCs on economic growth was led by exports of companies
in three manufacturing sectors dominated by US firms: chemicals, computers
and electrical engineering. These three manufacturing sectors alone accounted
for 40 per cent of Irish economic growth during the 1990s, and this does not
include the IT growth of software-related services and teleservices. They
were the only economic sectors that exceeded the average GDP growth rate
of 6.3 per cent in the 1990s, together growing annually by about 15 per
cent. But their pattern of growth indicates a source of vulnerability of Irish
growth. In each year since 1994, the output of two of these three sectors
grew rapidly (often by 30–50 per cent), while the third was relatively
stagnant. In 1995, for instance, output in computers grew by 49 per cent
and electrical engineering by 33 per cent, but chemicals grew by just 3.8 per
cent. In 1998, output in chemicals and electrical engineering both grew by
29 per cent but computers by only 4 per cent. And in 1999 computers
output grew by 33 per cent and chemicals output by 13 per cent, but output
in electrical engineering actually declined. Even a single product can have a
large effect on economic growth, as was the case in 1997/98 when Pfizer
introduced the drug Viagra on to the world market and 'Irish output' of
organic chemicals products rose by 70 per cent. The 1990s were a period of
historic expansion of US marketing efforts across the Atlantic economy
into Europe and an extended period of US economic growth that surprised
many experts. But a period of bust in the same products and services would
have a severe impact on the southern Irish economy, since its economic
growth record has become so dependent on these few sectors and companies.

One result of foreign domination was that the gap between GDP and
GNP, which opened after 1980, rose even further. Ireland is unique in
Europe to the degree that its gross *domestic* product exceeds its gross
national product because of the profits that are removed by foreign-owned
manufacturers. Unlike GDP, GNP does not include the profits, dividends
and interest that are removed from a country. GNP is a better measure of
the degree to which economic growth benefits a country as a whole because
it measures the resources that remain there as a result of its economic
efforts. GDP measures effort expended in the economic activities of a
country while GNP measures the returns these activities bring to the
country.

After 1980, TNCs were a large enough sector for their behaviour to
strongly affect the Irish economic structure. The amounts of profits received

and subsequently removed by TNCs became larger and larger. The state had also incurred a large foreign debt, the interest on which was also repatriated. In 1983, foreign profit repatriations made up just 3 per cent of GDP. By 1995, they were nearly 19 per cent. In 1999, they had risen to an astounding 40 per cent of GDP (48 per cent if incomes from royalties and licences are included)!

As the net amount of profits leaving Ireland grew, the gap between GDP and GNP widened. In 1980, southern Irish GNP and GDP were practically equal. From that time, however, the two began to diverge substantially as more foreign profits were repatriated so that GDP grew at a more rapid rate than GNP (a much smaller investment income flowed back into Ireland from abroad). In 1990, GDP was 11 per cent higher than GNP. By 1999, GDP exceeded GNP by nearly 18 per cent. In simple language, GDP overstated by nearly a sixth how much material wealth was created for Ireland by the economic activities of its people. Less and less of the fruits of Irish labour remained in the country and more flowed abroad.[6]

The important development is the degree to which a greater proportion of economic growth in the 1990s was made up of foreign profits, which are mainly repatriated. After a period of incubation as TNCs invested during the early 1990s, the proportion of TNC profits in GDP began to rise to an astonishing extent after 1997. In 1998, the growth of foreign profits was equivalent to 80 per cent of economic growth! During the two years 1997–99, the rise of TNC profits was equivalent to two-thirds of economic growth. Although accurate data for wages paid by TNCs are not yet available, the rise in TNCs' value-added in those two years – profits *and* wages – may have actually exceeded the rise in GDP.

Profit shifting

Arguably, Ireland's most important function within the Atlantic 'new economy' of the 1990s was as a site where US companies would shift their products into Europe, while accumulating profits in order to avoid taxation. TNCs regularly distort the internal prices at which their subsidiaries sell materials and components to each other so that they can shift their profits to countries with the lowest taxes (Emmanuel and Mehafdi 1994, pp. 55–88). Subsidiaries in low-tax countries like Ireland import components at artificially cheap prices, assemble them and sell them on at inflated prices, recording artificially high profit rates. Such practices are especially prevalent in sectors where components have no clear 'open-market prices', like electronic components or patented preparations for pharmaceuticals and soft drinks. Since taxing authorities find it difficult to impute a 'fair' or 'arm's length' price for such products, TNCs can sell them among their subsidiaries at vastly distorted prices (Wheeler 1990). Although TNC profit shifting was common knowledge for several decades, it was not until the mid-1990s that mainstream Irish experts became concerned about the practice (Mangan 1994; Murphy 1994).

Of course, TNCs keep their profit-shifting activities secret from tax authorities, so it is difficult to chart this behaviour accurately. But significant transfer pricing is indicated by inexplicably high TNC profit rates, output growth and rises of labour productivity in the sectors most prone to profit shifting. Tax authorities may also uncover uncommonly high numbers of cases of profit shifting among foreign corporations in specific sectors of a given economy.

Stewart (1988) used many of these indicators to establish widespread transfer pricing in Ireland in the 1980s. O'Hearn (1998a) presented data from unpublished surveys to show that in the sectors most prone to transfer pricing (computers, pharmaceuticals and soft drinks), US companies in Ireland regularly maintained profit rates as a percentage of sales of 35–70 per cent. Overall, profit rates of US companies were three times higher than those of other TNCs and up to ten times higher than the average among Irish-owned firms. According to the US Department of Commerce's *Survey of Current Business* (various years), US TNCs maintained profit rates during the 1990s that were five times greater than they were elsewhere in the world (up from two and a half times higher in the 1970s). These uncommonly high TNC profit rates were accompanied by rapid output growth, beyond what would have been expected from their rates of investment. In real terms, TNCs invested in the first half of the 1990s at less than two-thirds the rate they invested in the first half of the 1980s, even though their output was growing at a historic rate.

On the other hand, *even if* recorded Irish economic growth was vastly inflated in the 1990s by the activities of TNCs, it could continue to be rapid as long as foreign activity and related domestic activities continued to expand sufficiently. Early in the new century, foreign activities were still expanding, as the US economy continued to boom. But what of the indigenous economy?

The indigenous economy: following the European path?

The rise of a dynamic indigenous sector, tied directly or indirectly to the explosion of activity by TNCs in the 'new economy', would be the most important indicator that Ireland had reached a switching point in the 1990s. This would mean that dependent development within the Atlantic 'new economy' now enabled the country to piggyback on global expansion to develop a dynamic regional economy, unlike earlier periods when dependent growth combined limited industrial transformation with widespread *de*industrialisation. The transformations of Irish industry from woollen manufactures to provisions, and from cotton to linen, were both sectorally and geographically restricted. As I have shown, the new industries did little to create broadly linked economic activities. Their main effect on the island as a whole, therefore, was deindustrialisation. Apart from indicating a shift in Irish economic change, an integrated regime of foreign and indigenous growth, in the major innovative sectors, would also mean that Ireland had found an alternative to previous growth paths of small European states. If Senghaas (1985) is right, these required the development of an indigenous market, to support the development of an indigenous industry, which eventually began to export. The Irish model was very different, as it was clearly based on TNCs, with the hope that indigenous firms could piggy-back on their expansion.

Although rapid growth had been occurring for only a few years, O'Malley (1998) was already arguing that the 1990s were indeed different from earlier periods because a dynamic indigenous manufacturing sector had grown alongside the transnational sector. Where indigenous manufacturing employment fell by 22.6 per cent during 1980–88, it then rose again by 6.9 per cent during 1988–96. This, he argued, indicated a sort of rebirth of the indigenous economy in southern Ireland. Moreover, growth in exports by indigenous firms since 1988 was higher than the average growth of exports from the EU or OECD countries. And indigenous profit rates rose from 1 per cent of sales during the mid-1980s to 6 per cent in 1995 (although this was only a fraction of TNC profit rates and, as we shall see, they fell dramatically in 1998 and 1999). Other experts contended that the new expansion of TNCs in Ireland in the 1990s had a different effect on indigenous industry than had previous expansions. Not only were the new projects much bigger in terms of output and employment, but they were supposedly more 'rooted' in the Irish economy and were heavily linked to Irish suppliers. Barry *et al.* (1999), for example, estimate that Irish economy expenditures *per employee* by TNCs increased by more than 50 per cent between 1983 and 1995. This rise was particularly rapid in marketable services. Barry (1999) and Barry *et al.* (1999) also argue that the shakeout of indigenous industry in the 1970s and 1980s left a core of firms that were more dynamic and able to take advantage of these new opportunities and, sometimes, to grow into exporters in their own right.

Ó Riain (1999) gives a different account of indigenous growth. He claims that there were 'two globalisations' in Ireland in the 1990s. One was the outward movement of US capital through Ireland and into Europe. The 'second globalisation' was the development of an Irish indigenous sector that was dynamic and globally oriented. Its major actors were Irish entre-preneurs who were 'globalised' by their connections with IT TNCs, often in places like Silicon Valley. But they were also globalised in the sense that they were not just dependent sub-suppliers of TNC subsidiaries in Ireland, but were more often world-class exporters.

Ó Riain credits this Irish success to the *flexible* developmental policies of the Irish state. Unlike *bureaucratic developmental states* such as South Korea since the 1970s, the Irish state did not control corporate decisions either by direct political pressure or by manipulating market instruments like interest rates, exchange rates or prices. This kind of interventionist control of the developmental process, he argues, became outdated in the context of the flexible globalisation of the 1990s. Instead, Ó Riain suggests, southern Ireland's flexible developmental state intervened in more localised ways. It combined a neoliberal macro-economic environment, which attracted capital investments, with trilateral social partnership agreements, which enhanced flexibility. Fiscal restraint, low taxes and low wages were combined with targeted state programmes to foster key skills and provide infrastructure.

At the enterprise level, the Irish state performed everyday micro-intervention in the economy. State agencies used their good relations with foreign investors to identify opportunities for local entrepreneurs. As mentioned in chapter 6, in response to criticisms about the lack of linkages between the foreign and indigenous sectors, the Irish state set up a national linkages programme in 1985 to identify and encourage backward linkages from TNCs into the local economy. The programme was run by a separate agency called *Forbairt* (later 'Enterprise Ireland'), which was dedicated solely to local firms, on the understanding that they had different needs and interests than did the foreign clients of the IDA. In the early to mid-1990s, Forbairt attempted to create linkages between foreign and local companies by identifying opportunities and local entrepreneurs who were willing to exploit them. The state took the same approach to giving help and advice to individual companies or small groups of companies about exporting their products. Thus, the Irish state identified opportunities across a range of small local firms rather than prodding large business groups into new markets.

In reality, the glowing accounts of an indigenous revival in the 1990s are distinctly overblown. Enterprise Ireland had only limited success in its linkage programme, principally because putting real pressure on TNCs to link locally would have undermined the basic attractiveness of Ireland as a deregulated, hands-off state. In 1996, out of 2,667 indigenous firms that employed ten or more people, only 174 were sub-suppliers to TNCs. The sectoral distribution of these firms was hardly high tech. Most provided routine supplies like packaging and printed materials: 114 were in plastics, fabricated metals or paper/printed products. Just thirty-three were in electrical engineering or computers and only three were in the chemicals sector (Breathnach and Kelly 1999).

Although official reports and some economists make a great deal of substantial rising linkages between foreign and local firms, it is by no means clear that this occurred after 1990. Ruane (1999) cites data that show backward linkages of foreign firms rising from IR£627 million in 1990 to IR£1,490 million in 1996. On the other hand, the proportion of raw materials that were purchased locally by TNCs hardly rose at all, from 18.8 per cent in 1990 to 19.1 per cent in 1996. The absolute rise in local purchases was purely an effect of rising TNC output in Ireland – they were not buying local inputs in greater proportions. Even so, an absolute rise in backward linkages would have provided substantial business opportunities for local firms.

In reality, however, TNC purchasing patterns were shifting radically. They were buying more of their inputs from *other TNC subsidiaries* in Ireland. To use one of the examples I have already introduced, Dell was buying Intel computer processors in a big way. Official figures called these 'local purchases', although both were giant global companies rather than Irish sub-suppliers. The same was true of a whole raft of TNCs that began to buy from each other after they located in the Dublin-area computer agglomeration after 1992. Forfás (1997) estimated that two-thirds of 'local purchases' in the electronics sector actually consisted of one TNC subsidiary buying from another. Moreover, Enterprise Ireland found that, in the 1990s, TNCs were insisting on globally integrated component supply, which was beyond the capacity of most Irish producers and essentially cut them out of the market for supplying TNCs (Breathnach and Kelly 1999). The net result was that TNCs were buying a substantially *smaller* share of their material supplies from Irish firms in the year 2000 than they had in 1990.

But there was another side to the story of indigenous Irish industry. This was Ó Riain's *second globalisation*, which was concentrated in the software sector. Software was already a significant and growing sector by 1994. By 1996 many experts considered it to be a real Irish success story, the place where 'the new breed of entrepreneur – the Celtic Tiger' was best represented (Lucey 1996). During 1993–95, software exports from the south of Ireland rose by nearly 60 per cent, from IR£1.8 billion to IR£2.8 billion. Total output grew by 50 per cent, to IR£3 billion. The country was one of the top five software producers in the world. By the year 2000, it was the second largest exporter of software behind the US, having surpassed Israel and India. Nor were the 400 indigenous software firms just local subcontractors to the big TNCs. According to Ó Riain (1999), the rise of indigenous software in the 1990s had only indirect ties to the influx of foreign computer firms at the same time: 82 per cent of Irish software companies had no alliances of any kind with TNCs (the other 18 per cent that did were concentrated in low-end activities like localisation, translation and assembly). Nearly 80 per cent of Irish software companies exported some of their product and nearly half exported most of their product (Forbairt 1996).

Whereas TNCs had maintained a 90 per cent share of the Irish electronics sector since its emergence in the 1980s (and more than a 95 per cent share of output), *half* of software employment in Ireland was in domestic

firms. In 1997, 108 foreign-owned software firms emplo
while 571 indigenous software firms employed 9,200 pe
employment, the two sectors tracked each other closely;
software employment had doubled from 4,448 and ind
ment had doubled from 4,495. The rise of employment i
companies is obviously connected to the massive inflow of
the reasons behind indigenous expansion are less obvious; the expansion of
indigenous software production has not been replicated in other high-tech
industrial sectors where TNCs dominate, like computer hardware and
pharmaceuticals.

The success in software was partly due to very special, even accidental
conditions that relate back to Irish educational policies. Although the Irish
state was primarily neoliberal in its approach to encouraging entrepreneurship, it actively intervened in two markets after the latest period of dependent
development began in the 1960s: incentives to foreign capital (as I have
already discussed) and the labour market. Irish education policy was defined
primarily by the perceived needs of export-oriented industry. A watershed
OECD-funded report of 1966 explicitly recommended that 'the educational
system would henceforth be assessed by its capacity to facilitate the achievement of these new economic objectives' (quoted in Clancy 1986, p. 125).
The report called for remedial action to avoid a shortage of technically
qualified personnel for exporting firms and from that time the main objective of Irish educational policy was to get more post-primary students to
take science and technical subjects. This attitude intensified during the
1980s and 1990s. A 1980 white paper contained only one criterion by
which to evaluate public education policy: 'higher education provision
must match labour market needs' (Clancy 1986, p. 126). The state doggedly
pursued this policy through the 1980s, despite the fact that most newly
qualified engineers and technicians immediately emigrated to find work. In
the 1990s, perhaps more by accident than design, Ireland found itself with
a huge surplus of low-waged English-speaking technicians and engineers
just as US computer firms began to seek locations from which to launch an
export assault on the European 'big market'. The state strengthened its
advantages by managing its social partnership agreements to maintain
wage restraint and relative labour peace.

The thousands of engineers and technicians who had qualified in Ireland
but emigrated, and others who stayed in Ireland but became dissatisfied
with their TNC employers, made up a pool of potential entrepreneurs, with
particular knowledge of the software industry and eager to set up as small
employers. Ó Riain (1999) calls these people *globalised Irish*, with the
skills, knowledge and experience required to compete globally. In the
rapidly growing IT sector of the 1990s, dominated by US capital, which
concentrated many of its European operations in Ireland, these prospective
Irish capitalists benefited from the insider knowledge that the IDA could

provide after years of associating with US TNCs. The result was rapid growth.

Despite the apparent success of the indigenous software sector, there are also weaknesses that raise questions about the sector's long-term sustainability. The industry is dominated by TNCs in every respect except employment. With half of software employees in 1995, TNCs accounted for 87 per cent of Irish software sales and 92 per cent of software exports from Ireland. Microsoft alone accounted for at least 40 per cent of exports (Forbairt 1996). The Irish side of the industry, on the other hand, consisted mostly of very small firms. In 1995, more than 250 of Ireland's 390 indigenous software companies employed fewer than ten people (the average indigenous firm employed fewer than fifteen). Of course, smallness in itself is not necessarily a bad thing, either economically or in terms of the conditions faced by workers in small firms as opposed to big ones. But it indicates that the software sector in Ireland, like the rest of the economy, is essentially dualistic – highly developed transnational giants alongside a scattering of very small domestic firms.

Yet there is a twist in the tail of software dualism, which has been one basis of local optimism. Unlike other sectors in which indigenous firms have a presence, Irish software firms appear to do things that are more technically sophisticated, if not more profitable, than their TNC counterparts. Software TNCs in Ireland primarily perform localisation activities: the adaptation of software that was already developed in the US to local languages and cultural and technical formats, so that they can be sold in other markets. TNC parent corporations keep practically all of their product development in the US: 'like the crown jewels … they won't let them go' (Ó Riain 1997, p. 16). In this respect Ireland's situation is similar to India's, where US TNCs 'generat[e] "software exports" by directing their local software engineers to routine tasks that US software people would like to avoid, like debugging existing software, extending the life of old operating systems, or porting existing applications to different platforms' (Evans 1995, p. 195). While such activities require substantial training, the actual work involved is more in the nature of repetitive assembly-line work. Both Lotus and Microsoft were attracted to Ireland because they required a European hub for localisation and distribution as the 1993 single market approached. Ireland provided among the lowest costs in the EU with a friendly political environment and, most importantly, low taxes (Ó Riain 1997, p. 10).

The indigenous software industry is different. While some domestic 'software' companies supply routine services for TNCs – providing instructions, providing translations, subcontracting routine programming – a fairly distinct and apparently growing local sector does small-scale software development, independently of the major TNCs. Many of these firms began by developing software services for firms in Ireland that were adopting computer systems, but they gradually developed their software applications into products they could sell in international niche markets. These companies, like small software companies elsewhere, survive by providing products whose turnover is too small to attract the major companies. Many began by supplying customised services to businesses and then developing them into products. Yet these activities are generally less productive or profitable even than routine TNC localisation activities. While indigenous software companies employed as many people as software TNCs in 1997, TNC revenues were *eight times* higher. Some Irish companies developed new software technologies but the most successful of them tended to be bought out by US firms, which removed their technologies to the US. The withdrawal of development functions to the US reinforces an existing tendency for low rates of research and development (R&D) in the indigenous software sector. Survey research shows that expenditures on R&D make up about 12.7 per cent of output, a level which one expert calls 'worrying' for companies in such a high-tech sector (Lucey 1996). Moreover, expenditure on training fell after 1993 from 3.1 to 2.4 per cent of revenues. Finally, in terms of size, indigenous software firms still account for less than 3 per cent of industrial employment in the south of Ireland. The Irish software sector, as Ó Riain puts it, 'cannot bear the burden of the huge expectations which have been placed on [it]' (1997, p. 24). The positive example of domestic Irish software, so far, is still too limited to counterbalance Ireland's rapidly increased dependence on a small concentration of foreign investors in electronics and pharmaceuticals.

Aside from a part of the indigenous software sector, then, indigenous expansion still often depends on the ability of companies to establish supply relationships with TNCs. These associations are not generally very positive. Jacobson (1999) found that giant software TNCs not only insisted on monopsonistic relationships with their local Irish suppliers of software manuals, but they also encouraged them to invest in specialised printing machinery even though they knew that they would soon replace them with non-Irish suppliers of CD-ROMs. As a result, local suppliers went through a quick life cycle of start-up, expansion and decline over less than a decade. Moreover, as the technologies of supply became more advanced, TNCs moved from local suppliers to other TNCs. Microsoft, for instance, replaced local manual suppliers with TNC CD-ROM pressers as it developed its network of sub-suppliers. By 1998, all of Microsoft's suppliers were other TNCs located in Ireland.

Although the relationships between TNCs and local suppliers may be short-lived and, in some cases, parasitical, it could still be the case that sub-suppliers of TNCs gain enough knowledge or other resources through the association for them to be in a better market position when the sub-supply relationship breaks down. Supplier firms might gain access to otherwise confidential or expensive technologies, sources of raw materials or market intelligence from their TNC client. Or they could be cajoled and helped by the TNC to manufacture sub-supplies to a higher specification than they might have for other clients. This was not the case, however, in 1990s Ireland. A study by Breathnach and Kelly (1999) of all indigenous establishments with ten or more employees asked whether local companies that act as subcontractors to TNCs are more likely to innovate in their products or production processes than companies who do not act as suppliers. The study found no statistical differences in the likelihood of innovation between the 174 companies with sub-supply relationships to TNCs and the 1,225 companies that did not supply TNCs. In fact, there was a weak indication that suppliers of TNCs were actually *less* likely to innovate.

According to the study, the main reason why contact with TNCs did not promote innovation was that TNC subsidiaries perform very little R&D in Ireland, so they do not have much to offer a sub-supplier by way of technology and knowledge transfer. This finding conflicts with the popular perception of the 'new TNCs' of the 1990s, which, according to Barry *et al.* (1999, p. 54), 'dramatically' increased their rates of R&D spending in Ireland. Renowned international economists like Jeffrey Sachs (1997) and Paul Krugman (1997), who also assert that the influx of high-tech foreign investments into Ireland in the 1990s brought a corresponding technology transfer, share this perception. But data collected by the state body Forfas show that R&D expenditures made up only 1.2 per cent of total TNC expenditures in Ireland, and 1.1 per cent of indigenous firms' expenditures, compared with an OECD average of 2.4 per cent. In electrical and electronic equipment (the sector including computers), the OECD average was 5.6 per cent, but computer firms in Ireland spent just 1.9 per cent of expenditures on R&D (Breathnach and Kelly 1999, table 11). Breathnach and Kelly conclude that TNCs 'may not be the storehouses of knowledge and expertise that they are often assumed to be' and that, 'as is the case in almost all aspects of Irish industrial policy, the headline statistics on innovation disguise considerable heterogeneity within the data' (p. 24). In his study of technical workers in TNC subsidiaries in Ireland, McGovern goes even further. He quotes a TNC manager who insisted that 'there is no genuine R&D in Ireland', and he concludes that this situation will remain 'so long as the best engineers, chemists and technicians are employed by the branch plants of multinational corporations' (1998, p. 162). This would not be such a surprise for critical development theorists with knowledge of the concept and structure of commodity chains in global production complexes. From that perspective, one would expect the more innovative links of commodity chains, like product design and R&D, to remain in the parent country or other core countries, while more routine operations are placed in regions like Ireland.

The power of the Irish state seems inadequate in the face of such TNC power, with the ability to manipulate suppliers, force them into monopsonistic

Table 7.3 Corporate profits received in southern Ireland by country of ownership, 1990–99 (IR£millions, current prices)[a]

Year	TNC profits	Irish corporate profits	Total corporate profits	TNC share of total corporate profits
1990	2,608	2,764	5,372	0.485
1991	2,538	3,053	5,591	0.454
1992	3,042	3,014	6,056	0.502
1993	3,355	3,793	7,148	0.469
1994	3,787	3,715	7,502	0.505
1995	4,193	5,524	9,717	0.432
1996	5,826	4,408	10,234	0.569
1997	7,382	5,458	12,840	0.575
1998	12,078	3,332	15,410	0.784
1999	16,249	1,794	18,043	0.901

[a]Profits do not include royalties and licence fees.
Source: national income and expenditure and balance of international payments data provided to author by the Central Statistics Office.

relationships and then cut them off as technologies change. While the state helped local entrepreneurs enter IT, and many of them became very rich, it could do little to keep them in business or expand over the long term. This is quite different from East Asia, where subcontracting networks are more stable and dynamic. Irish subcontracting is 'flexible' but, for this very reason, it is insecure and its long-term sustainability is questionable.

The sustainability of Irish indigenous industry became more questionable at the end of the 1990s. Table 7.3 shows the shares of corporate profits that went to TNCs and Irish companies between 1990 and 1999. As I have already shown, the rise of TNC profits was spectacular, with more than seven times more profits received in 1999 than in 1990. The indigenous share of profits fell from 51.5 per cent in 1990 to less than 10 per cent in 1999. More important, however, is the absolute profit-making performance of indigenous companies. While indigenous profits doubled in the first half of the 1990s, keeping pace with TNC profits, they began to fall thereafter. In 1999, indigenous companies received only two-thirds of the profits they received in 1990, and the fall was much greater in real terms. This falling rate of profit was reflected in a sharp rise in the numbers of company failures during 1999–2000 (Canniffe 2000).

This duality between a rapidly growing foreign sector and a stagnant indigenous one is shown most clearly in productivity figures for the 1990s. Output in the three US-dominated sectors of computers, electrical engineering and chemicals grew by 375 per cent during 1990–99 while employment grew by only 73 per cent. This means that output per employee grew by some 215 per cent or nearly 9 per cent annually, which is rapid by any standard. Yet in the rest of the economy – mainly Irish owned and dominated by services, construction and basic manufactures – output rose by just 55 per cent while employment grew by 40 per cent. Output per employee grew by less than 10 per cent over the decade, or by about 1 per cent annually, which is stagnation by any standard. By 1999, the average worker in the foreign sector produced nearly eight times more output by value than did the average worker in the rest of the economy. The foreign sector was growing in an intensive way, by producing much more output without much additional labour. This is a feature of innovative economies, although the real dynamism of this sector is questionable since much of its value-added was a result of profit shifting rather than real increases of productivity. On the other hand, the indigenous sector grew extensively, by adding on more labour at the existing level of productivity, which clearly indicates the absence of innovation.

The TNC profits explosion and inequality

Although there were success stories in indigenous Irish industry during the 1990s for those firms that 'hooked on' to the forces of globalisation, foreign economic activities – investments, exports, profits – were the main story of southern Ireland's rapid growth. Dwindling profits in Irish companies cast doubts on the sustainability of indigenous industry. This was an increasing characteristic of the southern Irish economy in the late 1990s, as foreign profit levels exploded to unprecedented levels. I have shown the uniquely dominant effect played in southern Irish economic dynamics by the production and trade flows that are central to the latest phase of accumulation in the Atlantic economy. US capital, seeking access to the European 'big market', found it most advantageous and profitable to use the open door that was provided by the Irish regime. Of course, GDP is a combination of flows, some inward and some outward. While the activities of TNCs and, particularly their profits, made up an increasing proportion of GDP, the difference between GDP and GNP was not as large as the amount of profits and debt interest that was repatriated. There were countervailing flows back into the Irish economy. Most importantly, several years of Celtic tiger growth encouraged a large rise in unearned incomes and professional fees, much of which was invested abroad by the richest segments of society. And a few Irish TNCs also invested abroad. In time, these began to make returns that were repatriated *into* Ireland. Although the inflows were never very great compared with the outflows, they made the economy in terms of GNP appear to be doing better than it actually was.

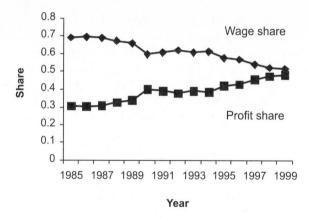

Figure 7.1 Changing factor shares of Irish income, 1985–99. Source of data: *National Income Accounts* (Central Statistics Office, various years).

Rapidly rising outflows of TNC profits combined with inflows of profits to the upper strata of the Irish population created a dynamic of class inequality that was unknown in southern Ireland before the 1990s. Before 1987, factor shares of non-agricultural income were relatively stable, with wages accounting for 70 per cent and profits for 30 per cent. Thereafter, factor incomes began to shift rapidly in favour of profits. As figure 7.1 shows, by 1999 for the first time in the history of the independent Irish state, the profits share from non-agricultural activities was virtually equal to the wage share.

The rapid changes in favour of capital in the class distribution of incomes meant that income growth was concentrated in profits and exports rather than in consumption, whether private or public. While national income grew annually in real terms by 6.4 per cent in the 1990s, private consumption grew by 4.9 per cent and public consumption by just 3.4 per cent. The share of personal consumption in GDP fell from about 60 per cent in 1990 to 52 per cent in 1999. Taking personal and public consumption together, the overall consumption share fell during that period, from 76 per cent to less than 65 per cent.

The overwhelming proportion of economic growth in the south of Ireland was from the production of exports, and this was dominated by computers and pharmaceuticals, which were in turn dominated by TNCs like Intel. Until they shot upward in 1998, foreign profits were practically equivalent to the export surplus, which drove economic growth. The predominant share of those profits was taken out of Ireland rather than being reinvested. Thus, the main recipients of the fruits of economic growth in Ireland were a *foreign* capitalist class rather than a domestic one. Therefore, Ireland in the 1990s was essentially in the same structural position as n the 1970s. It was dependent almost entirely on new incoming ctivities for its economic growth. It lacked the kinds of self-sustaining ships between investment, growth and a growing indigenous market that were so remarkable in other small European countries at the end of the nineteenth century, or in East Asia at the end of the twentieth. It sustained a high growth rate because foreign activities expanded so rapidly.

This form of dependent development contributed to class (factor income) inequality and also to international inequality, because it produced high returns primarily for a foreign class. Yet the removal of large profit incomes by US TNCs did not impoverish Ireland relative to richer regions. Ireland converged significantly with the wealthier European countries during the 1990s in terms of per capita output and incomes. This convergence was drastically overstated in official statistics by profit shifting, which artificially inflated GDP growth. It was also distorted because burgeoning computer exports, which were rapidly falling in price, inflated the calculations of *purchasing power parities*, by which national incomes are usually compared (O'Hearn 1998a). Still, Ireland's national income undoubtedly converged on the European average during the 1990s, so one could hardly argue that it had been impoverished by dependency as it had been in the 1980s. Rather, the agglomeration of global investments in Ireland created a form of dependent economic growth that raised average incomes *as long as TNC production continued to expand at a rapid rate.*

If a rapid inflow of foreign projects created a form of economic growth that raised Irish as well as foreign incomes, how did this form of dependent growth affect inequality *within* Ireland? Before the 1990s the removal of vast amounts of wealth ironically tended to dampen social inequality in Ireland because the class that received most incomes from economic growth was *foreign* capital, whose incomes did not show up in the Irish income distribution. Within Ireland, the main class benefactors from dependent growth in the 1970s and 1980s were the professional classes and some indigenous capitalists in finance and construction who serviced the foreign sector. Thus, during the 1970s and early 1980s individual incomes became slightly less unequal. During that time, income equalisation was also helped by the decimation of the protected Irish capitalist class, which reduced unearned incomes at the top end of the scale, and by the secular movement of farmers and agricultural workers into higher-paying industrial or service jobs (O'Hearn 1989). In the 1990s, however, these trends weakened since there were fewer indigenous capitalists left to go out of business and because most of the transfer of labour from farming to waged employment had already taken place.

New trends of the late 1980s and 1990s increased income inequality. The Irish labour market became more segmented during the growth phase of the 1990s, with a clear distinction between core and peripheral jobs. Peripheral jobs, typically in services and often filled by women working part time or on a fixed contract, were relatively low paying. Core jobs and especially professional positions, often filled by highly educated men, were higher paying. Economic growth created few new jobs before 1994, but thereafter employment grew rapidly. The numbers at work grew by a third between 1994 and 1999. But the vast majority of the 400,000 net new jobs were in services or construction. Manufacturing, the centre of TNC-led economic growth, created just 39,000 new jobs while mostly low-paid service employment grew by 293,000. Even within industry, there was a clear distinction between core and peripheral workers. Between a third and a half of new TNC workers were part-time or temporary contract workers, and most new employees were still routine production-line workers rather than the high-tech engineers who were promoted by the IDA and the Irish government as the public image of the Celtic tiger.

As this labour market segmentation became more pronounced, individual income distributions became more unequal. The available data show that both wages and personal incomes became more unequal after 1987. Between 1987 and 1995, direct incomes of the lowest decile actually fell in real terms. This was partly compensated by state transfers, so that their real disposable incomes grew annually by 1.33 per cent. Meanwhile, the incomes of the second, third and fourth poorest deciles of the population grew at less than 1 per cent annually. The disposable incomes of the richest four deciles of households, on the other hand, grew *twice as quickly* as those of the poorest four deciles.

One reason for increasing inequality was rising wage inequality. Nolan and Hughes (1997, p. 4) found that 'from 1987 to 1994 there was a consistent widening in dispersion for both weekly and hourly earnings, particularly at the top of the distribution'. In terms of hourly earnings, the average wages of the bottom quarter fell from 73 per cent of the median income in 1987 to 67 per cent in 1994. Average earnings for the top decile, on the other hand, rose from 196 per cent of the median income in 1987 to 226 per cent in 1994, a rather astounding increase in a period of just seven years. In terms of weekly earnings, the bottom quartile fell from 72 per cent to 68 per cent of the median income, while the top 10 per cent rose from 184 to 198 per cent (Nolan and Hughes 1997, p. 5). Earnings became more unequal for both men and women, and for both younger and older employees. In fact, the fall in hourly wages was especially large for the bottom 10 per cent of male workers, whose average wage fell from 53 per cent to 45 per cent of the median (Nolan and Hughes 1997, p. 6).

Rising inequality was directly connected to the nature of economic growth in the 1990s. Growth created some jobs for skilled and semi-skilled operatives in manufacturing, but many more for service and commerce workers with low pay. Three-quarters of low pay was accounted for by skilled and semi-skilled workers in manufacturing, clerical workers, service workers and employees in commerce, insurance and finance (Nolan and

Hughes 1997, p. 10). The proportion of southern Irish employees on low pay rose from 20 per cent to 24 per cent between 1987 and 1994 (Nolan and Hughes 1997, p. 7), compared with 12–13 per cent in the rest of the EU except Scandinavia, where 5–6 per cent of workers were on low pay.[7] Thus, Irish workers experience about twice as much low pay as the rest of the EU and more than four times as much as Scandinavia. There was also a rise in the incidence of relative poverty in the 1990s, with the proportion of families receiving less than 60 per cent of the average income rising from 28 per cent to 35 per cent during 1987–94 (Callan *et al.* 1996). Relative poverty appeared to increase further after 1994, with the proportion of the population receiving less than 40 per cent of average income rising from 7 per cent in 1994 to 10 per cent in 1997 (Wren 2000).

    This rising level of inequality and relative poverty during a period of rapid growth was not effectively countered by state policies. Indeed, the overriding ideological position of the 1990s in Ireland was that growth was the product of liberal policies, including privatisation and 'responsible' fiscal policies. Thus, state revenues rose annually by 9 per cent after 1990 but state spending rose by a mere 3.4 per cent per year. Many social services were run down. Most notably, a populist social housing regime that provided affordable and reasonable housing to successive generations of low-income households became the victim of privatisation and fiscal restraint (Fahey 1999). Moreover, since taxes were progressively reduced on capital, the burden of taxation fell heavier on workers and the poor. Nearly three-quarters (72 per cent) of the increased revenues of the 1990s came from taxes on incomes and expenditure while less than a fifth (18 per cent) came from corporate profits taxes, despite the fact that corporate profits made up such a large proportion of economic growth. Capital gains and wealth taxes each accounted for about 1 per cent of increased revenues. Thus, the Irish state got considerably richer during the 1990s, but it was largely at the expense of the Irish working (and consuming) public. To do otherwise, by taxing profits, would have been seen by Irish policy makers as 'killing the goose that laid the golden egg'.

Conclusions: evaluating the Celtic tiger

For the world economy and, within it, the Atlantic economy, the 1980s were a period of restructuring that enabled the long US-led expansion in the 1990s. From the previous Japanese expansion, US firms borrowed new patterns of production and foreign investment, chiefly the elements of flexible production that allowed them to produce smaller runs of products that were not only customised to the consumer but which could also change as the market changed. The most successful firms were more responsive to changing market demands and they were also able to push off onto their smaller suppliers many of the costs and risks that were involved in flexible production. Part of the new strategy was often to move the final production process close to the final market. This impelled numerous US firms to move production facilities into Europe in the early 1990s, in time for the opening up of the single market in 1993. The pattern of this move, however, was different from previous waves of investment. Rather than firms searching around on their own for the best deal – whether in terms of grants packages, taxes or government support – they moved together in *agglomerations*. A few sites, most notably Britain and the south of Ireland, became host to large proportions of the incoming firms from the US and Japan.

As a result, the 1990s were to the 1980s as day is to night for southern Ireland. The 1980s appeared to confirm the predictions of critical development theories: that peripheral areas are most unlikely to develop industrially while still dependent on TNCs. The 1990s appeared to show the opposite: that a region could develop industrially and attain upward mobility into the ranks of the wealthy countries if it could attract enough TNCs from key innovative sectors. This had been a feature of articles about the East Asian 'tigers' of the 1970s and 1980s, although they participated to a much higher degree than the Irish did in the leading sectors of Pacific economic expansion. Indigenous South Korean firms produced computer chips, cars, computers and an array of high-tech consumer durables. Indigenous Taiwanese firms, too, produced computers and sophisticated electronic machinery.

Ireland in the 1990s was different. Foreign companies that produced computers, computer parts and pharmaceuticals in Ireland dominated its overall economic growth. Indigenous Irish growth was practically limited to services, or at best to the software sector. The degree of linkages between foreign and indigenous firms decreased rather than increased. Most importantly, Irish companies were not 'breaking through' into innovative export activities, nor were TNCs locating their more innovative activities in Ireland. The Celtic tiger, despite its increasing concentration in high-tech IT sectors, was concentrating in the most routine segments of those sectors, whether assembly of components, localisation of software or call-centre servicing.

Yet southern Irish growth was high and consistent. Even into the opening years of the twenty-first century experts were predicting that it could continue for another decade (O'Leary 2000). If so, Irish per capita output would not only match the EU average, it could even reach the very top of the EU (at least in terms of purchasing power parities).

These things happened without any essential change in industrial strategy by the Irish state. As in the 1970s and 1980s, it targeted the leading sectors of global production – most importantly computers, pharmaceuticals and internationally traded services – and the economy rode on that growth. But there were important policy changes that had social side-effects, particularly by increasing inequality. A 'social partnership' kept a lid on wage increases so that a few people gained most from the effects of growth. The wealthy and some professionals became substantially wealthier from privatisation, tax cuts on profits and wealth, and by activities such as construction and speculating in housing (the prices of which skyrocketed). And the state refused or was unable to counteract inequality because its economic 'success' was directly associated with fiscal restraint.

As the years of high growth mounted, this association became stronger in the official 'expert' mind. The IMF's consultation report for 2000, for example, cited Ireland as a 'spectacular' example of the positive results that come from 'sound and consistent macroeconomic policies, a generally flexible labor market, a favorable tax regime, and the long-standing outward orientation of Ireland's trade and industrial policies' (IMF 2000, p. 2). It called on Ireland to tighten its fiscal policy further, to keep holding the line on wages and to increase its programme of deregulation and privatisation. This was widely reported by the press as 'vindication' of the Irish finance minister's strict neoliberal policies of wage and fiscal restraint (Suiter 2000). It was practically a universal conclusion among conventional economists and officials that wages and spending must be constrained for fear of 'overheating' the economy and making it 'uncompetitive'. This was despite the fact that wages made up a minuscule proportion of the costs of the TNCs that drove Irish economic growth and despite the fact that Ireland's was easily the lowest ratio of public spending to GDP in the EU. Thus, inequality was not just a side-effect of the rapid growth in Ireland during the 1990s: it was a direct consequence of the neoliberal economic model that was seen to be responsible for growth.

A more positive result of growth was the near elimination of southern Ireland's historically high unemployment rates, the one issue that plagued Irish society in the 1980s and into the first half of the 1990s. The incidence of relative poverty rose in the 1990s, as a greater proportion of the population failed to participate in the rapid rise of wealth and economic growth. But the intensity of poverty did not increase because so many poor families now had at least one and sometimes two or more jobs. Their individual earnings were low, but they exceeded the threshold for receipt of social welfare payments and several wages together made up family incomes that helped households avoid the worst levels of absolute poverty that had appeared in the 1980s. A relatively small number of jobs were created in the high-tech sectors that led the Irish surge of growth, and only some of them were relatively well paid. The vast majority of new jobs were in services, predominantly low paid and insecure.

Thus, Irish growth in the 1990s and after was *disarticulated*. It was not based, like that in small European economies which earlier developed to core status, on the development of a local market for products that could be the centre of innovation and expansion. It was driven by the rapid external growth of the 1990s, by the new investment patterns that were associated with it and by the European policies that increased its attractiveness as a market for US goods. To the extent that there was an indigenous turnaround from the 1980s, it appears to have been more parallel to the explosion of TNC activity in Ireland, a *second globalisation* with its own dynamic. But even this source of growth has been seriously overestimated by social scientists and business analysts who have studied or commented on Ireland. Although the mainstream economic experts refused to contemplate it, questions still remained as to whether this form of economic growth was sustainable or even socially desirable.

Ironically, from the standpoint of a well known 'dependency debate' of the 1990s, the recent Irish experience is not so surprising. O'Hearn (1990) distinguished between *flows* and *stocks* of TNC penetration, and found that investment flows had a net positive effect on economic growth while the stock of TNC investments was negatively associated with growth. In times of rapid inward investments, the flow effects outweighed the stock effects, and economic growth was likely to be high. Once investment flows slowed down, however, the *negative externalities* of a high presence of TNCs began to dominate and economic growth was stagnant. This was the basis of Dixon and Boswell's (1996) analysis of *negative externalities* from foreign capital penetration, which was part of a key debate in the sociological literature about the differential effects of foreign and domestic investments (see also Firebaugh 1992). If there is such a differential effect, and its nature is still hotly debated, then the rapid growth rates in 1990s Ireland should hardly be surprising. US companies located in the south of Ireland in unprecedented numbers, exporting output and aggregating profits there, and this led to a situation where the positive *flow effects* continued to swamp any negative *stock effects* throughout the 1990s and into the twenty-first century. The impact of the positive flow effect on economic growth was a result of the huge numbers of new US projects compared with the relatively small size of the country. The duration of the Irish expansion was a result of the surprisingly long duration of US expansion in the Atlantic and world economies beginning in the early 1990s.

Key questions as Ireland and the US entered the twenty-first century were how long the US-led 'new economy' would continue to expand and, once it slowed, whether new 'stock effects' (negative externalities) would again dominate the Irish political economy as they had in the 1980s. A repeat of US disinvestments in the new century could create another, possibly deeper, period of recession and decline. Irish economic experts and politicians did not take seriously the unique instabilities inherent in an economy where, in 1998 and 1999, TNC value-added was the overwhelming source of economic growth (as much as 85 per cent) and TNC profits alone accounted for half of economic growth. To the contrary, Barry and Bradley (1997) and Krugman (1997) argued hopefully that the south of Ireland had attracted a 'critical mass' of foreign firms that would now be self-sustaining as more and more TNCs located where their predecessors had already found conditions to be favourable.

Finally, even if Irish growth proved to be sustainable, it is highly questionable whether the model could be generalised. Countries on the EU periphery (Portugal, Spain, Greece), the eastern European periphery and much further afield looked to Ireland as a model of successful development. Yet southern Ireland 'succeeded' because it attracted up to a fifth of US manufacturing investments into the EU with just 1 per cent of the EU population. Next door, Britain attracted *two-fifths* of total foreign investments into the EU with nearly twenty times as many people. It hardly became a 'tiger' for doing it. The same limitations of the TNC-led model hold for Spain, with ten times more people than Ireland, or even Portugal, with triple the population. Moreover, other countries will find it hard if not impossible to follow the Irish path simply because there is not enough foreign investment available to sustain growth in more than one or two peripheral European zones. As the limitations of Irish-style neoliberal development become clearer, semi-peripheral countries may return to models based on more interventionist and regulatory forms of developmental state.

Notes

1   Speech to the Center for National Policy, reprinted at http://www2.whitehouse. gov/WH/EOP/OVP/speeches/cnp.html
2   For an analysis of how US producers regained market leadership in semi-conductors, see Macher *et al.* (1998).
3   Some of the more critical views of the US-led boom were collected on the website www:\itulip.com\, which compared the boom of the 1990s to the disastrously illusive Dutch tulip boom of the seventeenth century.
4   On social partnership, see Sabel (1996) and O'Donnell and Thomas (1998).
5   In the 1990s the EU decided that even this special tax rate for manufacturers was discriminatory, so the Irish state began a process of setting *all* corporate tax rates at 12.5 per cent (capital gains taxes were also halved). The Irish state stood by these low rates despite the fact that they were attracting large numbers of brass-plate companies and tax-avoidance scams. The Revenue Commissioners attempted to draft a formula for legislation that would ensure companies which were availing themselves of Irish tax breaks had 'real substance'. But this was difficult because measures such as employment creation were no longer reliable in the context of the 'new economy', where substantial paper profits could be gained with a minimal workforce (O'Kane 2000).
6   The difference between GDP and GNP was statistically reduced, however, when new ESA95 national accounting procedures were introduced in 1995 and 1997, at the behest of Eurostat. First, royalties and licences were treated as payments for services and included in GNP, where they had previously been treated as corporate profits and, when repatriated by TNCs, were

subtracted from GNP. Then, after 1997, several more changes were introduced
which substantially increased the statistical measure of fixed capital formation.
Software acquisitions and artistic originals were the most important items that
were moved from intermediate consumption to fixed capital formation.

7   Low-paid workers are those earning less than two-thirds of the median gross
wage of all full-year full-time workers.

Chapter 8

Comparing cycles of peripheral economic change

Economic cycles, hegemonic change and patterns of industrialisation

This book has concentrated on three cycles of Atlantic economy change and three associated cycles of industrialisation and industrial transformation in Ireland. The first cycle was associated with the British challenge of the Dutch-led world economy, the period through which Britain used its commercial and military superiority to move the centre of the world economy from the Baltic to the Atlantic. The second cycle began with the industrial revolution around cotton, during which England consolidated its superiority in manufactures by capturing world raw materials for its reorganised factory-based industry. The third cycle was associated with England's displacement as hegemon by the US, whose multidivisional industrial corporations became 'transnational', invoking a new form of foreign investment based on semi-peripheral manufacturing in TNC subsidiaries.

For each period, I identified and analysed a typical and repeated pattern of 'problem solving' between Ireland (as a peripheral region) and the prevailing hegemonic power, first Britain and then the US. Partly because of its proximity to the core, and partly because its early dominant peripheral classes were *from* the core, the Irish approach to problem solving at the beginning of each cycle was to try to copy the core processes of industrialisation. In the first two instances, the late seventeenth century and the late eighteenth century, Ireland's entrepreneurial classes, the colonial landed gentry and a more limited class of merchants, tried to replicate British success in specific industrial commodities: wool and cotton. For a time, the Irish industries succeeded. But they did so through a combination of state support and advantages in low labour costs and resources (such as plentiful waterpower). As I have shown most explicitly in the case of cotton, these advantages were in the nature of what Schumpeter (1947) called *adaptive responses* rather than *creative responses*. In other words, Irish industry could compete for a time by extending itself and taking advantage of its existing resources and patterns of productive organisation. However, as the core British industries innovated their organisation of production and distribution, and as they exploited their imperial advantages in material supply and market access, adaptive responses were insufficient for the Irish industries to survive.

Similarly, southern Irish ISI in the 1930s and 1940s relied on state protection and low labour costs to attain considerable success in an 'easy phase' of basic industrialisation. Yet the lack of *innovation*, reinforced by state policies that were *anti*-developmental insofar as they avoided inducing firms to change their behaviour after they were established and protected, meant that southern Irish industry could not (would not) expand beyond these easy phases. Capital deepening, trade deficits and insufficient foreign exchange earnings all became chronic, just as they would in the Latin American experiments with the same developmental model (O'Donnell 1978). If Senghaas (1985) is correct, such an outcome was not inevitable. Ireland *could have* followed the example of small European states by encouraging an agricultural revolution, building up its internal market and encouraging innovation in the production of capital goods and consumer goods that would first satisfy that market but eventually reach into export markets. O'Malley (1989) argues that the Irish state could have induced such a process of capital deepening in the 1950s.

There is, however, another side to the process of 'iterative problem solving' that repeatedly limited Ireland's attempts to industrialise. As a peripheral region within the Atlantic economy, Ireland was part of an economic system. It had to negotiate its economic strategies with other regions of the system, particularly with the dominant hegemonic power. Irish development was part of a larger process of 'iterative problem solving' for England and the US, as they created and reproduced the Atlantic economy as part of their hegemonic projects. Core competitors like France and Holland, and later the EU, also sought their own solutions. Thus, the transformation of Irish industries – woollens, cotton manufactures and import-substitution industries – was not simply a result of their 'failure' to innovate or even of their lack of 'endowed' resources. Transformation was ultimately the result of the regional system building of an Atlantic division of labour. Direct hegemonic policies that aimed to reduce and transform Irish industries were effective *enough* to bring about change that was, if contradictory, in the interests of the core hegemonic project of the time. The cattle bills, Woollen Act, Act of Union and the Marshall Plan were all central to the destruction of Irish industries that either competed with (in the cases of woollens and cotton) or were disruptive to the liberal world-system (in the case of import-substitution industries in general). Further positive policies to encourage provisions and linen production and, in the twentieth century, to open up Irish trade within the EU were all central to creating new (semi-)peripheral industries that were important to the success of the whole Atlantic economy and world-system. Irish provisions fed the English fleets and American colonies, Irish linen clothed the navy and colonies and, most recently, the southern Irish export platform provided US firms with a free route into EU markets and a low-tax site to accumulate profits.

No one could have foreseen *exactly* how these outcomes would help solve problems of hegemony and accumulation within the Atlantic economy, or the new problems they would create. Yet in every case, there is clear documented evidence that the hegemonic powers launched their projects in Ireland with the intent of creating the broad outcomes that eventually transpired. Then, their hegemonic power left them more able to resolve the conflicts and contradictions of policies, even turning them to their own advantage, as in the case where England used the withdrawal of Irish provisions as a weapon against hegemonic competitors.

Tracing specific hegemonic policies as elements of problem solving is important. But policies are surface representations of deeper hegemonic processes that, ultimately, have a critical influence on the ability of peripheral regions to industrialise successfully. I have argued throughout this book that specific policies like the Woollen Act or the Marshall Plan were successful because they were underpinned by longer-term processes which built up the institutions and infrastructures of hegemony. These deep processes are the basis of *path dependency* and, as such, cause the historical regularity that I have identified in Ireland's repeated cycles of industrialisation and industrial transformation. They began with Ireland's incorporation into the English regional system, a process that changed Irish class structures and introduced new economic and political institutions in ways that, however imperfectly and subject to resistance, subordinated Irish economic decisions to the interests of the emerging empire. While historians have fought over the nature of the subsequent social relations on the land, I have argued that the transformation of class relations in the town and particularly the removal of the native Irish commercial classes and merchant fleets were critical to the process of effective incorporation. Meanwhile, the wholesale confiscation of Irish lands, putting them under the control of settlers and collaborators, was crucial to England's subsequent ability to manage change in the country-side (again, imperfectly but *effectively enough*).

The processes that subordinated Irish economic relations to the institutions of the Atlantic economy, however, were the most important deep hegemonic processes that would affect Irish developmental outcomes for centuries. As Arrighi (1994) argued, England's imperial control of the Atlantic regions added a territorial logic of power to the world-system. By asserting direct colonial control where possible, and informal imperial control elsewhere, Britain marshalled the resources of the world to its economic project. It did this first by force, through naval supremacy and policies like the Navigation Acts. Then, after capturing competitive advantage, it controlled resources and markets through free trade and its superior commercial infrastructures. Such control made it possible for English industry and commerce to innovate. Access to consistent supplies of raw cotton of the right quality, for example, made English factory innovations profitable. Control of raw material supply on the front end of commodity chains was matched by advantages in commercial access to markets at the back end. Without stable sources of material supply or access to expanding markets, industrial aspirants in peripheral regions like Ireland had no choice but to compete for a time through *adaptive responses* like exploiting cheaper labour. But they eventually had to face the reality that they could not compete in the long run, and they rationally opted for more limited means of accumulating profits, whether through a return to agriculture or a more restricted line of industry.

These deep infrastructures influenced outcomes in the same direction over time: Irish classes repeatedly attempted to industrialise when opportunities appeared, were eventually unable to compete with core industry and moved back into agrarian production or subordinate industry. Even in the twentieth century, southern Ireland seized the opportunity given by decolonisation and world recession and attempted to industrialise by substituting indigenous products for imports. But its opportunities were limited by its small market, by its lack of access to materials and technologies, by hostility from Britain and by the free-enterprise orientation of the Irish state. In order to overcome these limitations and avoid isolation and impoverishment, Ireland became reincorporated into the new structures of the Atlantic economy after the Second World War. The price it paid, once again, was a subordinate and limited industrial role, this time as a dependent export platform for mainly US companies that desired access to the European market.

Despite the consistent pattern of resubordination of the Irish economy, the nature of the subordinate outcome changed in each cycle, particularly between British and US hegemony. To support its territorial advantages and control of Atlantic trade, Britain redirected and limited Irish industrial production and peripheralised the broad Irish agrarian economy. Direct exploitation at the point of production was largely an Irish matter, since a settler class owned most Irish industry. There was undoubtedly a substantial unequal exchange between low-profit, low-wage Irish exports and Irish imports of British industrial goods and British-distributed colonial goods. But the main consequence of British hegemony was economic oppression, which left large sections of the Irish population underemployed and in chronic subsistence crisis and eventually led to famine, emigration and depopulation. US competitive advantages were based on internalising transactions costs through the development of the multidivisional firm. After the Second World War this entailed the geographical reorganisation of firms, siting different subsidiaries and nodes of commodity chains where they would best help companies achieve their *global* strategies of production and distribution. The result in Ireland was substantial direct exploitation of southern Irish labour by external capital, which then removed its profit abroad. This appropriation of surplus was increased further by the degree to which the Irish population at large subsidised foreign profits through IDA grants and incentives, which were ultimately financed by taxing Irish workers and consumers. Economic oppression was more cyclical than it had been under Britain. The southern Irish economy attained periods of relatively high employment followed by high unemployment, although the northern economy went into chronic decline. Periods of net emigration cycled with periods of net immigration.

Where Ireland was transformed into a supplier of food and by a very limited range of industry under Britain, it was reintegrated under US hegemony into a global division of labour within TNCs. This finally transformed southern Ireland from a largely rural, agrarian country to an urban industrial and service economy. Ireland's twentieth-century *dependent industrialisation* raises the question of whether certain cycles, although ending once again in economic subordination, can leave a peripheral zone with greater long-term chances to develop and increase its national wealth. This has been a popular theme in the south of Ireland since the 1960s, but never more so than when the 'Celtic tiger' emerged in the 1990s.

Irish industry in a restructured Europe: what has changed?

I have analysed Ireland as an *intermediating periphery* within the Atlantic economy. It played an important systemic role in the Atlantic strategy of each hegemonic power. This role was an intermediate one between the hegemonic core economy and important economic processes on the other side of the Atlantic. For the first two cycles of industrialisation and industrial transformation, Ireland was transformed into a producer of critical industrial products for the British-centred Atlantic economy. These were vital for cross-Atlantic commerce and territorial control, although they involved relatively simple processing for limited markets. In the early phases these were primarily *Irish* products that were produced under the direction mostly of resident landed and merchant classes. Some were absentee landlords or split their residence between Ireland and Britain. Most of the direct beneficiaries of dependent development were indigenous classes, even if they spent or invested a large proportion of their wealth abroad. They included an industrial bourgeoisie, some of whose members had vied for a larger *core* industrial position in the early stages of the industrial cycle (and even for limited political autonomy) but who settled for a more limited but nonetheless profitable peripheral position in the transformed industries. They were, in Robinson's (1983) terminology, local *collaborators*, although they were collaborators who, as a class, sometimes aspired to higher station when the opportunity presented itself. The rise of an indigenous northern bourgeoisie, Ulster Scots by ethnic origin but British unionist by ideology, finally transformed the leading collaborators into a loyal class. But the concentration of semi-peripheral Irish industry in the north-east of the island also helped transform the wider project of industrialisation and economic development into a *national* one that was eventually equated with political independence. The two oppositional industrial projects, unionist and nationalist, were temporarily resolved by the forcible partitioning of the island into two economies and two polities after 1920.

The shift of the indigenous Irish development project to a nationalist one coincided with a much larger shift in the Atlantic economy, from British to US hegemony. Thus, the Irish *national* project of industrialisation arose in the 1930s and came into crisis just as the US was instituting a new global regime of open doors for a new international division of labour. Within this context, the Marshall Plan and subsequent programmes had the dual aim of reconstructing Europe as a market for US industrial products, while opening the former colonial regions as sources of raw materials and, later, cheap labour for US-based global corporations. The consolidation of a free trade area was an important part of this strategy, although the creation of a new Europe eventually had the contradictory outcome of creating a new competitor for world economic power (Thurow 1992).

Ireland was not a very important part of this US strategy. The southern Irish government practically had to beg the US to be included in the Marshall Plan and, once in, traded a substantial degree of its recently won autonomy in return for some moderate loans that it used to fund specific development programmes. But, as elsewhere in the then Third World, the post-war modernising project led by the US and joined by a unifying Europe had a powerful attraction for an Irish state whose development regime was in crisis. TNCs were instant modernisers, bringing a promise of industrialisation, which, to a degree, they delivered until they began to disinvest in the 1980s.

A changing Europe made Ireland more attractive in the 1970s. US computer corporations came there to exploit it as a point of entry into the European market. But this wave of investments consisted of US firms that were relatively small and discrete. They created few jobs and not only did they fail to link with Irish firms but they were not even linked with each other. Ireland was important to scores of individual US firms, but it was not yet a crucial export platform for access to Europe. It attracted projects mainly because it could offer a better package of grants and other incentives than other potential host regions. Meanwhile, the free trade regime that was necessary to attract these companies – with free imports of parts and materials and free exports of products and profits – also caused a wave of import penetration in consumer products that drove most of the indigenous import-substitution firms out of business. World recession, including disinvestment by US-based TNCs and general 'Eurosclerosis', caused the radically open and dependent Irish economy to go into a severe nosedive.

The new economy of the 1990s, with its agglomerated patterns of investment, brought the south of Ireland back to prominence as a critical intermediating periphery. Not only was the US economy booming, with its corporations searching for new markets, but reform in the EU had created a neoliberal deregulated 'big market' that was intended to be a launching pad for a revitalised Europe. In reality, the big market was even more important as a consumer of US-based IT goods and services. This time, it was not just discrete projects looking for a profitable place to produce goods for the European market that found their way into Ireland. Rather, whole US-based IT sectors based their European operations in Ireland. Digital, the largest foreign employer of the 1970s, provided 1,200 jobs in Ireland at its peak. At the end of the 1990s, ten US hardware corporations each employed more than that amount in a computer sector that exported product worth more than £3 billion. At the top end, Dell employed more than 5,000 people, Intel 3,600, IBM 3,300, Xerox 2,200 and Motorola 2,000. According to the US Department of Commerce, Ireland attracted 10–15 per cent of total US investments into the EU in the late 1990s (Duffy *et al.* 1999, p. 27). This included some *40 per cent* of US electronics investments into the EU.

Ireland was again playing an important intermediating role, as the point through which US products flowed into European markets and in which profits were accumulated and removed back to North America. Unlike previous cycles of industrialisation, however, the class that directly organised industry in Ireland was a global bourgeoisie rather than an Irish one. It was based mainly in the US and, therefore, had global production strategies that *still* located the most innovative stages of production overwhelmingly at home, even though some of the highest value-added stages of production were sited in Ireland to benefit from its low taxes. The restraining dynamic imposed by British hegemony on Irish industry was that it was restricted to certain non-competing products that were important to empire but had strictly limited markets and relatively basic technologies. Under US hegemony, Ireland participated in segments of the most expansive and innovative commodity chains of the global economy. The restraining dynamic of this relationship was that Ireland depended on the decisions of external capital regarding which productive segments would be placed in Ireland, where they would obtain their material inputs and sell their products, and how much they would expand or how long they would remain.

Industrial cycles and innovation

I have argued elsewhere (O'Hearn 1994) that innovation is the key characteristic that not only distinguishes peripheral industry from core industry, but also reinforces the hierarchy between them. Core states successfully localise innovation within their territories or corporations, capturing sectors that are or become centres of *creative response*. This enables them to achieve higher wages, higher capital intensity and higher profitability, while semi-peripheral regions rely on less profitable forms of *adaptive response*. Senghaas (1985) and Mjoset (1992) put a similar emphasis on systems of national innovation, or *autocentric development*. These enabled small European economies to attain core status by provoking virtuous cycles of agrarian reform, expansion of local markets and innovative industrial centres that could eventually attain global reach through export and even foreign investment.

Clearly, Ireland's early cycles of industrialisation and transformation did not create national systems of innovation. Provisioning the empire was profitable for some landholders and merchants, but it expanded primarily by extending outward to use more lands and labourers, the classic *adaptive response*. The provisions industry created few linkages to other industrial activities, save the destructive and self-limiting process of clearing woodlands for barrel staves and pasture. Likewise, linen was strictly limited in its market. In its early stages it expanded by extending its household-based production into new areas and new households. Although it went through a period of intensification to factory production after the fall of the Irish cotton industry, this was not an expansive process with outward linkages to new innovative industries. Rather, it was a process of geographical concentration that left the rest of the island even more peripheral and prone to subsistence crisis than before.

What of the third transformation: from ISI to ELI? This was a transformation that finally 'industrialised' the island of Ireland to an extent that it had never been industrialised before. Had Ireland finally achieved, under US hegemony, the development path it had sought so many times before? In the 1980s, critical analysts of development had substantial evidence to argue that it had not. Crotty (1986, n.d.) argued that Ireland still suffered from the continuity of 'individualist capitalist colonialism', which, as in centuries before, was run by an inept colonised state that ruled for the benefit of a few and to the detriment of the masses. Since the 1950s, this state elite had borrowed from its citizens to subsidise export growth, and borrowed further abroad on the basis of its rapidly growing exports. The state taxed neither landowners nor capital, but instead replicated the 'traditional capitalist colonial condition' of making land and capital cheap and labour relatively dear. Instead of substituting cattle and sheep for labour as in the nineteenth century, this time companies were substituting capital for labour, causing unemployment and emigration. Crucially, with regard to whether Ireland had now graduated into core industrialisation, Crotty argued that export growth had little to do with efficiency but was simply subsidised through grants, tax relief and cheap capital. Exports created too few jobs, which were insecure since capital was footloose. And

exports were attained at the 'too great' cost of import dependence. Subsidising exports diverted resources from production for the home market
into production for foreign ones, adding to the cost of goods consumed or
invested in Ireland and reducing the well-being of the Irish people.

Other critical analysts agreed that Ireland was still stuck in a peripheral
developmental path. O'Malley (1989) argued that the indigenous sector
was still underdeveloped and had failed to achieve the high-tech, capital-
intensive large scale that dominated the core European economies. Munck
(1993) situated Ireland in the context of dependent uneven development,
arguing that, as an enclave economy, periods of expansion would be
followed by periods of abrupt capital withdrawal, unemployment and
emigration. O'Hearn (1989) argued that the liberal model that allowed
penetration by TNCs had also created negative externalities that caused the
destruction of local industry and any real possibility of local innovation,
without creating substantial new opportunities through linkages or spin-
offs. And a 1991 conference in Dublin asked the question, 'Is Ireland a
Third World country?'

One of the most important, and still provocative, critical approaches of
this time was Mjoset's (1992) analysis of a 'post-war vicious circle of Irish
industrialisation'. Building on the work of Senghaas (1985) and Amin
(1975), Mjoset argued that southern Ireland's liberal ELI strategy gave the
state little capacity for policy implementation. As a result, it had a weak
national system of innovation that was characterised by a disarticulated
economy and that gave generous privileges to a decentralised structure of
foreign firms that was beyond its control. Not only did these firms keep
their innovative activities in their home countries, but the state's inability to
induce linkages between them and indigenous firms meant that there was
no internal system of innovation. Instead, southern Irish society was characterised by the threat of marginalisation, emigration and population decline.
Most crucially, the state's low capacity to implement policy left it at the
mercy of the foreign sector, which it continued to subsidise to a rising
degree.

Interestingly, Mjoset was most critical of the state's emerging policy of
using consensual national agreements to resolve distributional conflicts,
which many experts later credited as a major factor behind the successes of
the 'Celtic tiger' (for example O'Donnell and Thomas 1998). He argued
that European success was not based on consensus, which Ireland had
already tried during the 1970s. Rather, 'if a general formula is needed
concerning the relations between institutions and growth, it should focus
on the inter-relationship between the broader institutional system and the
"national system of innovation" surrounding the "development blocks" –
the clusters of important firms – of a particular economy' (Mjoset 1992,
p. 16). The crux was the lack of indigenous industry and the unsophisti-
cated degree of processing of raw materials. Unlike other European countries,

Ireland had not developed effective manufacturing industries supported by national systems of innovation. It had tried to import a foreign system of innovation by subsidising TNCs, but they continued to be disarticulated, with weak linkages and no real effect on national innovation.

As we saw in chapter 7, few of the characteristics that underlay Mjoset's analysis of low innovation and disarticulation in the Irish economy changed in the 1990s. If anything, TNCs bought a smaller proportion of their material inputs in Ireland. And the amount of spending on R&D remained very low in foreign and domestic firms alike. What *did* change was that Ireland attracted 'clusters of important firms' around Intel, Microsoft and, perhaps, Pfizer. These were sufficient to drive a very rapid growth of exports and output. Whether a national innovative cluster was created in software is debatable (see Ó Riain 2000). But I have argued here and elsewhere (O'Hearn 2000) that this sector was small, vulnerable and not particularly productive, as it produced an eighth of the output of the foreign-owned software sector, with as many workers.

What is at issue, and this is crucial from the standpoint of development theory, is whether it is possible to achieve a highly industrialised and highly wealthy economy *without* a national system of innovation as prescribed by Senghaas or Mjoset. Experts from within Ireland and outward to the OECD and IMF appear to argue that such an outcome is possible, and that Ireland has successfully managed a 'switching point' from its previous cycles of underdevelopment to full core status. Yet, despite half a decade of extremely high growth rates, the experiences of other regions of the Atlantic economy over the past several hundred years indicate that innovation has been crucial to upward mobility from semi-peripheral to core status. Neo-classical economists like O'Rourke and Williamson (1999) have attempted to show that convergence is possible through free trade only, but they fail to show that the cyclical convergence of incomes is matched by a long-term developmental convergence that makes possible such an upward leap into the core. Lack of national innovation in countries like Ireland, Portugal and Spain impeded such upward mobility. These and many other historical examples cast doubt on the long-term sustainability of Irish growth in the late twentieth and early twenty-first centuries. On the side of sustainability are a near decade of very rapid, if dependent, growth and the conviction among most orthodox experts that the world and Ireland *had* actually entered a *new* economy sometime in the 1990s.

There is, however, another and more important side to articulation than the technical aspect of clustered firms or whether US TNCs are now more 'grounded' in Ireland. This is the question of social articulation. Even if growth is sustained, the path to economic growth *does* matter. There is still the central question of whether growth is or can be equitable. As de Janvry asked with regard to Latin America: is growth articulating? 'Does growth in disarticulated export enclaves or in import-substitution industrializing countries lead ... to gradual changes in the production structure that result in *social articulation?*' (1981, p. 265, my emphasis).

De Janvry answers his own question in terms of social class alliances. Dominant alliances, he argues, have their own 'laws of reproduction' and they use their control of the state to attempt to perpetuate the status quo. Therefore, there is no reason why disarticulated growth should resolve itself by subsequent articulation. It is more likely that a resolution to the contradictions of disarticulated accumulation – unequal distribution – will be postponed by calling further on foreign capital and imports; by intensifying inequality; by increasing outward orientation; and by 'co-option, segment-ation, separation, and repression' (de Janvry 1981, p. 265).

Back in the European context, however, Katzenstein (1985) seems to have a different and more hopeful answer than de Janvry. He maintains that social articulation can compensate for the economic disarticulation that necessarily arises when small countries are dependent on export markets. Regardless of their success in promoting national innovation for export, continental Europe's small open economies still could not influence world markets or insulate themselves from their effects. They have had to internalise the costs of economic restructuring that are imposed from without. Accord-ing to Katzenstein, these states have compensated domestic classes for flexibly adjusting to the fluctuations of external markets by erecting and maintaining effective welfare states that create greater equality and social protection. This has been achieved through a national system of 'social partnership' in which consensus emerges from continuous political bargaining among interest groups, state bureaucracies and political parties. Compen-satory social protection has been institutionalised in this way to the degree that quick and significant retrenchments of the welfare state in response to international forces are unlikely. Thus, for Katzenstein social democracy and equality are necessary elements of the continuing economic success of small European states.

The term 'social partnership' invites comparison with the corporatist bargaining structures that emerged in southern Ireland after the 1960s. But I have argued along with others (Allen 2000; Ó Cinnéide 2000) that, in spite of its adopted name, Irish social partnership is about wage flexibility without the degree of either democracy or social protection that Katzenstein found in other small European states. Rather, in the years of the Celtic tiger, the main compensatory trend has been full employment, albeit generally with low wages and low security. Rather than the previous European model of democratic corporatism and social protection analysed by Katzenstein, Ireland's social partnership is more like the new European social model that Streeck (1999) calls 'competitive solidarity'. According to Streeck, the new European social model is based on achieving equality on the supply side, through investment in training and infrastructure, rather than equality of outcomes through social protection. Because of the increasing intensity of competition in international markets, most states no longer seek, for the sake of national solidarity, to avoid high wage disparities between higher-productivity manufacturing and low-productivity public and service sectors. Nor is the dampening of inequality between the highest salary receivers and the unemployed, through liberal social welfare provisions, a basis of solidarity. Such social protection is constrained by a pervasive and increasingly competitive international market and by supranational institutions devoted to safeguarding that market. National regimes seek solidarity 'through *joint competitive and productive success* ... gradually replacing *protective* and *redistributive* with *competitive* and *productive* solidarity' (Streeck 1999, p. 5, emphasis in original).

This analysis fits the Celtic tiger like a glove. It is widely agreed that the main success of social partnership has been its role in dampening labour demands for higher wages and broader social demands for more public services and social protection. Public investment, while falling rapidly as a proportion of national income, has been redirected into 'competitive' projects like physical infrastructure and technical education while the state's provision of health care, housing and general education has eroded to the bottom of the EU scale. And the budget is determined *not* by bargaining between the state and the public legs of social partnership but by the government and its finance minister working to the neoliberal constraints of the international market as expressed in the demands of the TNCs in Ireland and prospective TNC entrants. This model has created sufficient national solidarity to enable flexibility so long as compensation has been provided by high employment from the influx of new foreign investments and the construction projects and services that accompanied the 'boom' of the 1990s. But the future of 'competitive solidarity' as a basis for national consensus was already beginning to come apart as southern Ireland entered the twenty-first century.

Research elsewhere indicates that the continental European developmental models are possibly unique in their social democratic outcomes. The more likely outcome where dependent states attempt to erect social democracies is that they eventually lose their relative autonomy and capacity, enabling dominant classes to reintroduce the disarticulated accumulation regimes that de Janvry describes (Evans 1985; on Mexico, see Hamilton 1982).

As a now industrialised, indeed in many ways a *post*-industrial service economy, Ireland differs in obvious ways from the mixed industrial/peasant societies that de Janvry observed but it also differs fundamentally from the continental European models. Although many Irish workers have been proletarianised and their jobs are often insecure and poorly paid, they do not retain ties to the land and subsistence production to the same degree as is characteristic of many parts of Latin America. Moreover, Ireland is, as it has been for centuries, more thoroughly integrated into the core industrial circuits of the Atlantic economy, situated between the two great core regions and performing intermediating activities that tie the two regions together. It participates in nodes of high-tech commodity chains that are not at the beginning stages of processing but toward the end, organised by the most advanced world corporations and often involving highly educated engineers, even if their engineering work is routine. The Irish are full members not just of the EU but of Western culture; they have 'become white' not just in US society (Ignatiev 1995) but in European and world society.

Despite this, Ireland's open accumulation regime is characterised by many of the elements of disarticulation that de Janvry describes, with a dynamic that suggests a continuation of that historical path rather than articulation. Irish growth is *still not* articulating, either in Senghaas's economic sense or in de Janvry's broader social sense. Economically, Irish growth is based more than ever on a distinct enclave of US-based exporters that are less rooted than ever in the broad Irish economy, even though they are more rooted *in each other in Ireland*. Despite the micro-management of state bodies like Enterprise Ireland, the small amount of indigenous innovation that has occurred is in parallel to rather than linked to the foreign sector (Ó Riain 1999). This does not indicate a dynamic that would lead to articulation. Instead, the very basis of Irish growth is deregulation and free trade, and the Irish state has consistently lost its capacity to make economic policy because of its membership of the EU. The class alliance that has driven Irish economic growth is led by global capital, whose interests are primarily in further economic disarticulation rather than articulation.

It is at the social level that the 'Celtic tiger' accumulation regime has most displayed historical continuity rather than change. Growth has gone hand in hand with inequality, poverty and social division. Division has been papered over by the so-called consensus politics of 'social partnership'. But, close up, the partnership process looks more like de Janvry's description of 'co-option, segmentation, separation, and repression'. Its main purpose is to restrain demands for wages and social spending by incorporating trade unions and social organisations into the negotiation processes of the social partnership agreements. It has done little to resolve the problems that cause discontent. Rather, in the 1990s promises of rapid economic growth and the reality of falling unemployment muted what Allen (2000) called the Celtic tiger's 'discontented majority'. Even so, discontent grew, as the inequities of the Irish growth model became more apparent. By the late 1990s trade unions threatened to abandon partnership because wage increases had not even kept up with inflation, much less increased productivity. Each successive state budget of the late 1990s promised more and gave less to low-paid workers, to the economically disadvantaged and to the regions outside Dublin that had gained little from economic growth. Social services were run down, cities were gridlocked and a severe housing crisis left tens of thousands of people without adequate accommodation.

In the end, the Irish approach to development has been to give the best possible deal to core capitals in the hope of attracting them in the greatest possible numbers, so that the wealth they generate will 'trickle down' to the local population. When growth is rapid enough, as it was in the late 1990s, the trickle becomes a stream. But without a new dynamic toward social articulation, the latest cycle of industrialisation and industrial transformation in Ireland will surely prove to be another, if different, form of peripheralisation rather than a switching point from dependent peripheral development to full membership of the core of the Atlantic economy.

The best hope for a transformation toward an articulated development strategy may be if discontent is transformed into widespread mobilisation for social change. Social change requires a strong incentive to break out of the neoliberal growth strategy, which, since the 1960s and especially since 1990, was inextricably tied to inequality and disarticulation. In the 1990s the Irish regime achieved labour flexibility not through social democracy and social welfare, as Katzenstein claims happened in continental Europe, but through high growth and rising employment. Compared with the 1980s this represented a substantial achievement for many Irish workers, who were employed rather than unemployed, albeit at very low wages and on insecure terms. But it was unlikely that economic growth and employment alone could sustain widespread public support for a regime that was not providing a better quality of life in many other respects. In the year 2000, the emergence of inflation at twice the average EU level provoked scepticism among wider sections of the trade union movement about whether social partnership in its current form could satisfy the interests of Irish workers. Public questions continued to be raised about the unequal nature of Irish economic change and about the social consequences of policies that favoured growth over social inclusion. Political opinion polls showed rising support for minority political parties and independent political candidates with platforms that were critical of social bases of the Celtic tiger.

Arguably, the continuing weakness of indigenous innovation and the lack of substantial organic links between innovations in different sectors, such as agriculture and industrial processing, cast a shadow even over the sustainability of economic growth and high employment. Even if the social bases for equality were enhanced, there are still significant questions about Ireland's ability to transform its growth pattern from being an export enclave of US IT companies to a more sustainable pattern of interlinked autocentric growth. By and large, orthodox economists have not been very concerned about these problems and have continued to take solace from forecasts of continuing rapid growth (for example IMF 2000). But more critical analysts still see a need for a transition from Ireland's historical pattern of development, which I have described here as a long and repeated historical pattern. Ó Riain (1999, 2000) bases his hopeful expectations for Ireland on the future success of indigenous innovation, partly because of the return to Ireland of a 'globalised' population. I would argue, however, that he overestimates the vitality of this reverse diaspora and underestimates the persistence of deep historical processes. Munck and Hamilton (1993, 1998), while critical, try to analyse how a future articulated pattern of development could come about. Their hopes are based partly on policies that encourage indigenous development. But they argue that broader developments like Irish unification could also increase social articulation throughout the island of Ireland while increasing the general strength of the Irish economy and easing technical problems associated with Ireland's small market. Unification could increase scale economies, enable the further improvement of island-wide infrastructures and strengthen Ireland's entrepreneurial bases in civil society. Another possible reason for hope would arise if the social democratic elements of EU integration proved more powerful than its liberalising competition strategies, something that had not yet been the case at the beginning of the twenty-first century. In the end, however, Munck and Hamilton argue that sustainable growth would depend on redistribution and a more radical democratic framework than Ireland has developed heretofore. In other words, politics not economics is in command.

Historical paths: self-reinforcing or breakable?

The enduring theme of this book is the examination of the nature of historical regularities that are established in the process of creating and reproducing regional power economies like the Atlantic economy. A repeated theme is whether or under what conditions small regions can erect strategies to break out of the historical patterns that limit their possibilities of developing articulated economies. Two related but distinct problems continually arise. First, there is a 'technical' problem of creating a pattern of economic growth that is interlinked and based on innovation, so that it may be sustained. Second is the 'social' problem of whether growth, even sustained growth, can enable greater equality and inclusion of the mass of people in the processes of social decision making. Although many critical development analysts have concentrated on the first problem, the two sets of problems are interrelated. This is not simply because of the Marxian argument that a sustained high-growth economy would still exploit the masses of a society if innovation were based only on high profitability. It is also because the processes of sustainable innovation-based growth and equality are connected. The northern European experience suggests that the connection may be greater for small countries than for large ones, partly because large countries may have other options for solving problems of openness to world market forces, for example by fostering their infant industries to greater competitiveness before entering export markets.

The development problem for peripheral regions in the Atlantic economy and the broader world-system throws up the following problem: to be socially articulating, a significant part of surplus profits must be used to sustain an equalising social compromise. This is not, as neo-Keynesian development theory suggests, because it is necessary to create greater home demand for innovative indigenous products. For better or worse, the repeated historical experiences of regions like Ireland indicate that small countries must participate in export markets if they are to develop and sustain dynamic and innovative economic sectors (even if export participation is preceded by a period of protected import substitution). Social articulation is necessary primarily because such a country must mobilise a labour force that not only has a stake in responding to changing conditions in export markets but which is consistently involved in upgrading its skills and its practices.

Yet, as I have argued in Ireland's case, the consistent pattern of peripheral development, whether in a colonial relationship with Britain or a dependent one with the US and Europe, is disarticulating. To the extent that industry is encouraged it is restricted, not just to specific sectors like provisions or linen but even to specific nodes of the commodity chains that make up a sector (cotton weaving under the putting-out system, computer assembly or software localisation). Innovative nodes like R&D or product design are the *least* likely economic activities to flow from core economies to peripheral ones. Even if dependent industrialisers attract clusters of projects as in the Celtic tiger, they still find it difficult to attain the broad linkages that characterise Amin's *autocentric* development or Senghaas's national systems of innovation. Without sustained autocentric development, liberal policies must be employed to attract a continual inflow of foreign investments that is sufficient to sustain economic growth. I have argued in the Irish case that these developmental strategies are by definition disarticulating because policies like privatisation and fiscal restraint impede the development of social welfare and equality.

The Irish experience casts doubt on whether social democracy is a realistic developmental alternative to de Janvry's expectation of intensifying inequality and dependence. To be an alternative, it would seem, the initial growth strategy must be based on innovation and upgrading rather than on the accumulation of a restricted capitalist class (whether indigenous or foreign). Capital must have a recognised interest in social democracy and the state must have the capacity to implement social democratic policies to compensate the population for its sacrifices to the global market. The class basis *and* the international competitive basis of a given growth strategy must encourage rather than impede policies that reduce inequality and social exclusion.

This brings us back to history and path dependency. Comparing the success of small European states, beginning at the end of the nineteenth century, and Ireland's still-questionable 'success' at the end of the twentieth, one conclusion seems unavoidable: it *does* matter when a country or region attempts to achieve upward mobility within the world-system. Small northern European states attempted to construct national systems of innovation at a historical time when indigenous upgrading and social corporatism were possible. But Ireland was unable to attempt such an experiment as long as it was constrained by its position within the British-led Atlantic economy, as its industrialisation experiments had already been constrained in preceding centuries. After a short-lived flirtation with indigenous industrialisation based on protection of the local market but without any effective regulation of the behaviour of the Irish capitalist class, southern Ireland was finally drawn into ELI after the Second World War, this time within a US-centred Atlantic economy. In this phase of globalisation, however, the economic basis of growth was constrained by policies of openness to disarticulated foreign investment, while the social basis of growth was constrained by the competitive demands of the international market rather than the compensatory concerns of the indigenous working and unemployed classes.

Conclusions: the limitations of dependent growth

In an insightful comparative analysis of theories of economic change, So (1990, pp. 256–60) finds hope in studies that concentrate on specific cases. By looking at specific cases, some of the more orthodox students of modernisation have realised that the countries of this world are not all destined to achieve 'modernity' and wealth if they follow Western-style strategies of being and acting modern. And critical theorists like world-systems analysts who work at the national level have continued to examine the cyclical rhythms of the world economy, but have given national states and actors greater scope for acting in ways that can create positive change. So's own analysis of the South China silk district not only shows how world-systemic processes penetrate local economies, but also how the multiple forms of class struggle that they trigger can create new opportunities for local change (So 1986). The current analysis of the Atlantic economy has tried to achieve a similar end, although I have found historical patterns and processes to be more limiting than opportunistic from the perspective of local change.

Yet one should end on an optimistic note. One such note is obvious, although in some ways superficial: dependent industrialisation is clearly preferable to colonial underdevelopment as a form of peripherality. As the old saying goes, most people *will* prefer being exploited to not being exploited, if the latter means being unemployed and economically marginalised. Dependent industrialisation under US hegemony enables the average low-waged Irish service worker to achieve a considerably higher material standard of living than the average tenant under British hegemony could have ever hoped for. Being employed during a period of rapid investments like the 1990s is infinitely preferable to being unemployed during a period of disinvestment like the 1980s.

Yet mobilising for change requires a realistic analysis of the social and economic limitations of dependent growth, which, even under the Celtic tiger, are too restrictive. Historical paths are deep and solid. Fundamental change involves much more than clever local strategies to exploit the opportunities of the world-system better than other, competing regions. Rather, the persistence of world-historical processes indicates that fundamental change must, surely, be systemic. It must take place at the levels of Europe, of the Atlantic and global economies, and in the organisation of whole commodity chains. This is not to say that local mobilisation, resistance and change are a waste of time. Rather, local movements must take aim at systemic targets, albeit with increasing attention to making coalitions with like-minded movements for change in other localities. Marx, although writing at a time when single localities like Ireland were more crucial to the whole capitalist system, clearly understood the relationship between local action and global change when he wrote in 1870 of Ireland's position relative to Britain's within the Atlantic economy (Marx and Engels 1971, p. 388):

> To accelerate the social development in Europe, you must push on the catastrophe of official England. To do so, you must attack her in Ireland. That's her weakest point. Ireland lost, the British 'empire' is gone, and the class war in England, till now somnolent and chronic, will assume acute forms. But England is the metropolis of landlordism and capitalism all over the world.

References

'66 Business Conference (1967), *Business Representation in Irish National Affairs: The Report of a Study for the '66 Business Conference*, Dublin, Harbridge House Europe.

Agnew, J. H. (1994), *The Merchant Community of Belfast, 1660–1707*, PhD dissertation, Belfast, Queen's University.

Albion, R. (1926), *Forests and Sea Power: The Timber Problem of the Royal Navy, 1652–1862*, Cambridge, Harvard University Press.

Allen, K. (2000), *The Celtic Tiger: The Myth of Social Partnership*, Manchester, Manchester University Press.

American Tariff League (1942), *How High Are American Tariffs?*, New York, American Tariff League, Inc.

Amin, A. (1992), 'Big firms versus the regions in the Single European Market', in M. Dunford and G. Kafkalis (eds), *Cities and Regions in the New Europe*, London, Belhaven Press.

Amin, S. (1975), *Unequal Development*, New York, Monthly Review Press.

Armstrong, D. L. (1951), 'Social and economic conditions in the Belfast linen industry 1850–1900', *Irish Historical Studies*, 7, 28.

Arrighi, G. (1994), *The Long Twentieth Century*, London, Verso.

Arrighi, G. and J. Drangel (1986), 'Stratification of the world-economy: an explanation of the semiperipheral zone', *Review*, 10:1, 9–74.

Arthur, W. B. (1988), 'Self-reinforcing mechanisms in economics', in P. Anderson, K. Arrow and D. Pines (eds), *The Economy as an Evolving Complex System*, Santa Fe, Santa Fe Institute.

Baines, E. (1835), *History of the Cotton Manufacture in Great Britain*, London, Fisher, Fisher and Jackson.

Bairoch, P. (1976), 'Europe's gross national product: 1800–1975', *Journal of Economic History*, 5:2, 273–340.

Baran, P. (1957), *The Political Economy of Growth*, New York, Monthly Review Press.

Barham, B., S. Bunker and D. O'Hearn (eds) (1995), *States, Firms and Raw Materials: The World Economy and Ecology of Aluminum*, Madison, University of Wisconsin Press.

Barnard, T. C. (1979), *Cromwellian Ireland: English Government and Reform in Ireland 1649–60*, Oxford, Oxford University Press.

Barry, F. (1999), 'Irish growth in historical and theoretical perspective', in F. Barry (ed.), *Understanding Ireland's Economic Growth*, London, Macmillan.

Barry, F. and J. Bradley (1997), 'FDI and trade: the Irish host-country experience', *Economic Journal*, 107:445, 1798–811.

Barry, F., J. Bradley and E. O'Malley (1999), 'Indigenous and foreign industry: characteristics and performance', in F. Barry (ed.), *Understanding Ireland's Economic Growth*, London, Macmillan.

Beddy, J. P. (1943–44), 'Comparison of the principal economic features of Eire and Denmark', *Journal of the Statistical and Social Inquiry Society of Ireland*, 17:2, 189–220.

Bell, D. (1974), *The Coming of Post-industrial Society: A Venture in Social Forecasting*, London, Heinemann.

Berg, M. (1994), *The Age of Manufactures 1700–1820: Industry, Innovation and Work in Britain*, London, Routledge.

Bergesen, A. (1983), 'The class structure of the world-system', in W. R. Thompson (ed.), *Contending Approaches to World System Analysis*, Beverly Hills, Sage.

Bergesen, A. and R. Schoenberg (1980), 'Long waves of colonial expansion and contraction, 1415–1969', in A. Bergesen (ed.), *Studies of the Modern World-System*, New York, Academic Press.

Bergsten, C. F. (1987), 'Economic imbalances and world politics', *Foreign Affairs*, 65:4, 770–94.

Bielenberg, A. (1998), 'The Irish brewing industry and the rise of Guinness, 1790–1914', in R. G. Wilson and T. R. Gourvish (eds), *The Dynamics of the International Brewing Industry since 1800*, London, Routledge.

Blaug, M. (1961), 'The productivity of capital in the Lancashire cotton industry during the nineteenth century', *Economic History Review*, 13:3, 358–81.

Block, F. (1977), *The Origins of International Economic Disorder*, Berkeley, University of California Press.

Bornschier, V. (1992), 'The European Community's uprising: grasping towards hegemony or therapy against national decline in the world political economy?', paper presented at the First European Conference of Sociology, Vienna, 26–29 August.

Bornschier, V., C. Chase-Dunn and R. Rubinson (1978), 'Cross-national evidence of the effects of foreign investment and aid on economic growth and inequality: a survey of findings and a reanalysis', *American Journal of Sociology*, 84:3, 651–83.

Borooah, V. (1993), 'Northern Ireland: typology of a regional economy', in P. Teague (ed.), *The Economy of Northern Ireland: Perspectives for Structural Change*, London, Lawrence and Wishart.

Bottigheimer, K. S. (1971), *English Money and Irish Land: The 'Adventurers' in the Cromwellian Settlement of Ireland*, Oxford, Oxford University Press.

Boyle, E. (1979), *The Economic Development of the Irish Linen Industry, 1825–1913*, PhD dissertation, Belfast, Queen's University.

Bradley, J. (1990), 'The legacy of economic development: the Irish economy, 1960–1987', in J. McCarthy (ed.), *Planning Ireland's Future: The Legacy of T. K. Whitaker*, Dublin, Glendale.

Bradshaw, B. (1978), 'Sword, word and strategy in the reformation in Ireland', *Historical Journal*, 21, 475–502.

Braudel, F. (1984), *The Perspective of the World*, New York, Harper and Row.

Breathnach, M. and D. Kelly (1999), 'Multinationals, subcontracting linkages and the innovative performance of indigenous firms: some Irish evidence', paper presented at the European Network on Industrial Policy International Conference, Dublin, 9–10 December.

Brenner, R. (1977), 'The origins of capitalist development: a critique of neo-Smithian Marxism', *New Left Review*, 104, 25–92.

Brenner, R. (1993), *Merchants and Revolution: Commercial Change, Political Conflict, and London's Overseas Traders, 1550–1653*, Cambridge, Cambridge University Press.

Buckley, P. J. (1974), 'Some aspects of foreign private investment in the manufacturing sector of the economy of the Irish Republic', *Economic and Social Review*, 5:3, 301–21.

Bunker, S. and D. O'Hearn (1993), 'Strategies of economic ascendants for access to raw materials: a comparison of the United States and Japan', in R. A. Palat (ed.), *Pacific-Asia and the Future of the World-System*, Westport, Greenwood Press.

Burawoy, M. (1979), *Manufacturing Consent*, Chicago, University of Chicago Press.

Butler, W. F. T. (1917), *Confiscation in Irish History*, Dublin, Talbot Press.

Callan, T., B. Nolan and B. Whelan (1996), *Poverty in the 1990s: Evidence from the Living in Ireland Survey*, Dublin, Oak Tree Press.

Canniffe, M. (2000), 'Company failures up 65% in second quarter 2000', *The Irish Times*, 14 July.

Canny, N. (1978), 'The permissive frontier: the problem of social control in English settlements in Ireland and Virginia', in K. R. Andrews, N. P. Canny and P. E. Hair (eds), *The Westward Enterprise*, Liverpool, Liverpool University Press.

Canny, N. and A. Carpenter (1991), 'The early planters: Spenser and his contemporaries', in *The Field Day Anthology of Irish Writing*, vol. 1, Derry, Field Day.

Carter, C. (1957), 'The Irish economy viewed from without', *Studies*, 46:182, 137–43.

Central Bank (1951), *Report of the Central Bank of Ireland for the Year Ended 31 March 1951*, Dublin, Stationery Office.

Central Statistics Office (1928), *Census of Population of Ireland, 1926. Volume II: Occupations*, Dublin, Stationery Office.

Central Statistics Office (1947), *Trade and Shipping Statistics 1945, 1946, 1947*, Dublin, Stationery Office.

Central Statistics Office (1954), *Census of Population of Ireland, 1951. Volume III: Occupations*, Dublin, Stationery Office.

Central Statistics Office (various years), *National Income Accounts*, Dublin, Stationery Office.

Central Statistics Office (various years), *Statistical Abstract of Ireland*, Dublin, Stationery Office.

Chandler, A. (1962), *Strategy and Structure: Chapters in the History of the Industrial Enterprise*, Cambridge, MIT Press.

Chandler, A. (1977), *The Visible Hand: The Managerial Revolution in American Business*, Cambridge, Belknap Press.

Chandler, A. (1990), *Scale and Scope: The Dynamics of Industrial Capitalism*, Cambridge, Belknap Press.

Chase-Dunn, C. (1989), *Global Formation: Structures of the World Economy*, London, Blackwell.

Chubb, B. (1963), '"Going about persecuting civil servants": the role of the Irish parliamentary representative', *Political Studies*, 10:3, 272–86.

Clancy, P. (1986), 'Socialisation, selection and reproduction in education', in P. Clancy, S. Drudy, K. Lynch and L. O'Dowd (eds), *Ireland: A Sociological Profile*, Dublin, Institute of Public Administration.

Clark, S. and J. Donnelly (eds) (1983), *Irish Peasants: Violence and Political Unrest 1780–1914*, Dublin, Gill and Macmillan.

Clark, W. A. G. (1934), *Linen, Jute and Hemp Industries*, cited in D. L. Armstrong, 'Social and economic conditions in the Belfast linen industry 1850–1900', *Irish Historical Studies*, 7, 28.

Coase, R. (1937), 'The nature of the firm', *Economica* (n.s.), 4:15, 386–405.

Coe, W. E. (1969), *The Engineering Industry of the North of Ireland*, Belfast, Institute of Irish Studies.

Cohen, M. (1990), 'Peasant differentiation and proto-industrialization in the Ulster countryside: Tullylish, 1690–1825', *Journal of Peasant Studies*, 17:3, 413–32.

Colgan, J. and E. Onyemadum (1981), 'Spin-off companies in the Irish electronics industry', *Journal of Irish Business and Administrative Research*, 3:2, 3–15.

Collins, B. (1982), 'Proto-industrialization and the pre-famine emigration', *Social History*, 7:2, 127–46.

Collins, B. (1997), 'The loom, the land, and the marketplace: women, weavers, and the family economy in late nineteenth and early twentieth century Ireland', in M. Cohen (ed.), *The Warp of Ulster's Past: Interdisciplinary Perspectives on the Irish Linen Industry, 1700–1920*, New York, St. Martin's Press.

Committee on Industrial Organisation (1965), *Final Report*, Dublin, Stationery Office.

Connor, J. M. (1977), *The Market Power of Multinationals: A Quantitative Analysis of U.S. Corporations in Brazil and Mexico*, New York, Praeger.

Council on Foreign Relations (1946), *The War and Peace Studies of the Council on Foreign Relations, 1939–1945*, New York, Harold Pratt House.

Courtney, D. (1995), 'Demographic structure and change in the Republic of Ireland and Northern Ireland', in P. Clancy, S. Drudy, K. Lynch and L. O'Dowd, *Irish Society: Sociological Perspectives*, Dublin, Institute of Public Administration.

Crafts, N. F. R. (1985), *British Economic Growth during the Industrial Revolution*, Oxford, Oxford University Press.

Crawford, W. H. (1969), 'The rise of the linen industry', in L. M. Cullen (ed.), *Formation of the Irish Economy*, Cork, Mercier.

Crawford, W. H. (1972), *Domestic Industry in Ireland: The Experience of the Linen Industry*, Dublin, Gill and Macmillan.

Crawford, W. H. (1988), 'The evolution of the linen trade in Ulster before industrialization', *Irish Economic and Social History*, 15, 32–53.

Crotty, R. (1966), *Irish Agriculture: Its Volume and Structure*, Cork, Cork University Press.

Crotty, R. (1986), *Ireland in Crisis*, Dingle, Brandon.

Crotty, R. (n.d.), *Individualist Capitalist Colonialism*, unpublished manuscript.

Cullen, L. M. (1967), *The Emergence of Modern Ireland, 1600–1900*, London, Batsford.

Cullen, L. M. (ed.) (1969), *Formation of the Irish Economy*, Cork, Mercier.

. M. (1972), *An Economic History of Ireland since 1660*, London, rd.

, B. (1987), 'The origins and development of the Northeast Asian political my: industrial sectors, product cycles, and political consequences', in F. C. Deyo (ed.), *The Political Economy of the New Asian Industrialism*, Ithaca, Cornell University Press.

Davis, R. (1962), *Rise of the English Shipping Industry in the Seventeenth and Eighteenth Centuries*, Newton Abbot, David and Charles.

de Janvry, A. (1981), *The Agrarian Question and Reformism in Latin America*, Baltimore, Johns Hopkins University Press.

de Paor, M. and L. de Paor (1958), *Early Christian Ireland*, London, Thames and Hudson.

Deane, P. (1968), 'New estimates of gross national product for the United Kingdom, 1830–1914', *Review of Income and Wealth*, 14:2, 104–7.

Deane, P. and W. A. Cole (1969), *British Economic Growth 1688–1959*, Cambridge, Cambridge University Press.

Department of Industry and Commerce (1926), *Trade and Shipping Statistics*, vol. 3, no. 4. Dublin, Stationery Office.

Department of Industry and Commerce (1935), *Shipping and Trade Statistics 1934*, Dublin, Stationery Office.

Department of Industry and Commerce (various years), *Census of Industrial Production*, Dublin, Stationery Office.

Dickson, D. (1976), 'Aspects of the Irish cotton industry', in L. M. Cullen and T. C. Smout (eds), *Comparative Aspects of Scottish and Irish Economic and Social History*, Edinburgh, Donald.

Dixon, W. J. and T. Boswell (1996), 'Dependency, disarticulation, and denominator effects: another look at foreign capital penetration', *American Journal of Sociology*, 102:2, 543–62.

Dobb, M. (1963), *Studies in the Development of Capitalism*, London, Routledge and Kegan Paul.

Dowling, M. (1999), *Tenant Right and Agrarian Society in Ulster*, Dublin, Irish Academic Press.

Duffy, D., J. Fitzgerald, I. Kearney and D. Smith (1999), *Medium-Term Review 1999–2005*, Dublin, Economic and Social Research Institute.

Durie, A. (1976), 'The Scottish linen industry in the eighteenth century: some aspects of expansion', in L. M. Cullen and T. C. Smout (eds), *Comparative Aspects of Scottish and Irish Economic and Social History*, Edinburgh, Donald.

Edie, C. A. (1970), 'The Irish cattle bills', *Transactions of the American Philosophical Society*, 60:2, 1–66.

Edwards, M. M. (1967), *The Growth of the British Cotton Trade*, Manchester, Manchester University Press.

Ellison, T. (1886), *The Cotton Trade of Great Britain*, London, Wilson.

Emmanuel, A. (1972a), *Unequal Exchange: A Study of the Imperialism of Trade*, New York, Monthly Review Press.

Emmanuel, A. (1972b), 'White settler colonialism and the myth of settler imperialism', *New Left Review*, 73, 35–57.

Emmanuel, C. and M. Mehafdi (1994), *Transfer Pricing*, London, Academic Press.

Eolas (1989), *Electronics Manpower Study: Trends in the Irish Electronics Manufacturing Industry up to 1995*, Dublin, Eolas.

Evans, P. (1985), 'Transnational linkages and the economic role of the state: an analysis of developing and industrialized nations in the post-World War II period', in P. Evans, D. Rueschemeyer and T. Skocpol (eds), *Bringing the State Back In*, Cambridge, Cambridge University Press.

Evans, P. (1995), *Embedded Autonomy*, Princeton, Princeton University Press.

Fahey, T. (1999), *Social Housing in Ireland: A Study of Success, Failure and Lessons Learned*, Dublin, Oak Tree Press.

Fanning, R. (1978), *The Irish Department of Finance 1922–58*, Dublin, Institute of Public Administration.

Fanon, F. (1968), *The Wretched of the Earth*, New York, Grove Press.

Farnie, D. A. (1979), *The English Cotton Industry and the World Market, 1815–96*, Oxford, Oxford University Press.

Federation of Irish Manufacturers (1949), *Annual Report*, Dublin, Federation of Irish Manufacturers.

Firebaugh, G. (1992), 'Growth effects of foreign and domestic investment', *American Journal of Sociology*, 98:1, 105–30.

Firth, C. H. (1962), *Cromwell's Army*, London, Methuen.

Fitzgerald, G. (1959), 'Mr. Whitaker and industry', *Studies*, 48:190, 146.

Fitzgerald, G. (1968), *Planning in Ireland*, Dublin, Institute for Public Administration.

Fogarty, M. P. (1973), *Irish Entrepreneurs Speak for Themselves*, Dublin, Economic and Social Research Institute.

Forbairt (1996), *National Software Directorate Irish Software Industry Survey 1995: Results*, Dublin, Forbairt.

Forfás (1997), 'Optimising purchasing linkages in the Irish economy', mimeo, Dublin, Forfás.

Foster, R. F. (1988), *Modern Ireland 1600–1972*, London, Penguin.

Frobel, F., J. Heinrichs and O. Kreye (1980), *The New International Division of Labor*, Cambridge, Cambridge University Press.

Gallagher, J. and R. Robinson (1953), 'The imperialism of free trade', *Economic History Review*, 6:1, 1–15.

Galtung, J. (1971), 'A structural theory of imperialism', *Journal of Peace Research*, 8:2, 91–154.

Gardiner, K. (1994), 'The Irish economy: a Celtic tiger?', *Ireland: Challenging for Promotion*, Morgan Stanley Euroletter (1 August), 9–21.

Geary, F. (1981), 'The rise and fall of the Belfast cotton industry: some problems', *Irish Historical Studies*, 8, 30–49.

Geary, F. (1989), 'The Belfast cotton industry revisited', *Irish Historical Studies*, 26, 250–67.

Geary, R. C. (1951), 'Irish economic development since the treaty', *Studies*, 40, 399–418.

George, S. (1992), *The Debt Boomerang*, London, Pluto.

Gibson, D. B. (1995), 'Chiefdoms, confederacies, and statehood in early Ireland', in B. Arnold and D. B. Gibson (eds), *Celtic Chiefdom, Celtic State*, Cambridge, Cambridge University Press.

Gill, C. (1925), *The Rise of the Irish Linen Industry*, Oxford, Clarendon.

Gray, J. (1993), 'Rural industry and uneven development: the significance of gender in the Irish linen industry', *Journal of Peasant Studies*, 20:4, 590–611.

Gray, J. (1997), 'The Irish and Scottish linen industries in the eighteenth century: an incorporated comparison', in M. Cohen (ed.), *The Warp of Ulster's Past: Interdisciplinary Perspectives on the Irish Linen Industry 1700–1920*, New York, St. Martin's Press.

Green, E. R. R. (1944), *The Lagan Valley*, London, Faber and Faber.

Griffith, A. (1918), *The Sinn Fein Policy*, Dublin, Sinn Fein.

Habakkuk, H. J. (1962), 'Public finance and the sale of forfeited property during the interregnum', *Economic History Review*, 15:1, 70–88.

Hall, T. (1986), 'Incorporation in the world-system: toward a critique', *American Sociological Review*, 51:3, 390–402.

Hamilton, N. (1982), *The Limits of State Autonomy: Post-revolutionary Mexico*, Princeton, Princeton University Press.

Harper, L. A. (1939), *The English Navigation Laws: A Seventeenth-Century Experiment in Social Engineering*, New York, Octagon Books (reprinted 1964).

Haydu, J. (1998), 'Making use of the past: time periods as cases to compare and as sequences of problem solving', *American Journal of Sociology*, 104:2, 339–71.

Hederman, M. (1983), *The Road to Europe: Irish Attitudes 1948–61*, Dublin, Institute of Public Administration.

Hill, C. (1967), *Reformation to Industrial Revolution: A Social and Economic History of Britain, 1530–1780*, London, Weidenfeld and Nicolson.

Hirschman, A. (1958), *The Strategy of Economic Development*, New York, Norton.

Hogan, M. (1987), *The Marshall Plan*, Cambridge, Cambridge University Press.

Hopkins, T. and I. Wallerstein (1986), 'Commodity chains in the world economy prior to 1800', *Review*, 10:1, 157–70.

Hunter, R. J. (1971), 'Towns in the Ulster plantation', *Studia Hibernica*, 11, 40–79.

Hymer, S. (1972), 'The multinational corporation and the law of uneven development', in J. N. Bhagwati (ed.), *Economics and World Order*, New York, Macmillan.

Ignatiev, N. (1995), *How the Irish Became White*, New York, Routledge.

IMF (2000), 'IMF concludes Article IV consultation with Ireland', Public Information Notice No. 00/61, 10 August.

Irish Customs (1763–1824), *Exports and Imports of Ireland, 1763–1824* (original volumes in the National Library of Ireland).

Irish Railway Commissioners (1837), *Second Report of the Commissioners Appointed to Consider and Recommend a General System of Railways for Ireland* (original volume in the National Library of Ireland).

Isles, K. S. and N. Cuthbert (1957), *An Economic Survey of Northern Ireland*, Belfast, HMSO.

Israel, J. (1989), *Dutch Primacy in World Trade, 1585–1740*, Oxford, Clarendon Press.

Jacobson, D. (1977), 'The political economy of industrial location: the Ford Motor Company at Cork, 1912–26', *Irish Economic and Social History*, 4, 36–55.

Jacobson, D. (1999), 'The evolution of networks around the subsidiaries of software MNEs in Ireland', mimeo, Dublin, Dublin City University Business School.

Jenkins, R. (1987), *Transnational Corporations and Uneven Development*, London, Methuen.

Katzenstein, P. (1985), *Small States in World Markets*, Ithaca, Cornell University Press.

Kearney, H. F. (1959), 'The political background to English mercantilism, 1695–1700', *Economic History Review*, 11, 484–96.

Keena, C. (2000), 'Growth predictions to rise following boom in exports', *The Irish Times*, 11 August.

Kelleher, P. (1987), 'Familism in Irish capitalism in the 1950s', *Economic and Social Review*, 18:2, 75–94.

Kelly, P. (1980), 'The Irish Woollen Export Prohibition Act of 1699: Kearney revisited', *Irish Economic and Social History*, 7, 22–44.

Kennedy, K. (1991), 'Linkages and overseas industry', in A. Foley and D. McAleese (eds), *Overseas Industry in Ireland*, Dublin, Gill and Macmillan.

Kennedy, K. and B. R. Dowling (1975), *Economic Growth in Ireland: The Experience since 1947*, Dublin, Gill and Macmillan.

Kennedy, L. (1996), *Colonialism, Religion and Nationalism in Ireland*, Belfast, Institute of Irish Studies.

Killeen, M. J. (1979), 'The electronics revolution: its impact on Ireland', address to the Royal Institution of Chartered Surveyors, mimeo.

Kinealy, C. (1995), 'Beyond revisionism: reassessing the Great Famine', *History Ireland*, 3:4, 28–34.

Krasner, S. D. (1976), 'State power and the structure of international trade', *World Politics*, 28:3, 317–47.

Kriedte, P., H. Medick and J. Schlumbohm (1981), *Industrialization before Industrialization*, Cambridge, Cambridge University Press.

Krugman, P. (1997), 'Good news from Ireland: a geographical perspective', in A. Gray (ed.), *International Perspectives on the Irish Economy*, Dublin, Indecon.

Labour Relations Commission (various years), *Annual Report*, Dublin, Stationery Office.

Laclau, E. (1971), 'Feudalism and capitalism in Latin America', *New Left Review*, 67, 19–38.

Landes, D. (1969), *The Unbound Promethius: Technological Change and Industrial Development in Western Europe from 1750 to the Present*, Cambridge, Cambridge University Press.

Lange, O. (1943), 'A note on innovations', *Review of Economic Statistics*, 25, 19–25.

Lazonick, W. (1991), *Business Organization and the Myth of the Market Economy*, Cambridge, Cambridge University Press.

Lee, J. (1973), *The Modernisation of Irish Society 1848–1918*, Dublin, Gill and Macmillan.

Lee, J. (1981), 'Irish economic history since 1500', in J. Lee (ed.), *Irish Historiography 1970–79*, Cork, Cork University Press.

Lee, J. (1989), *Ireland 1912–1985: Politics and Society*, Cambridge, Cambridge University Press.

Lenin, V. (1916), *Imperialism: The Highest Stage of Capitalism*, Moscow, Progress Publishers (reprinted 1965).

Lewis, W. A. (1954), 'Economic development with unlimited supplies of labour', *Manchester School of Economic and Social Studies*, 22, 139–91.

Lucey, K. (1996), 'Ireland's software industry poised for next leap', *The Irish Times*, 9 December.

Luxemburg, R. (1951), *The Accumulation of Capital*, New York, Monthly Review Press.

Lynch, P. (1969), 'The Irish economy since the war, 1946–51', in K. B. Nowlan and T. D. Williams (eds), *Ireland in the War Years and After*, Dublin, Gill and Macmillan.

Lyons, F. S. L. (1973), *Ireland Since the Famine*, Glasgow, Fontana.

MacCormack, J. R. (1956), 'The Irish adventures and the English civil war', *Irish Historical Studies*, 10, 21–58.

Macher, J. T., D. C. Mowery and D. A. Hodges (1998), 'Reversal of fortune? The recovery of the U.S. semiconductor industry', *California Management Review*, 41:1, 107–36.

Maddison, A. (1995), *Explaining the Economic Performance of Nations*, Aldershot, Edward Elgar.

Mallory, J. P. and T. E. McNeill (1991), *The Archaeology of Ulster from Colonization to Plantation*, Belfast, Institute of Irish Studies.

Mandel, E. (1975), *Late Capitalism*, London, Verso.

Mangan, O. (1994), 'No longer a joke', *Davy Stockbrokers Weekly Market Monitor*, 22 July.

Mann, J. A. (1860), *The Cotton Trade of Great Britain*, London, Simpkin, Marshall and Co.

Marx, K. and F. Engels (1971), *Ireland and the Irish Question*, Moscow, Progress Publishers.

Mass, W. and W. Lazonick (1990), 'The British cotton industry and international comparative advantage: the state of the debates', *Business History*, 32:4, 10–65.

McAleese, D. (1977), *A Profile of Grant-Aided Industry in Ireland*, Dublin, Institute of Public Administration.

McAleese, D. and D. McDonald (1978), 'Employment growth and the development of linkages in foreign-owned and domestic manufacturing enterprises', *Oxford Bulletin of Economics and Statistics*, 40:4, 321–39.

McCarthy, C. (1977), *Trade Unions in Ireland 1894–1960*, Dublin, Institute of Public Administration.

McCormick, T. (1989), *America's Half-Century: United States Foreign Policy in the Cold War*, Baltimore, Johns Hopkins University Press.

McCracken, E. (1971), *The Irish Woods since Tudor Times: Distribution and Exploitation*, Newton Abbot, David and Charles.

McGovern, P. (1998), *HRM, Technical Workers and the Multinational Corporation*, London, Routledge.

McMichael, P. (1990), 'Incorporating comparisons within a world-historical perspective', *American Sociological Review*, 55, 385–97.

McMichael, P. (1996), *Development and Social Change: A Global Perspective*, Thousand Oaks, Pine Forge Press.

McNeill, W. H. (1982), *The Pursuit of Power: Technology, Armed Force, and Society since A.D. 1000*, Oxford, Blackwell.

Meenan, J. (1970), *The Irish Economy since 1922*, Liverpool, Liverpool University Press.

Mjoset, L. (1992), *The Irish Economy in a Comparative Institutional Perspective*, Dublin, National Economic and Social Council.

Modelski, G. and W. R. Thompson (1988), *Sea Power in Global Politics, 1494–1943*, Seattle, University of Washington Press.

Mokyr, J. (1983), *Why Ireland Starved: A Quantitative and Analytical History of the Irish Economy, 1800–1850*, Boston, Allen and Unwin.

Monaghan, J. J. (1942), 'The rise and fall of the Belfast cotton industry', *Irish Historical Studies*, 3:9, 1–17.

Moody, T. W. (1939), *The Londonderry Plantation 1609–41*, Belfast, Mullan.

Munck, R. (1993), *The Irish Economy: Results and Prospects*, London, Pluto.

Munck, R. and D. Hamilton (1993), 'Alternative scenarios', in R. Munck, *The Irish Economy: Results and Prospects*, London, Pluto.

Munck, R. and D. Hamilton (1998), 'Politics, the economy and peace in Northern Ireland', in D. Miller (ed.), *Rethinking Northern Ireland*, London, Longman.

Murphy, A. (1994), *The Irish Economy: Celtic Tiger or Tortoise?*, Dublin, Money Markets International.

Murray, A. E. (1903), *Commercial and Financial Relations Between England and Ireland From the Period of the Restoration*, London, P. S. King and Son.

Murray, J. (1870), *Handbook for Shropshire, Lancashire and Cheshire*, London, Murray.

Musson, A. E. and E. Robinson (1969), *Science and Technology in the Industrial Revolution*, Manchester, Manchester University Press.

Neeson, E. (1991), *A History of Irish Forestry*, Dublin, Lilliput Press.

Nef, J. (1934), 'The progress of technology and the growth of large-scale industry in Great Britain, 1540–1640', *Economic History Review*, 5:1, 3–24.

Nolan, B. and G. Hughes (1997), 'Low pay, the earnings distribution and poverty in Ireland', working paper no. 84, Dublin, Economic and Social Research Institute.

Northern Ireland Economic Council (1983), *The Duration of Industrial Development Assisted Employment*, report no. 40, Belfast, NIEC.

Ó Cinnéide, S. (2000), 'Understanding the programme for prosperity and fairness', *Poverty Today*, 47, 4–5.

Ó Cróinín, D. (1995), *Early Medieval Ireland 400–1200*, London, Longman.

Ó Gráda, C. (1994), *New Economic History of Ireland*, Cambridge, Cambridge University Press.

O hUiginn, P. (1972), *Regional Development and Industrial Location in Ireland. Volume I: Locational Decisions and Experiences of New Industrial Establishments 1960–1970*, Dublin, An Foras Forbartha.

Ó Riain, S. (1997), 'The birth of a Celtic tiger', *Communications of the ACM*, 40:3, 11–16.

Ó Riain, S. (1999), *Development and the Global Information Society*, PhD dissertation, Berkeley, University of California.

Ó Riain, S. (2000), 'The flexible developmental state: globalization, information technology, and the "Celtic tiger"', *Politics and Society*, 28:2, 157–94.

O'Brien, G. (1919), *Economic History of Ireland in the Seventeenth Century*, Dublin, Maunsel.

O'Brien, G. (1987), *Anglo-Irish Politics in the Age of Grattan and Pitt*, Dublin, Irish Academic Press.

O'Brien, R. (1985), 'Technology and industrial development: the Irish electronics industry in an international context', in J. Fitzpatrick and J. Kelly (eds), *Perspectives on Irish Industry*, Dublin, Irish Management Institute.

O'Donnell, G. (1978), 'Reflections on the pattern of change in the bureaucratic-authoritarian state', *Latin American Research Review*, 13:1, 3–38.

O'Donnell, P. (1963), *There Will Be Another Day*, Dublin, Dolmen Press.

O'Donnell, R. and D. Thomas (1998), 'Social partnership in Ireland, 1987–1997', paper presented to the seminar Social Partnership in Western Europe, Cardiff, 11–13 September.

O'Donovan, J. (1940), *The Economic History of Live Stock in Ireland*, Cork, Cork University Press.

O'Hagan, J. W. and G. J. Foley (1982), *The Confederation of Irish Industry: The First Fifty Years 1932–82*, Dublin, Confederation of Irish Industry.

O'Hearn, D. (1987), 'Estimates of new foreign manufacturing employment in Ireland (1956–1972)', *Economic and Social Review*, 18:3, 173–88.

O'Hearn, D. (1988), *Export-Led Industrialization in Ireland: A Specific Case of Dependent Development*, PhD dissertation, Ann Arbor, University of Michigan.

O'Hearn, D. (1989), 'The Irish case of dependency: an exception to the exceptions?', *American Sociological Review*, 54:4, 578–96.

O'Hearn, D. (1990), 'TNCs, intervening mechanisms and economic growth in Ireland: a longitudinal test and extension of the Bornschier model', *World Development*, 18:3, 417–29.

O'Hearn, D. (1994), 'Innovation and the world-system hierarchy: British subjugation of the Irish cotton industry, 1780–1830', *American Journal of Sociology*, 100:3, 587–621.

O'Hearn, D. (1998a), *Inside the Celtic Tiger: The Irish Economy and the Asian Model*, London, Pluto.

O'Hearn, D. (1998b), 'The two Irish economies: dependencies compared', in J. Anderson and J. Goodman (eds), *Dis/Agreeing Ireland: Contexts, Obstacles, Hopes*, London, Pluto.

O'Hearn, D. (2000), 'Globalization, "new tigers", and the end of the developmental state? The case of the Celtic tiger', *Politics and Society*, 28:1, 67–92.

O'Kane, P. (2000), 'IDA fears abuse of 12.5% tax', *The Irish Times*, 25 June.

O'Leary, J. (2000), 'New economic traffic heading to Ireland', *The Irish Times*, 4 August.

O'Malley, E. (1980), *Industrial Policy and Development: A Survey of Literature from the Early 1960s*, report no. 56, Dublin, National Economic and Social Council.

O'Malley, E. (1989), *Industry and Economic Development: Challenge for the Latecomer*, Dublin, Gill and Macmillan.

O'Malley, E. (1998), 'The revival of Irish indigenous industry 1987–1997', *Quarterly Economic Commentary*, April, 35–60.

O'Rourke, K. and J. Williamson (1999), *Globalization and History: The Evolution of a Nineteenth-Century Atlantic Economy*, Cambridge, MIT Press.

OECD (1992), *Economic Outlook*, no. 51, Paris, OECD.

OECD (1993), *Ireland: Country Report*, Paris, OECD.

Pawson, E. (1979), *The Early Industrial Revolution: Britain in the Eighteenth Century*, London, Batsford.

Peillon, M. (1982), *Contemporary Irish Society*, Dublin, Gill and Macmillan.

Persuad, R. and C. Lusane (2000), 'The new economy, globalisation and the impact on African Americans', *Race and Class*, 42:1, 21–34.

Petras, J. (1978), *Critical Perspectives on Imperialism and Social Class in the Third World,* New York, Monthly Review Press.

Polanyi, K. (1957), *The Great Transformation: The Political and Economic Origins of Our Time,* Boston, Beacon Press.

Quinn, D. B. (1945), 'Sir Thomas Smith (1513–1577) and the beginnings of English colonial theory,' *Proceedings of the American Philosophical Society,* 89:4, 543–60.

Rabb, T. K. (1967), *Enterprise and Empire: Merchant and Gentry Investment in the Expansion of England, 1575–1630,* Cambridge, Harvard University Press.

Redford, A. (1934), *Manchester Merchants and Foreign Trade,* Manchester, Manchester University Press.

Renfrew, C. (1984), *Approaches to Social Archaeology,* Edinburgh, Edinburgh University Press.

Resnick, S. and R. Wolff (1987), *Knowledge and Class: A Marxian Critique of Political Economy,* Chicago, University of Chicago Press.

Revenue Commissioners of Ireland (various years), *Annual Report,* Dublin, Stationery Office.

Robinson, R. (1983), 'Non-European foundations of European imperialism: sketch for a theory of collaboration', in R. Owen and Bob Sutcliffe (eds), *Studies in the Theory of Imperialism,* New York, Longman.

Rosenstein-Rodin, P. N. (1943), 'Problems of industrialization of Eastern and South-Eastern Europe', *Economic Journal,* 55, 202–11.

Rothery, B. (1977), *Men of Enterprise,* Dublin, Institute for Industrial Research and Standards.

Rowthorn, B. (1987), 'Northern Ireland: an economy in crisis', in P. Teague (ed.), *Beyond the Rhetoric,* London, Lawrence and Wishart.

Rowthorn, B. and N. Wayne (1988), *Northern Ireland: The Political Economy of Conflict,* Cambridge, Polity.

Ruane, F. (1999), 'Whither Ireland's industrial policy?', paper presented to a conference of the European Network on Industrial Policy, Dublin, 10 December.

Ryan, W. J. L. (1948–49), 'Measurement of tariff levels for Ireland, for 1931, 1936, 1938', *Journal of the Social and Statistical Inquiry Society of Ireland,* 18:2, 109–32.

Sabel, C. (1996), *Ireland: Local Partnerships and Social Innovation,* Paris, OECD.

Sachs, J. (1997), 'Ireland's growth strategy: lessons for economic development', in A. Gray (ed.), *International Perspectives on the Irish Economy,* Dublin, Indecon.

Sawers, L. (1992), 'The Navigation Acts revisited', *Economic History Review,* 45:2, 262–84.

Schumpeter, J. (1939), *Business Cycles,* New York, McGraw-Hill.

Schumpeter, J. (1947), 'The creative response in economic history', *Journal of Economic History,* 7:2, 149–59.

Senghaas, D. (1985), *The European Experience,* Leamington Spa, Berg.

Sheridan, A. (1986), 'Porcellanite artefacts: a new survey', *Ulster Journal of Archaeology,* 49, 19–32.

Shoup, L. and W. Minter (1977), *Imperial Brain Trust,* New York, Monthly Review Press.

Simms, J. G. (1956), *The Williamite Confiscation in Ireland 1690–1703,* Westport, Greenwood.

So, A. (1986), *The South China Silk District*, Albany, SUNY Press.

So, A. (1990), *Social Change and Development: Modernization, Dependency, and World-System Theories*, Newbury Park, Sage.

Staley, E. (1937), *Raw Materials in Peace and War*, New York, Council on Foreign Relations.

Steensgaard, N. (1974), *The Asian Trade Revolution of the Seventeenth Century: The East Indian Companies and the Decline of the Caravan Trade*, Chicago, University of Chicago Press.

Stewart, J. C. (1976a), 'Foreign direct investment and the emergence of a dual economy', *Economic and Social Review*, 7:2, 173–97.

Stewart, J. C. (1976b), 'Linkages and foreign direct investment', *Regional Studies*, 10:2, 245–58.

Stewart, J. C. (1988), 'Transfer pricing: some empirical evidence from Ireland', *Journal of Economic Studies*, 16:3, 40–56.

Streeck, W. (1999), 'Competitive solidarity: rethinking the "European Social Model"', working paper 99/8, Koeln, Max Planck Institute for the Study of Societies.

Suiter, J. (2000), 'McCreevy vindicated by IMF', *The Irish Times*, 11 August.

Survey Team (1967), *Survey of Grant-Aided Industry*, Dublin, Stationery Office.

Sweezy, P. (1942), *The Theory of Capitalist Development*, New York, Monthly Review Press.

Takei, A. (1994), 'The first Irish linen mills, 1800–1824', *Irish Economic and Social History*, 21, 28–38.

Telesis Consultancy Group (1982), *A Review of Industrial Policy*, report no. 64, Dublin, National Economic and Social Council.

Thurow, L. (1992), *Head to Head: The Coming Economic Battle among Japan, Europe and America*, New York, Morrow.

Trevor-Roper, H. (1964), 'The fast sermons of the long parliament', in H. Trevor-Roper (ed.), *Essays in British History Presented to Sir Keith Feiling*, London, Macmillan.

Tyson, L. D. (1999), 'Old economic logic in the new economy', *California Management Review*, 41:4, 8–16.

Upgren, A. (1940a), 'Internal influences on imports of the United States', in *Studies of American Interests in the War and the Peace*, E-B11, New York, Council on Foreign Relations.

Upgren, A. (1940b), 'A pan-American trade bloc', in *Studies of American Interests in the War and the Peace*, E-B12, New York, Council on Foreign Relations.

Upgren, A. (1940c), 'The future position of Germany and the United States in world trade', in *Studies of American Interests in the War and the Peace*, E-B18, New York, Council on Foreign Relations.

Upgren, A. (1941), 'Problems of bloc trading areas for the United States', in *Studies of American Interests in the War and the Peace*, E-B31, New York, Council on Foreign Relations.

US Department of Commerce (various years), *Survey of Current Business*, Washington, DC, US Department of Commerce.

Useem, M. (1984), *The Inner Circle: Large Corporations and the Rise of Business Political Activity in the U.S. and U.K.*, New York, Oxford University Press.

Wallerstein, I. (1979), *The Capitalist World-Economy*, Cambridge, Cambridge University Press.

Wallerstein, I. (1980), 'One man's meat: the Scottish great leap forward', *Review*, 3:4, 631–40.

Wallerstein, I. (1984), *The Politics of the Capitalist World-Economy*, Cambridge, Cambridge University Press.

Wallerstein, I. (1988), *The Modern World-System III: The Second Era of Great Expansion of the Capitalist World-Economy*, New York, Academic Press.

Warren, B. (1980), *Imperialism: Pioneer of Capitalism*, London, New Left Books.

Wexler, I. (1983), *The Marshall Plan Revisited: The Europeam Recovery Plan in Economic Perspective*, Westport, Greenwood.

Wheeler, J. E. (1990), *Hearings on Tax Underpayments by Foreign-Owned US Subsidiaries*, Washington, DC, House Ways and Means Oversight Subcommittee of the United States House of Representatives.

Whitaker, T. K. (1948–49), 'Ireland's external assets', *Journal of the Statistical and Social Inquiry Society of Ireland*, 18, 192–211.

Williamson, O. (1970), *Corporate Control and Business Behavior*, Engelwood Cliffs, Prentice Hall.

Woodward, D. (1973), 'The Anglo-Irish livestock trade of the seventeenth century', *Irish Historical Studies*, 18:72, 489–515.

Wren, M. (2000), 'Relative poverty deepens despite Celtic tiger', *The Irish Times*, 19 May.

Wright, E. (1983), 'Giddens' critique of Marxism', *New Left Review*, 138, 11–35.

Wright, E. (1985), *Classes,* London, Verso.

Young, A. (1780), *A Tour in Ireland*, London, George Bell (reprinted 1882).

Archival sources

University College Dublin Archives (Patrick McGilligan papers)

P35b/10, Department of Industry and Commerce memorandum, 'Preliminary notes on planned economies' (1927).

P35b/10, Memorandum by Gordon Campbell, 'Industrial development' (19 July 1927).

P35b/52, Department of Finance memorandum to T. K. Whitaker (later sent to minister of finance), 'IDA report on export corporation' (6 October 1949).

P35b/52, Letter from J. E. Corrigan, chief of ECA mission to Ireland, to minister for external affairs Sean MacBride (7 December 1949).

P35b/52, M. Breathnach (principal officer, Department of Finance), 'On memorandum of foreign affairs' (4 May 1950).

P35b/57, Department of Agriculture, 'Memorandum for cabinet committee: liberalisation of trade' (22 February 1955).

P35b/57, Department of External Affairs, 'Memorandum for cabinet committee: extension and stabilisation of liberalisation of trade' (22 February 1955).

P35b/57, Department of Industry and Commerce, 'Memorandum for cabinet committee: OEEC liberalization of trade' (4 March 1955).

P35b/75, Department of Finance holograph, 'Memorandum on proposed Industrial Development Board' (1949).

P35b/75, Minister for external affairs Sean MacBride's memorandum, 'Irish currency counterpart of ECA loans' (30 December 1948).

P35c/2, Sean MacBride, letter to the government attached to Department of External Affairs' 'Memorandum for the government' (16 December 1948).

P35c/2, Secretary of finance James McElligott, letter to minister of finance Patrick McGilligan (17 December 1948).

P35c/2, Department of Industry and Commerce comments on Department of External Affairs' 'Memorandum for the government' (16 December 1949).

P35c/8, T. K. Whitaker, letter to minister of finance Patrick McGilligan (24 August 1949).

P35c/11, Minister of finance Patrick McGilligan's notes on a lecture by Paul Bureau, assistant city editor, *News Chronicle*, to Irish Institute of Bankers, Dublin (28 October 1948).

P35c/42, Department of External Affairs, 'Memorandum to government on proposal for establishment of a Land Development Authority' (16 February 1949).

P35c/47, Department of Finance memorandum (T. K. Whitaker), 'Financial policy' (26 November 1949).

P35c/47, T. K. Whitaker, 'Financial policy' (26 November 1949).

P35c/47, Letter from taoiseach John Costello to minister of finance Patrick McGilligan concerning T. K. Whitaker's memorandum 'Financial policy' (26 November 1949).

P35c/47, Department of Finance (T. K. Whitaker) memorandum, 'Financial policy' (26 November 1949).

P35c/47, Letter from J. E. Corrigan, chief of ECA mission to Ireland, to minister for external affairs Sean MacBride (7 December 1949).

P35c/117, Department of Finance, 'most confidential' memorandum, 'The economic situation' (9 December 1955).

P35c/117, General correspondence between parliamentary secretary to the government John O'Donovan and minister of finance Gerald Sweetman (January 1956).

P35c/117, Secretary of finance James McElligott's letter to taoiseach John Costello (10 September 1956).

P35c/117, Taoiseach John Costello, speech, 'The policy for production' (5 October 1956).

P35c/117, T. K. Whitaker, 'secret' memorandum to the minister of finance (10 October 1956).

S14106, US State Department, *The European Recovery Programme. Country Studies, Chapter 8: Ireland* (1948).

S14106H, Minutes of the Interdepartmental ERP Committee meeting (7 September 1951).

Irish State Papers Office, Dublin

S11987, Department of Industry and Commerce explanatory memorandum, 'On proposed legislation to establish an industrial efficiency bureau and to amend the Control of Prices Acts in certain respects' (1946).

S11987B, Department of Industry and Commerce, 'Memorandum of industrial development for An Taoiseach' (October 1945).

S11987B, Department of Industry and Commerce, 'Proposals to enact legislation for the better control of wholesale and retail prices of goods and services and for the promotion of efficiency in certain industrial undertakings' (15 January 1947).

S11987B, Department of Industry and Commerce, 'Memorandum for submission to the government on Paragraph 7 (Industrial Development) of Statement of Government Policy' (22 October 1951).

S14106C, Joint report of delegation to the U.S.A. 18–28th May, 1948 (minister for external affairs Sean McBride, secretary of finance James McElligott, secretary of external affairs F. H. Boland, Department of Finance officer G. P. S. Hogan).

S14106H, Interdepartmental ERP committee meeting (minutes) (7 September 1951).

S14299, Department of External Affairs, 'Submission to the government concerning interdepartmental and staff organisation required for the administration of the European Recovery Plan' (28 April 1948).

S14474A, Correspondence between L. Crawford, secretary of the Congress of Irish Unions, and minister for industry and commerce Daniel Morrisey (March 1949).

S14474A, Letter to minister of industry and commerce from the Federation of Irish Manufacturers (24 March 1950).

S14474A, Letter to minister of industry and commerce from the Association of Chambers of Commerce (27 March 1950).

S14474A, Drapers Chamber of Trade, letter to minister of industry and commerce (April 1950).

S14474A, Department of the Taoiseach memorandum, 'Deputation received by taoiseach from Irish Trade Union Congress' (23 May 1949).

Public Records Office, Kew

CO 852/877/1 #4, Letter from minister of state to secretary of state Caine (26 July 1947).

CO 852/877/1 #16, Notes on #15 by Glover (31 October 1947) and T. W. Davies (4 November 1947).

FO 371/71822, Letter from Gorell-Barnes to T. L. Rowan (Treasury) (5 August 1948).

FO 371/82937, Letter from Oliver Franks (British Ambassador to US) to Foreign Office (31 December 1949).

Unsigned newspaper and magazine articles

'24th annual meeting: Federation of Irish Manufacturers', *Irish Industry*, 26:3 (March 1958), pp. 24–5.

'Annual meeting of Cork Regional Group of Federation of Irish Manufacturers', *Irish Industry*, 25:6 (June 1957), p. 25.

'Discussion on free trade proposals', *Irish Industry*, 26:3 (March 1958), pp. 49–65.

'Federation of Irish Manufacturers: annual general meeting', *Irish Industry*, 25:2 (February 1957), p. 31.

'Ireland for the – foreigner', *Irish Industry*, 26:11 (November 1958), p. 1.

'Management talks with Kevin McCourt', *Management*, 25:3 (March 1978), p. 30.

'Openings for industry', *The Irish Times* (10 March 1950), p. 5.

'Symposium on proposed Free Trade Area', *Irish Industry*, 25:3 (March 1957), pp. 65–88.

'The Federation of Irish Industries: annual general meeting', *Irish Industry*, 27:2 (February 1959), pp. 15–40.

'The Federation of Irish Manufacturers', *Irish Industry*, 27:1 (January 1959), pp. 3–4.

'The imminence of the free trade area', *Irish Industry*, 25:11 (November 1957), p. 3.

'Will you come into my parlour?', *Irish Industry*, 25:2 (February 1957), p. 3.

Index

231